Feminism and Intersectionality in Academia

Stephanie Anne Shelton · Jill Ewing Flynn
Tanetha Jamay Grosland
Editors

Feminism and Intersectionality in Academia

Women's Narratives and Experiences in Higher Education

Editors
Stephanie Anne Shelton
University of Alabama
Tuscaloosa, AL, USA

Tanetha Jamay Grosland
University of South Florida
Tampa, FL, USA

Jill Ewing Flynn
University of Delaware
Newark, DE, USA

ISBN 978-3-030-08049-5   ISBN 978-3-319-90590-7 (eBook)
https://doi.org/10.1007/978-3-319-90590-7

© The Editor(s) (if applicable) and The Author(s) 2018
Softcover re-print of the Hardcover 1st edition 2018
This work is subject to copyright. All rights are solely and exclusively licensed by the Publisher, whether the whole or part of the material is concerned, specifically the rights of translation, reprinting, reuse of illustrations, recitation, broadcasting, reproduction on microfilms or in any other physical way, and transmission or information storage and retrieval, electronic adaptation, computer software, or by similar or dissimilar methodology now known or hereafter developed.
The use of general descriptive names, registered names, trademarks, service marks, etc. in this publication does not imply, even in the absence of a specific statement, that such names are exempt from the relevant protective laws and regulations and therefore free for general use.
The publisher, the authors and the editors are safe to assume that the advice and information in this book are believed to be true and accurate at the date of publication. Neither the publisher nor the authors or the editors give a warranty, express or implied, with respect to the material contained herein or for any errors or omissions that may have been made. The publisher remains neutral with regard to jurisdictional claims in published maps and institutional affiliations.

Cover image: © aelitta/iStock/Getty Images Plus
Cover design by Tom Howey

Printed on acid-free paper

This Palgrave Macmillan imprint is published by the registered company Springer International Publishing AG part of Springer Nature
The registered company address is: Gewerbestrasse 11, 6330 Cham, Switzerland

Acknowledgements

We thank the panelists and discussant from the first NCTE session: Heidi Jo Jones, Audrey Lensmire, and Amanda Haertling Thein. We also acknowledge the other friends who helped inspire the session, including Candance Doerr-Stevens, Jessie Dockter Tierney, and Stephanie Rollag.

We acknowledge Audrey Lensmire's and Amy Tondreau's roles in the second NCTE session, which were key to this book's coming-to-be.

We are grateful for all of Maureen A. Flint's behind-the-scenes work, which helped to make this book possible.

Stephanie celebrates the moments that brought her and her co-editors together, and is so grateful for their tireless work, brilliant insight, and constant humor. She thanks the authors for their willingness to trust the editors with their narratives. She is grateful to her colleagues at the University of Alabama, particularly those who are a part of the #UAQUAL Crew. And, finally, thank you to Mama, Belle, Tray, Laurie, and the munchkins for being an impossibly supportive family.

Jill thanks her colleagues at the University of Delaware—several of whom appear in this volume—for their support and listening as she enthusiastically recounted each stage of the creation of this book. She is grateful for the sharp minds of her co-editors, who were a joy and privilege to work with. Finally, she thanks her parents, husband, and son.

Tanetha Jamay expresses her sincere gratitude to her co-editors for their leadership and to the contributors for sharing their beautiful stories. She appreciates the opportunity to work and learn with such a strong group of women who all pulled together to make this book happen. She also thanks her mother and others in her family for their courage.

CONTENTS

1 Introduction: The Moments That Became a Book—The Need for Intersectional Women's Narratives in Academia 1
Stephanie Anne Shelton, Jill Ewing Flynn and Tanetha Jamay Grosland

Part I The Superwoman Complex: The Challenges of Family Life for Women in the Academy

2 "I Would Never Let My Wife Do That": The Stories We Tell to Stay Afloat 15
Amy Tondreau

3 Building a Compass: Leaving, Loss, and Daughterhood in Academia 25
Maureen A. Flint

4 The Undecided Narratives of Becoming-Mother, Becoming-Ph.D. 37
Kelly W. Guyotte

5 Showing Up 49
Sarah R. Hick

6   Superwoman Goes Camping: The On-Going Quest
    to Right-Size My Life   61
    Sharon I. Radd

Part II   The Less Traveled and Less Valued Pathways:
          Examining the Devaluation of Women's
          Contributions to the Academy

7   There and Back and There Again: Notes
    on a Professional Journey   75
    Cheryl R. Richardson

8   A Woman's Worth: Valuing Self, Risk, and (Re)vision   85
    Tanetha Jamay Grosland

9   The Ancestral Double Dutch: From Cotton Myths
    to Future Dreams   95
    Stephanie P. Jones

Part III   The Importance of Intersectionality: Exploring
           the Diversities of Women in the Academy

10 Honest and Uncomfortable: A Loving Look
    at My Exclusive Campus   103
    Lisa M. Dembouski

11 Afro-Puerto Rican Primas: Identity, Pedagogy,
    and Solidarity   117
    Erica R. Davila and Ann M. Aviles

12 Lessons on Humility: White Women's Racial Allyship
    in Academia   131
    Daniela Gachago

13 Living with Three Strikes: Being a Transwoman
    of Color in Education   145
    Aryah O. S. Lester

Part IV Vulnerability in the Academy: Women Explore
         Emotionality, Affect, and Self-Care

14 You Can't Un-See Color: A Ph.D., A Divorce,
    and *The Wizard of Oz*   155
    Meghan E. Barnes

15 Doctor of Vulnerability and Resilience   167
    Janine de Novais

16 Teaching and Learning Within Feminist Dystopias   179
    Alyssa D. Niccolini

17 Re-introducing the Phoenix Within   193
    Cheryl E. Matias

Afterword   201

Index   203

CHAPTER 1

Introduction: The Moments That Became a Book—The Need for Intersectional Women's Narratives in Academia

Stephanie Anne Shelton,
Jill Ewing Flynn and Tanetha Jamay Grosland

Though we did not know it at the time—in fact did not all know one another yet—this book began while casually socializing in November 2014 at the National Council of Teachers of English (NCTE) Annual Convention. Co-editor Jill Ewing Flynn joined several graduate school friends for libations and, as night fell and temperatures dropped, conversations turned to work, family, research, and teaching—with each woman reflecting on how her choices after completing a Ph.D. led her on a different journey than the others. Those women, all recognized on our Acknowledgements page for their importance to this book's existence, agreed, "THIS conversation could be a session at the conference!"

S. A. Shelton (✉)
University of Alabama, Tuscaloosa, AL, USA

J. E. Flynn
University of Delaware, Newark, DE, USA

T. J. Grosland
University of South Florida, Tampa, FL, USA

© The Author(s) 2018
S. A. Shelton et al. (Eds.), *Feminism and Intersectionality in Academia*,
https://doi.org/10.1007/978-3-319-90590-7_1

Fast forwarding one year, co-editor Stephanie Anne Shelton sat as an audience member in an overly air-conditioned hotel conference room at NCTE in November 2015, while Jill and co-editor Tanetha Jamay Grosland sat at a front table as co-speakers with the friends with whom the session was planned in the previous year. The all-women panel aimed to discuss female academics' personal and professional experiences, with the speakers representing a range of institutions, job titles, and individual identities. Though an early morning session, there was standing room only as women filled the room's chairs and then began to file along the walls to hear the panel. The session was structured so that each speaker shared her unique trajectory, a discussant wove the various narratives into an overall consideration of the ways that women navigated male-dominated academia, and then the participants invited audience members to share their own experiences within the contexts that the panel had offered. The panelists provided a range of gendered topics for consideration, including the complexities of motherhood, the challenges of being first-generation college graduates, the difficulties of finding an academic career that was a good "fit," and the realities of being racially underrepresented in higher education. Each presenter discussed how she had experienced the demands of her Ph.D. program and her life as an academic while working to maintain a personal life outside the university setting. Emphasizing the theme of "pathway," they shared their journeys to their current positions and the different routes that they had taken. Once the remaining time was yielded to those in attendance, dozens of hands reached into the air as women eagerly sought to raise comments and questions.

The energy in the room, buzzing with collective support and sympathetic outrage, empowered women to share a range of experiences and to question a multitude of inequalities. After several minutes, the conversation shifted to focus on what one attendee referred to as "mommy guilt." Once she introduced this term and reflected aloud on how she often felt torn between the societal expectations of being a successful mother and of being a successful academic, numerous others took up the same thread. For nearly the remainder of the time allotted to audience discussion, those who spoke focused on the seeming impossibility of being both a scholar and mother. This discussion was wonderful, in that it is one that rarely receives true attention in academic settings, and it was clear in many women's body language that they felt celebration and relief in finally being heard, finally being understood.

However, Stephanie sat in her chair frustrated, fearing the possibility of a backlash if she offered a critique of the trajectory of the discussion. As the session's scheduled time neared its end, however, she tentatively raised her hand and offered,

> I recognize the challenges of motherhood for any woman in our society, and of all of the ways that academia is unkind to mothers. I have absolute respect for all of you who raise children. But, I'm really bothered that the room's discussions have shifted to focus only on that aspect of what it means to be a woman. I don't plan to have children, but I certainly share realities with all of you, like being underpaid, undervalued, overworked. And, focusing only on motherhood excludes a lot of different kinds of women.

Issues of child rearing and being a wife had dominated the collective narrative and centered traditional notions of womanhood as heterosexual, as cisgender, and as married partners raising children. Others began to nod; faces registered recognition and agreement. And then, the session was over. Another panel was waiting for the room. As the previously packed space began to empty, Audrey Lensmire, one of the panelists, hastily invited any who were interested in continuing the discussion to gather outside.

That is when we met. Jill, Tanetha, and Audrey left the raised platform and joined Stephanie and chapter author Amy Tondreau in one of the convention center hallways. We each thanked the others for their contributions to the discussion and agreed that considering women's experiences both within and beyond notions of parenting was important. We agreed that we would submit a revised and expanded NCTE proposal for the following year that would again examine women's experiences in academia, but with a more intentional emphasis on intersectionality. That was our beginning, and it was one that was strongly committed to exploring a diversity of women's experiences, identities, and understandings in higher education. And thus the plan for the book was born.

THE POLITICAL CONTEXTS OF WOMEN'S EXPERIENCES

In the year following when we three met, the US 2016 Presidential Election was in full force, and it unquestionably shaped us, the places we live and work, and this book. Primary elections winnowed the field down to two major candidates: Hillary Clinton, the first female Presidential candidate to be nominated by a major US political party, and Donald J. Trump, whose controversial, and often derisive, comments regarding a number of groups (e.g., women, those with disabilities, immigrants, Muslims) galvanized the nation's political landscape. When the three of us met again for our session on women's experiences in academia at NCTE, it had been less than two weeks since Trump had been declared the next President. This context made our session, which had already been important to us, feel incredibly relevant in new ways.

The discussions that we brought to the conference were proudly feminist, but Trump's election had thrown the traditional notions of feminism into question. Prior to the election, numerous polls had confidently predicted Clinton's win (e.g., Rhodan and Johnson 2016; Westcott 2016). In the aftermath, the inevitable sifting through the election data began in an effort to understand how the election had gone so differently than expected. One of the most significant findings was that a cornerstone of Trump's electorate had been women—specifically, college-educated White women (Featherstone 2016; Scott 2017). Such a result seemed counterintuitive, that women would select Trump as their political voice, when "he was recorded bragging about…grab[bing] women's genitals without their permission…made degrading comments about a female political rival…[and] has a history of making sexist comments about his employees" (Scott 2017, para. 6). As former First Lady Michelle Obama put it, women who voted for Trump arguably "voted against their own voice" (Hansler 2017).

However, as the nation worked to understand how election predictions had been so inaccurate, many racially minoritized US women were not perplexed, were not at all surprised. The election result was not the origination of the term "White Feminism," but it was a moment when the term had a clear frame of reference. Author Tamara Winfrey Harris (2016) wrote, "The triumph of President-elect Donald Trump represents the failure of many things. One of them is white feminism" (para. 3). White Feminism is, at its heart, characterized by "the needs of straight, white, middle-class American women" (para. 4) while ignoring the realities and needs of women with multiple intersections, such as racially minoritized women, transwomen, queer women, low-income women, rural women, and disabled women. It is a claim of feminism made by the women who most benefit from the status quo, and that contention is anti-feminist and ultimately hurts *all* women and *all* of society.

It was within this sociopolitical context that we gathered to discuss women's experiences in academia at NCTE. Our initial proposal for our panel had intended to promote women's self-advocacy within higher education, while examining women's experiences including and beyond motherhood. As we presented, sitting and talking with other women in our session who were similarly working to understand the election and the simultaneous mobilization and problematization of "White Feminism," our discussions actively underscored intersectional understandings of women in academia. The previous year's panel had been intentionally diverse, without an overt emphasis on intersectionality, but this year was different—there was a need to deliberately discuss feminist concepts as constantly intersecting, rather than risking any form of slippage back to "White Feminism," which had masqueraded as an investment in women's experiences while only interested in specific versions of womanhood.

As our session came to a close, several of those present reflected on the range of ways that we had and might have discussed women in higher education. With earnestness and fervor, we heard over and over again, "This session ought to be a book." We left the session, gathered around a bench, and began to plan to do just that. We had all agreed with others' assertions that "there ought to be a book about this stuff"; now, we would ensure that there was one. And, we would work intentionally so that our book was mindful of the diversity inherent in the term "women" and respectful to the ranges of experiences that women might have in academia.

INTERSECTIONALITY AND WOMEN IN ACADEMIA

From the beginning, we operated within a feminist theoretical framework and continuously returned to Kimberlé Crenshaw's (1989) concept of "intersectionality" as a guiding tenet. As Gloria Steinem pointed out following the 2016 election, "There is no such thing as 'white feminism.' Because if it's white, it's not feminism. It's either talking about all women, or it's not" (Blay 2017, para. 7). We would extend Steinem's statement to say that feminist work, in working to represent and support *all* women, is necessarily and unceasingly intersectional. Specifically, we understand intersectionality to refer to the interconnectedness of social and identity categories, including but not limited to race, ethnicity, socioeconomic class, gender identity, gender expression, sexual orientation, language, geography, and able-bodiedness. As we moved from the planning stages to making the book a reality, we specifically adopted Crenshaw's concept of challenging a "single-axis framework" as a means of supporting intersectional understandings of identities and experiences (1989, 139). Crenshaw points out that a dominant tendency in any form of social justice-oriented scholarship has been inadvertently to reinscribe oppressive discourses by ignoring the multifaceted nature of personal identities. An example of this single axis could be "White Feminism," which centers the experiences of White women to "represent" those of all women, while ignoring the ways that, for example, racially targeted women face oppressions from which White women are exempt.

Feminism, Intersectionality, and This Book

This book adopts an intersectional approach in an effort to be as inclusive and applicable to the diversity of women in higher education as is possible, without ever claiming to be comprehensive. We acknowledge that we have not included every possible perspective or issue that is important to women academics, as doing so is arguably impossible, but we have worked diligently to offer a variety of voices, trajectories, identities, and perspectives. For example, the narratives found here feature the experiences of graduate students, adjunct faculty, clinical faculty, tenure-track faculty; women of varying socioeconomic backgrounds; racially minoritized women; women outside the USA; LGBTQ+ women.

In addition to the demographic diversity that is integral to this project, we have included a wide range of topics in its narrative-based chapters. This emphasis on narrative-based writing is an effort, informed by feminist researchers, to blur the boundaries between academic and personal accounts, and to emphasize the personal as being both political and worthy of academic attention (e.g., DeVault and Gross 2007; Hainisch 1970; Smith 1987). The women in this book discuss, through their personal narratives, topics such as power dynamics in personal relationships, emotionality as a perceived weakness in academics, and the taken-for-grantedness of women's labor as integral aspects of women's identities in academia. We would add that a narrative-based approach has provided opportunities here for often excluded and disenfranchised women to share their higher education experiences in a space that decenters standard research writing (e.g., Hinton 1966; McLaren 2000), while simultaneously making these materials accessible to a range of readers, including those both inside and outside academia.

We were deliberate about both the book's sections' and chapters' order. Each of the four parts reflects major elements of the conversations that we have had and have encountered—from our conference interactions, our discussions with colleagues and one another, our daily lives, and the authors' input—that provide broad organizational threads that weave the various chapters together in complementary but unique narratives of women's diverse experiences in higher education.

PART I: THE SUPERWOMAN COMPLEX: THE CHALLENGES OF FAMILY LIFE FOR WOMEN IN THE ACADEMY

The starting point for the book's narratives is the place where we three met several years ago: a discussion of women's familial roles. However, in response to the discussion that we had in 2015, this section offers a variety of considerations of what it means for a woman to simultaneously navigate family life and the academy. The section opens with Amy Tondreau's chapter, a version of which was a part of our NCTE 2016 session, written from her perspective as a graduate student. She explores the concept of a "trailing spouse" and the fragility of marriage when it is the wife who pursues the advanced degree, not the husband. Maureen A. Flint's chapter follows and considers the ways that loss, pain, and love shape a daughter's "becoming" in graduate school in the wake of her mother's death. Kelly W. Guyotte's chapter offers a raw reflection on navigating motherhood as an early career faculty member, while wrestling with the uncertainties of being a mother. Sarah R. Hick offers a narrative that balances humor and frustration, as she supports her wife in the delivery room while considering her former insistence on a child-free life. Sharon I. Radd offers camping as a literal and metaphorical image to discuss the freedom and joy that she has found through both her family and her profession. This section offers a range of professional trajectories, from graduate programs through an established academic career, and it insists on a variety of ways to understand both "family" and the ways that women might navigate these ties within the academy.

Part II: The Less Traveled and Less Valued Pathways: Examining the Devaluation of Women's Contributions to the Academy

Research has confirmed that, as is the case in most facets of society, women in academia typically work harder than men but earn substantially less (AAUP 2016; Jaschik 2011). The academy is a space where a growing number of women are finding positions, but they continue to find their presences and contributions devalued. This section provides a rare space for women to explore the ways that their paths in higher education have been less traveled, in that they took—by design or by force—routes that deviate from the more well-worn roads and the ways that those less-frequented pathways have been undervalued by colleagues, partners, families, society, and sometimes themselves. Cheryl R. Richardson's narrative describes an international professional adventure with a number of obstacles along the way, including battling self-doubt, but ultimately guided by a commitment to the notions of "career" and racial equity. Tanetha Jamay Grosland, one of the book's editors, shares her journey—one that some would deem winding and aimless—as purposeful in its self-searching and self-finding. Stephanie P. Jones explores the ways that an ancestry of enslavement both pains and empowers her to draw from the past as she crafts a future both based on her heritages and of her own making. This section centers the narratives that are rarely given space and attention: those that focus on the realities of pain, of gendered choices, and of women's journeys as always tied to pasts and futures that are simultaneously individual and collective.

Part III: The Importance of Intersectionality: Exploring the Diversities of Women in the Academy

Intersectionality runs throughout this book, with each chapter exploring the ways that various components of authors' identities mattered in their recounted experiences and continue to matter in their everyday lives. These chapters are unique in their discussions of intersectionality, in that the authors here explicitly examine why intersectionality is so critical for them and for higher education. Lisa M. Dembouski's chapter begins this section and offers a difficult yet humorous consideration of deafness as an important factor in her lived experiences, her scholarship, and her daily interactions with colleagues and her institution. The challenges that she faces in insisting on equal access for all on her campus set up the overarching theme in this section of the necessity of and consistent resistance toward intersectionality, even in well-meaning and social justice-oriented settings. Erica R. Davila and Ann M. Aviles, co-authors and cousins, take up this thread in their chapter's discussion on their efforts to honor their identities as Afro-Puerto Rican women, as they teach themselves and their students to honor ancestries and histories, while faced with the realities of racism, patriarchy, and anti-immigrant sentiments in the USA. Continuing this necessary examination of race and racism in higher education, Daniela Gachago offers an honest and sometimes painful critique of her coming to terms with her own White privilege and identity as a White woman in South Africa. Closing this section is Aryah O. S. Lester's narrative exploring the complexities of being an educator who is a transwoman of color, and the physical and professional risks that come with her multifaceted identity. Her chapter closes with an important call that echoes throughout this section for more substantial efforts to integrate intersectional understandings and approaches into education and into discussions of women's experiences.

PART IV: VULNERABILITY IN THE ACADEMY: WOMEN EXPLORE EMOTIONALITY, AFFECT, AND SELF-CARE

We made a very deliberate decision to close the book with a section focusing on vulnerability. Often, and particularly in much of academia, emotionality and honest vulnerability are characterized as "weak," "unprofessional," and most of all, "feminine," which is nearly always equivalent with "less than." The pervading attitude is that moments of openness, of personal hurt, belong outside the office and the classroom. Here, those narratives are given a place of distinction—because they matter; because they are important. Meghan E. Barnes's chapter sets this section's tone, as she recounts the grief of navigating her doctoral program while coping with betrayal and divorce. Janine de Novais considers her own efforts to manage her responses to others' pressures and assumptions while a single mother completing a doctoral program far from home. Alyssa Niccolini's chapter draws on metaphor to examine the realities of her expendability as an adjunct instructor. All three of these chapters offer a form of resolution, but they are all heavy with hurt and uncertainty. Cheryl E. Matias closes this section and the book by offering the image of a reborn phoenix as a means of demonstrating the ways that her and others' moments of vulnerability may ultimately lead to renewed strength and self-worth.

Honoring Hidden and Suppressed Narratives

This book's exploration of the diversities and complexities of women's experiences in higher education is invaluable, as this range of narratives celebrates stories that are often hidden and suppressed. While each author's experiences are unique, we argue that those diversities present a meaningful and cohesive overall narrative of the complexities of womanhood in academia. Taken as a whole, the book highlights the importance of rejecting a single-axis framework of understanding women in academia and of reaffirming intersectionality in a way that honors often devalued and derided characteristics, such as emotionality and professional vulnerability. We now invite you to hear the stories of the women in these pages.

References

AAUP: American Association of University Professors. 2016. "Women in the Academic Profession." *AAUP Issues*. December 20, 2017. https://www.aaup.org/issues/women-academic-profession.

Blay, Zeba. 2017. "Gloria Steinem on Why There Is No Such Thing as 'White Feminism.'" *Huffington Post*. May 5, 2017. https://www.huffingtonpost.com/entry/gloria-steinem-on-why-there-is-no-such-thing-as-white-feminism_us_590b5136e4b0d5d90499fce8.

Crenshaw, Kimberlé. 1989. "Demarginalizing the Intersection of Race and Sex: A Black Feminist Critique of Antidiscrimination Doctrine, Feminist Theory, and Antiracist Politics." *University of Chicago Legal Forum*: 139–167.

DeVault, Marjorie L., and Glenda Gross. 2007. "Feminist Interviewing: Experience, Talk, and Knowledge." In *Handbook of Feminist Research: Theory and Praxis*, edited by Shirley Nagy Hesse-Biber, 173–198. Thousand Oaks: Sage.

Featherstone, Liza. 2016. "Elite, White Feminism Gave Us Trump: It Needs to Die." *Verso Books*. November 12, 2016. https://www.versobooks.com/blogs/2936-elite-white-feminism-gave-us-trump-it-needs-to-die.

Hanisch, Carol. 1970. "The Personal Is Political." In *Notes from the Second Year: Women's Liberation: Major Writings of the Radical Feminists*, edited by Anne Koedt Shulamith, 76–78. New York: New York Radical Women.

Hansler, Jennifer. 2017. "Michelle Obama: 'Any Woman Who Voted Against Hillary Clinton Voted Against Their Own Voice.'" *CNN Politics*. September 27, 2017. http://www.cnn.com/2017/09/27/politics/michelle-obama-women-voters/index.html.

Harris, Tamara Winfrey. 2016. "Some of Us Are Brave: The Failure of White Feminism." *Bitch Media*. November 16, 2016. https://www.bitchmedia.org/article/some-us-are-brave-0.

Hinton, William. 1966. *Fanshen: A Documentary of Revolution in a Chinese Village*. New York: Monthly Review Press.

Jaschik, Scott. 2011. "The Enduring Gender Gap in Pay." *Inside Higher Ed*. April 5, 2011. https://www.insidehighered.com/news/2011/04/052/the_enduring_gender_gap_in_faculty_pay.

McLaren, Anne E. 2000. "The Grievance Rhetoric of Chinese Women: From Lamentations to Revolution." *Intersections: Gender, History and Culture in the Asian Context* 4 (17). http://intersections.anu.edu.au/issue4/mclaren.html.

Rhodan, Maya, and David Johnson. 2016. "Here are 7 Electoral College Predictions for Tuesday." *Time*. November 8, 2016. http://time.com/4561625/electoral-college-predictions/.

Scott, Eugene. 2017. "Millions of American Women Disagree with Michelle Obama: Donald Trump Is Their Voice." *The Washington Post*. September 28, 2017. https://www.washingtonpost.com/news/the-fix/wp/2017/09/28/millions-of-american-women-disagree-with-michelle-obama-donald-trump-is-their-voice/?tid=sm_fb&utm_term=.90789a3d4abd.

Smith, Dorothy E. 1987. *The Everyday World as Problematic: A Feminist Sociology*. Boston: Northeastern University Press.

Westcott, Lucy. 2016. "Presidential Election Polls for November 1, 2016." *Newsweek*. November 1, 2016. http://www.newsweek.com/presidential-election-polls-november-1-clinton-trump-515705.

PART I

The Superwoman Complex: The Challenges of Family Life for Women in the Academy

CHAPTER 2

"I Would Never Let My Wife Do That": The Stories We Tell to Stay Afloat

Amy Tondreau

DISSATISFACTION

My husband and I grew up at opposite ends of the smallest state in the nation. Rhode Island can be an insular place, one that many of its residents don't leave. It's a small-town mentality taken state-wide, one large experiment of seven degrees of separation. As wide-eyed high school sweethearts, Matt and I ventured as far as Boston for college, then graduated, and settled into a Boston suburb less than an hour's drive from both my parents and my in-laws.

From the outside, I imagine it looked like we were living the suburban American dream. Married a bit over two years, Matt and I enjoyed our life together. I spent my days in a colorful 4th-grade classroom reading and writing with precocious kids on the verge of middle school, across the hall from a mentor teacher who was like my second mother. I was in a great district with the kind of job that I could hold for the next thirty years. Matt was moving up the corporate ladder in a Fortune 500 company. We rented a cute apartment with a backyard, an easy drive north to our friends in Boston or south to our family in Rhode Island.

A. Tondreau (✉)
Teachers College, Columbia University, New York, NY, USA

On Saturdays, Matt went golfing, and I'd hit Target and get a pedicure, or we'd catch my nephew's baseball game. Some sunny Sunday mornings when the mood struck us, we'd visit open houses and talk about buying a place. Everything was comfortable. We were happy.

Except.

Except for the nagging feeling that something wasn't right. It started out small enough that I could ignore it—a bad day, a rough month. But across several years, my sense of claustrophobia grew and grew until it took over. I felt like I was suffocating. I looked around and realized that I didn't want to buy a house and have a baby. I didn't want to welcome another crop of 4th graders every year until my current crop was middle-aged. It felt selfish, but I wanted…more.

But, as much as I knew that I wanted something else, I wasn't really sure what that something else might be. What else was I qualified to do? I was finishing a master's degree that would allow me to become a reading specialist, but that seemed like a different version of the same story. Administration seemed like too much budgeting and facilities management, and seven years into teaching, it felt too late to choose a different career and start over. So, when my advisor in my master's program suggested a doctoral program, I was surprised. When he suggested that I could attend a top-tier institution, I was shocked. I'd always been a good student, and I genuinely loved learning, but academia was for older gentlemen in tweed jackets with suede elbow patches or for scientists who loved laboratories and spreadsheets. No one in my family or circle of friends had pursued that path, and I had never considered it a space that was open to me.

Still, my advisor was encouraging, and he coached me through the application process. When Matt and I talked it over, he echoed my advisor's confidence. While my main concern remained whether or not I could even get into these programs, Matt's main concern was the finances of it all, which we couldn't seem to get any candid answers about. After our initial research, we decided to test the waters. I applied to exactly three schools, all in northeastern cities where we already had friends or family. I imagined it as a way of calling my advisor's bluff, and after the rejections rolled in and proved that academia wasn't for me, I could readjust my expectations or look for another path forward. Imposter syndrome is real, friends.

The first sign that things might not be quite as straightforward as I'd imagined came when I sat down with my advisor toward the end of the application process. I assumed he might have some last-minute feedback on my essay or tips on recommendation letters. When he began asking about my husband, I was taken aback. *Was my marriage strong?* His question rebounded around my brain as he explained that doctoral programs often lead to divorce (see also Barnes, this volume). *His* doctoral program had led to *his* divorce. I stammered some version of my condolences. "I don't mean to scare you, but it's really hard on a marriage. Divorce happens more than you'd think," he said. "You should take that into consideration as you make your decisions over the next few months." Still imagining there would be no decision to make, I wasn't *too* concerned. But the question stuck with me. And when two acceptance letters arrived, that question demanded an answer.

Permission

Thankfully, I married a man who treated me as a partner and supported my ambitions. He analyzed the pros and cons of each program with me, gave me pep talks when I thought that I couldn't possibly hold my own academically, and figured out our budget when we decided on a school. At work, he negotiated to spend two days a week in the office in Massachusetts and work the rest of the week from our new home. Together, we decided to pick up and move our lives to New York City. We talked through every choice along the way, as a team. That's not to say there weren't arguments and anxiety and tears (there were plenty), but we felt as though we were making thoughtful, responsible decisions. We would quickly learn, however, that not everyone agreed with our assessment.

Most of the initial pushback came from Matt's colleagues. When he explained our plans to move, some asked invasive questions about our plans for a family. Others asked equally invasive questions about our finances, openly calculating the expected "return on investment" for my education, and finding it wanting. But the responses that surprised me most had to do with permission.

One colleague, upon hearing our plans, looked Matt in the eyes and said, "Man, that's crazy. I would never let my wife do that."

Matt met this man's gaze and replied, "Well, I guess you haven't met my wife. I don't *let* her do anything."

In a way, that story became our identity. That moment, those phrases, became our mantra as we slogged through the challenges of relocating—packing, apartment hunting, the mountains of paperwork required for a New York City rental agreement—and the process of figuring out what our lives in the city would look like once we got there. We'd retell the story to each other to prove that we were the ones in on the joke, brave enough to venture out and disrupt the status quo. We were the ones who didn't need permission to live our lives as we chose. That story became armor we didn't even know we would need for the battles yet to come.

INITIATION

I entered into my first semester as a doctoral student with a great deal of privilege and support. I was able to attend school full-time, to focus on classes and my fellowship, while my husband commuted across hours and states, back and forth each week. So, I also entered that semester with a great deal of guilt. Transitioning from working full-time to taking out loans and asking my partner to make such sacrifices felt awful. I feared that I wouldn't (or couldn't) make it through the first year of doctoral work, which culminated in a make it or break it examination. The potent combination of guilt and fear made that first year a caffeine-fueled blur of anxiety.

The state of that first year was epitomized by our Tuesday evenings. Matt would drive back from Boston after work on Tuesdays. I had six hours of classes, stacked back to back until 9:00 p.m., on Tuesday nights. (*"Won't it be nice to get all of those classes done at once?"* my precious, naïve former self had thought.) Matt and I would meet up in our new neighborhood, exhausted and cranky, and attempt to find a parking space that would not earn us another ticket. It was the perfect recipe for a screaming match, every single week. I began to understand what my advisor had been talking about.

Of course, Tuesday night fights were not the only issue that arose. While I was able to build a new social network in the city through my classes and roles at the university, Matt was spending half of his week in another state, and the rest separated from his previous social circle without many opportunities to build a new one. We also juggled new distributions of the chores and errands that made up daily life. I couldn't carry groceries back from the store by myself, let alone find the time to plan and cook dinners every night, as I had done before our move. Matt was out of state for part of the week, leaving me to manage laundry, bill paying, the post office, or whatever else came up on those days. Who dealt with the landlord? Who dealt with the cockroaches? New responsibilities and old ones began to overwhelm us. It felt like our life in New York was temporary, a test we needed to pass until life could return to "normal." We were barely keeping our heads above water, and the doubt crept in.

PERFORMANCE

In the midst of our practical concerns, we overlooked some of the larger issues that animated our struggles. Not only were we grappling with the challenges of orienting to newly divided responsibilities and a new city, we were also grappling with our gender roles. Despite our story about standing up to sexist co-workers, we had never really escaped the patriarchy. Specifically, the role of a trailing spouse, or the spouse who relocates for his or her life partner's career, is typically cast as female (Cooke, 2001, 419). While men's work is historically viewed as important enough to uproot a family, women's professional roles have not been valued in the same way. When a woman relocates for her male partner, the hegemonic gendered notion remains that her work is in their new home (Bailey and Cooke, 1998, 101). The care work traditionally taken on by women is portable, able to be done wherever the home (and/or children) might be. When we sought out resources for trailing spouses, we found blogs and articles like, "Fighting the Expat Blues: 5 Tips for Expat Wives Abroad" (Reilly, n.d.) or the writer of "Memoirs of a Trailing Spouse," who bemoaned, "few ever think of the frazzled... mom (commonly known as the trailing or accompanying spouse) with toddlers in tow, left to fend for themselves in a foreign land and foreign language, while her husband goes off to long days at the office or on extended business trips" (Wilcox, 2013). None of it seemed to fit our experience.

Matt's coping mechanism was to try to play a "tough guy" role. He tried to roll with the punches, to pretend that he liked living in a big city and that he could handle the stress of his weekly commute. He didn't want to admit how much he disliked work, particularly now that he was the sole breadwinner. How could he look for a new job when we needed his paycheck to make rent? With a social network at home that had proven it didn't understand our choices, and no new social network built up, to whom could he have admitted his struggles?

At the time, though, I was unaware that my husband was having difficulty adjusting. This was partly because he was trying to hide it, and partly because I was too busy drowning in my own concerns. Judgment of my choices was both implicit and explicit, both self-imposed and inflicted in the careless remarks of family members, Matt's co-workers, or even strangers. According to Bolton (2000), the "third shift" consists of the self-doubt and anxiety a woman can feel about the way she handles her conflicting obligations, following her "first shift" at work and "second shift" at home. My guilt grew each time we needed to order takeout, the dishes went undone, or we ran out of something I "should" have remembered to pick up at the store. I felt selfish for taking the time that I needed to camp out in the library, reading and writing and thinking, when I "should" have been working, cooking, or cleaning. I felt even more selfish moving away from my aging parents and hearing about my father's dialysis or my niece and nephew's soccer games from several states away. Even our United Parcel Service (UPS) delivery guy shook his head disapprovingly when he asked what *exactly* it was I was going to school for and laughed when I told him how long it would take.

My perceived failings in my "second shift" at home and the self-doubt of my "third shift" placed extra pressure on my "first shift": school. The anxiety inherent in the competition and intensity of doctoral work was a sea that sometimes threatened to drown me but always surrounded me, battering me with wave after wave. Afraid that each opportunity offered to me might be the last, I said yes to everything. Guilt over my decreased financial contribution coupled with my undying need to prove my intellectual competence made each individual decision seem easy. Yet, it quickly became clear that my (arguably gendered) inability to say no and desire to please were liabilities. I took on too much. I began placing other obligations, such as meeting with students well beyond my teaching assistant (TA) office hours or taking the subway to distant schools that no one else wanted to travel to for coaching or supervision, ahead of moving my own work forward. Worse, I began to burn myself out. By the end of my second year, I started to consider the possibility that I might not finish the program.

Days passed, and we muddled our way through. I would start crying in the middle of otherwise quotidian conversations. Matt's temper flared up over seemingly trivial things. We began drinking with dinner each night, something we hadn't done before the move; some nights we started drinking even earlier. We worried and wallowed and raged in seemingly equal parts.

Of course, looking back now, it seems like a case study out of a textbook. The patriarchy, imposter syndrome, social isolation, depression, and anxiety each played its stereotypical part. In that first year, though, I didn't have the vocabulary to name any of them. No one else in my cohort seemed to be struggling, and I didn't want to be the one to bring it up. I thought it was just me. Just us. *Was my marriage strong?*

REVISION

I wish I could identify a turning point, one event that turned things around. Instead, it was a more gradual realization that we couldn't stay so miserable. And for anything to change, we had to take action. So, in moments a bit too raw and personal to recount here, we began to confess our fears and unhappiness to one another and began trusting that we could help each other through them. Once we were honest with one another, it was easier to be honest with ourselves about what we needed. The most crucial first step was that, with the help of our doctors, we pursued therapy and medication for the mental health issues that we faced. Accepting help didn't come naturally to either of us, and we had to experiment and give ourselves time to figure out what each of us could be comfortable with. We started reading books on communication, mindfulness, anxiety, vulnerability, and happiness; tweeting and emailing articles back and forth; or reading passages aloud to each other. We explored our "love languages" and Myers-Briggs types, dove headfirst into Brené Brown books about having the courage to be vulnerable, and tried the Marie Kondo method and meditation. Our attempts were haphazard at first, but we gradually developed more purpose as we learned what resonated with us, what worked, and what didn't. We learned vocabulary to name what we felt and why, and increased our awareness of the discourses that circulated in and around us. We tried to accumulate all the tools we could, individually and together, to pull ourselves out of the water and onto solid ground again.

It was slow, meandering progress. Thankfully, both of us stuck it out and did the work. Some of it was independent, and some of it was together. First, we landed on lasting solutions with our doctors; I stuck with medication for my anxiety; and Matt stuck with therapy for his depression. Then, we could address more practical matters. We got rid of the car and moved to a new apartment. Matt found a new job that he hated, then another new one that he loves. We named my third year in the doctoral program "The Year of No," and I worked on being more intentional with my time; after the year was over, I was ready to defend my dissertation proposal. I had to learn to say no to things other people wanted me to do in order to say yes to my own work.

In short, Matt and I were able to re-narrate our New York City academia experience by centering ourselves as agentive actors in the story (Johnston, 2004). As Connelly and Clandinin (1990) argue, "humans are storytelling organisms, who, individually and socially, lead storied lives" (2). From a narrative perspective, we had to see that our story could be rewritten, and that we were the ones who needed to begin revising it. We also had to see each other (and ourselves) as multifaceted, fluid characters. Despite our now seven years of marriage and sixteen years together, or perhaps because of it, we are not the same people we once were. Our identities have shifted and multiplied, conflicting and constantly becoming (Moje and Luke, 2009). The city, the distance from our families, the new jobs, and new experiences challenged and changed us. We had to make space in our relationship for that change. We had to relearn each other and ourselves—an academic and a trailing spouse, a yogi and a runner, introverts, New Yorkers. It's this work that we took on together, and continue to take on, that ultimately allows me to answer the question my advisor posed years ago: Yes, my marriage is strong. Maybe it wasn't, really, back when he posed the question. But we've built it that way, choice by choice.

Continuation

This story—my story—might seem like a linear victory narrative, but I assure you that it is not. It's a constructed representation that follows the purposeful path of a story arc, ingrained as it is as a way to make coherence from the chaos of life. But this story is very much still being written. Beginning year five of my doctoral program, I'm trying to persist to graduation and avoid the dreaded all-but-dissertation (A.B.D.) label. There is, again, mounting pressure to start a family. I've mainly avoided the questions over the past few years, but graduation will also mean a resurgent interest in my uterus. Matt still doesn't like New York City, and I fall more in love with it each day. I feel a ticking countdown clock on my time here and sometimes cry in the midst of conversations about leaving. Our "Two-Body Problem" remains. As Wolf-Wendel et al. (2004) argue, the difficulty of two professional life partners obtaining jobs in the same location (or a reasonable commuting distance from one another) often forces a "no-win" situation: Either one individual may be forced to abandon a career for the other, or the relationship may falter due to the distance between the spouses' jobs. Consequently, Matt and I still aren't sure how to decide where to go next. Do we move for my career again? Is it Matt's turn to choose a place he'd like to live? Can we afford to wait here until I get a "real" job? Will I ever pay back my loans?

It's messy. It's been messy, and it will continue to be messy. What matters, I think, is admitting to the mess and letting others see it. It's uncomfortable, but it's the only way that we're not in the mess alone. It's hard, but it's the only way we know that our messes are not unique. It's complicated, but it's the only way we can break down our isolation and be in this together. I don't have all the answers, but I do have my story, and I'll work to create spaces where more of us can share our stories with one another.

References

Bailey, Adrian J., and Thomas J. Cooke. 1998. "Family Migration and Employment: The Importance of Migration History and Gender." *International Regional Science Review* 21, no. 2 (August): 99–118.

Bolton, Michele. 2000. *The Third Shift: Managing Hard Choices in Our Careers, Homes, and Lives as Women*. San Francisco: Jossey-Bass.

Connelly, F. Michael, and D. Jean Clandinin. 1990. "Stories of Experience and Narrative Inquiry." *Educational Researcher* 19, no. 5 (June): 2–14.

Cooke, Thomas J. 2001. "'Trailing Wife' or 'Trailing Mother'? The Effect of Parental Status on the Relationship Between Family Migration and the Labor-Market Participation of Married Women." *Environment and Planning* 33, no. 3 (March): 419–430.

Johnston, Peter. 2004. *Choice Words: How Our Language Affects Children's Learning*. Portland: Stenhouse.

Moje, Elizabeth Birr, and Allan Luke. 2009. "Literacy and Identity: Examining the Metaphors in History and Contemporary Research." *Reading Research Quarterly* 44, no. 4 (October): 415–437.

Reilly, Rachel K. n.d. "Fighting the Expat Blues: 5 Tips for Expat Wives Abroad." *InterNations*. Accessed December 8, 2017. https://www.internations.org/guide/global/fighting-the-expat-blues-5-tips-for-expat-wives-abroad-16471.

Wilcox, Quenby. 2013. "Introduction," Memoirs of a Trailing Spouse. *Global Expats Blog*, November 13, 2013. https://globalxpatsblog.wordpress.com/.

Wolf-Wendel, Lisa, Susan B. Twombly, and Suzanne Rice. 2004. *The Two-Body Problem: Dual-Career Couple Hiring Practices in Higher Education*. Baltimore: John Hopkins University Press.

CHAPTER 3

Building a Compass: Leaving, Loss, and Daughterhood in Academia

Maureen A. Flint

When I picture my mother, she is laughing, her head tilted back, hair pushed back from her face, eyes alight. My mother, who taught her three daughters how to explore the world with curiosity and creativity, to take up space, talk back, take a seat at the table, and stand up for injustices, big and small. As I navigate my way toward a doctoral degree, my mother and her womanhood have guided that journey, building compasses to chart the way. My mother, who died on a Sunday morning in April, four years after she was diagnosed with Lou Gehrig's disease [amyotrophic lateral sclerosis (ALS)]. My mother, who continues to become woman in the actions of her daughters, our performances of womanhood that intertwine and echo her (Butler 1990).

French philosophers Deleuze and Guattari (1987) describe the micro-movements of becoming woman as a femininity that is particular, fluid, and specific. Through these small negotiations and performances (unconsciously tucking hair behind ears, biting my bottom lip to concentrate), woman replicates and becomes different and particular through repetition. I am echoing my mother as I twist her ring around my finger, contemplating the next sentence, even as this repeating of a small

M. A. Flint (✉)
University of Alabama, Tuscaloosa, AL, USA

action becomes part of my womanhood. As I become woman, I am at once replicating my mother as I am becoming in a way that is specific and distinguishable from her: I am becoming daughter. Reflecting on my journey into academia, I find that my compasses of womanhood are produced through the memories and moments of my mother, or who I remember her to be. Becoming daughter: Stopping the car to gather armfuls of goldenrod in September, hanging up pink flamingo lights around the porch in the summertime, singing out of tune to the radio. Never finishing a knitting project, coming home from work smelling like oil paint, and stubbornly supporting liberal candidates in a relentlessly conservative town. Becoming woman is fleeting, transitory, wrapped up in moments of daughterhood and motherhood that are specific to places and times.

Several years ago, I was making dinner with a friend from my master's degree cohort whose mother had also passed away. As we waited for the food to bake, she asked me a question that has stuck with me since, reverberating through the map of choices that have led me toward a Ph.D. program, my becoming woman/daughter in academia. She asked me,

> do you ever feel like everything you've done since your Mom passed away, everything you will do, all the things you're going to accomplish... mean nothing because she's not there to share it with?...
>
> ...
>
> ...

"Nothing" is an aching, hollow word, and even now, years after this conversation, there's no denying that to lose your (my) mother creates an emptiness that is more than body. Does another body ever fill that place? Who do you look to for support, for encouragement, for advice? How do you become woman in academia (and beyond) without a mother? How do you navigate the journey toward a Ph.D. without a compass? Building a map from memories that are fading at the edges, memories that might be dreams or just photographs, a process of becoming daughter.

Following these micro-moments of becoming woman/daughter follows feminist scholar Rosi Braidotti (2006, 2011), who advocates for a politics of location that zigzags through multiple time zones, charting nonlinear paths of transpositions and becoming(s). To chart my becoming woman/daughter in academia is to follow a zigzagging voyage from New York to Alabama, a journey of leavings (my hometown, "The City," career path(s), relationships) that are intertwined with my mother and woman/daughterhood, at the same time as they are ethically and emotionally wrapped up with my family: my sisters and my Dad. This is the journey I map and the compasses I build in this chapter, a narrative of becoming woman/daughter in academia.

Leaving

Five years ago, I moved from New York City to Tuscaloosa, Alabama. With this move, two years after my mother passed away, I left my family in Western New York and a career path as a patternmaker in the fashion design industry for a master's degree in higher education. During my time in Alabama, as I've moved my way through finishing my master's, working three years as a full-time staff member in student life (taking classes on the side), and most recently, making the decision to leave the track to success that is marked out in student affairs (from coordinator to assistant director to director and beyond) to become a full-time doctoral student, the narrative of leaving and navigating this path has been (and continues to be) shaped by daughterhood. The divergence of this narrative is particularly noticeable when you ask my Dad and my younger sisters, Leah and Amelia, how I ended up in Alabama to begin with:

Dad: It was because of that guy
Maureen: They were paying my tuition
Amelia: I was always kind of confused about the whole thing… and I think everyone thought, you were in New York City and were going to be a fashion designer, like you always said you would, and then suddenly you were moving to Alabama…
Maureen: The fashion industry just wasn't right for me
Leah: You know, it seemed really fast, but I was in a similar place at the time [changing my mind about what I wanted to do] so I figured, you had to do what you had to do…
Maureen: I just had to get away

Despite my persistent denial, my Dad isn't wrong. I ended up in Alabama in part because of a relationship. I never would have considered

The University of Alabama (it was an unlikely choice for someone who'd never been south of Pennsylvania for more than a week), had it not been for the urging of a long-distance love interest who lived in Birmingham, Alabama. This has always been hard for me to admit. How do I reconcile a feminist, independent, stubborn, career-motivated sense of self when/if I confess that I made a major life choice in part because of a relationship—because of a man? I've always been reticent to admit this when the inevitable question is asked (What brought you to Alabama?), anticipating judgement, being coded as not serious, weak. So, I turn the narrative, hedging and pointing to a generous assistantship working in residential life, the fact that I was ready to leave New York, a city that increasingly felt impersonal and unwelcome, a city that I'd lost my connection to. My family does not have this reticence, dredging up the (now defunct) relationship whenever the question of my unlikely move comes up. To them, perhaps the story of following makes sense, makes the pieces fit—I'd grown up never wavering from my telescoped narrative, that I was going to be an artist, like my Mom, that I was going to move to New York City. Suddenly, none of that was the case, and my family was deeply confused. Who was I if I wasn't following the compass I'd so adamantly set for myself? Lingering in the intersection of our narratives is the (never asked) statement that is at once an answer and a question: *if your mother was still here…*

Building Multiple Compasses

Dorothy Allison (1995) writes, "Two or three things I know for sure… of course it's never the same things and I'm never as sure as I'd like to be" (5). The narrative of my journey from New York to Alabama, from fashion design to academia, is one of those stories I never know if I know for sure, and I'm never as sure as I'd like to be. It is a story of multiple compasses, a journey that is fragmentary, shifting, and partial, intersected by multiple and simultaneous happenings and potential influences, a remembering that I continue to return to, rewrite, a snapshot in this moment and time. Becoming daughter as a map in creation (re)shaped through returning and remembering. I tell my journey of becoming daughter through compasses, embracing the multiple definitions of the term; an instrument that can help you find your bearings or, in another sense, a tool to draw circles and arcs that traverse space and time.

My narrative of becoming daughter in this way forgets to forget by jumping back in time (and space), following my zigzagging journey of building compasses, (re)turning to where I am from (Braidotti 2011).

FROM

I grew up in a small rural town in Western New York. Nestled at the foot of the Finger Lakes, Bath is isolated from the tourism that hits the region in the summer by a fifteen-mile stretch of vacant country highway. I was born in a small community hospital on that highway, about five minutes from the center of town, and grew up walking across the street to school every morning. Upon graduating high school, I not only knew the names of each one of the hundred and thirty people in my graduating class, but any number of intimate details surrounding their personal lives and family histories.

Mom was diagnosed the summer before my senior year of high school. My parents brought us together in the living room, a family meeting where they shared what they had only recently learned: that her loss of balance at the beach earlier that year and her sporadic trouble walking up the stairs were the initial stages of muscle atrophy and degeneration that characterize ALS. I remember crying, asking questions, researching the strange new series of words "Amyotrophic Lateral Sclerosis" on the family computer (and in vain and with increasing trepidation "cure" and "recovery"), not knowing who to tell, what to say, or how to explain it. By the time I started my senior year of high school in the fall, it seemed like everyone knew.

When I told my high school guidance counselor that I wanted to go to college in New York City she looked at me, surprised. "Still?" she asked. I reeled, *Was I doing the right thing?* A good daughter stays, she takes care of her family (see also Tondreau, this volume). A good woman makes sacrifices (Steedman 2010). My Mom and I talked, and she assured me, again and again, that she was fully behind me continuing with my dream of going to art school in New York City. For my family, there was never any doubt that I would go to New York City, and she was so adamant about my continuing on that in some way it was for her that I started applications to three schools in the city that fall. When I was accepted to Pratt, early admission in December, she danced around the living room with me, an elation that lasted both of us for weeks.

Leaving

At Pratt, I found an escape from the expectations of a small town, the role of the daughter of a dying woman. A small art and design school located in the heart of Brooklyn, Pratt is a bubble, a fenced-in city block of artists and idealism surrounded by Hasidic communities, subsidized housing, and the ever-encroaching gentrification of white-collar neighborhoods. Looking back on it, my time at Pratt fluctuated among feelings of guilt for leaving, exhilaration at the newness and adventure of the city, feelings of imposter syndrome and insecurity as an artist and designer, as well as an ever-developing sense of style that included a rotating rainbow of hair colors.

> *Dad*: That's not contagious, is it? (commenting on my [light purple] hair as we pulled into the house at Christmas)

Perhaps it was because of those tumultuous feelings that now much of my first three years are a blur. I worked hard; I remember that, homework most nights, sewing until early hours of the morning. I threw myself into class work. I made ridiculous and extravagant things, like a sleeping bag shaped like a life size bison (complete with silkscreened organ pillows), and a menswear collection parodying past boyfriends. I applied to be a resident advisor when I was a sophomore, and after that, residential life became a huge part of my life. I dated haphazardly, without commitment or real intention. I had a large and close group of girlfriends; we made dinner together and went on adventures through the city. I was rash and made mistakes, forging a compass for myself away from the confines of my small town.

All this time she was getting sicker. Sometimes I forgot to call, so wrapped up in working to forget, in maintaining a safe distance from seeing her deteriorate. My Dad would send me e-mails with the subject line "call your mother" from his office in between caring for her. Our house changed in small yet noticeable ways, the ramp built for her wheelchair off the side door, the accessible van in our driveway. It was hard to go home, especially that last Christmas, when she was immobile, helping my sisters and me through the holiday baking by painstakingly spelling out directions using a silver dot on her glasses as a pointer for her computer. She kept up with my projects and classes, showing off pictures of garments I'd made to her friends, and telling everyone she'd met about my patternmaker internship with a well-known designer. Did I do it for her? I think about that sometimes, even now, over ten years after dancing around the living room, elated together at my acceptance. Pratt was my idea, my dream, but she championed it, made it possible. At some point, doing it for her, doing it because of her became inseparable from doing it for me.

Loss

She passed away on a Sunday morning in April of my junior year. I had thought about it for so long, prepared for it, that everything seemed surreal for months, and I forgot how to talk to people for a while, feeling adrift and not knowing how to navigate the conversation of what it felt like to lose my mother. (Because was she really lost, or was it me?) Somehow, I made it through finals, and I floated through that summer in the city, a nomad. My compass of becoming woman shifted, different things becoming visible in my relationships and encounters. I looked at the women I worked with in my internship and realized that they had families they rarely saw, or had few relationships outside of their work, and I wasn't sure if that was what I wanted. I lost motivation and enthusiasm for my schoolwork, going through the motions of designing my senior collection, directionless.

Meanwhile, I'd moved from my role as a resident advisor into a leadership role as a hall director in residence life. My supervisor in the position, Grace, was understanding and thoughtful, checking in with me and supporting me unobtrusively. She would invite me over to make dinner and watch an episode of *The Good Wife* with her, and we'd sit in comfortable silence, not having to worry about what to say. Eventually, I began talking to Grace about what a career in higher education was like, and different things stuck out to me, different becomings became resonant, and I began to think of student affairs as a career path where I could focus on relationships with others, where I could have some kind of impact on the world, like my Mom had had on hers. It was with trepidation that I called my Dad one evening from my office,

Maureen: I'm thinking about going to graduate school, for higher education…
Dad: Okay, wow…
I'm going to support you in whatever you do…
…remember I don't pay for second degrees (or weddings)

I was still unsure about whether I was making the right decision about the change of career or moving to a new place. I was moving too quickly to let myself pause and think about the ever-present question. *Would you? If your mother was still here...* echoed as I applied to master's programs, was admitted to The University of Alabama, and accepted an assistantship. My Dad quietly supported me through it all, helping me to buy a car, driving to and from the city multiple times to help me move back home for a few weeks, and eventually, helped pack my small hatchback with a fraction of my belongings for the fifteen-hour drive from New York to Alabama. I told my sister Amelia that I had to get away, get out of the city, become differently because everything I was: artist/woman/daughter was so wrapped up in grief that I wasn't sure how to move forward.

Shift

Geographically, my journey of becoming woman has been one of leaving that is intertwined and intersected with my mother, her diagnosis, and death. Leaving my hometown and my Mom's diagnosis to New York City, leaving the city and my Mom's death to Alabama. Jumping forward into the present, I find myself in a different leaving, another shift in my compass, moving away from student affairs, the career path that brought me to Alabama, into the role of a full-time student, researching and writing toward a doctorate in educational research, a becoming as a qualitative scholar.

> *Amelia:* I just think everyone wonders, why are you still in school? You've been in school forever

This becoming has also meant a remaking of my map, as I venture into further uncharted territory and move further beyond the understood and safe identity and expectations my family had/has for me. The thing with leaving is that when you return, or join up again, you find that everything else has moved on, has become differently without you, and that you also no longer fit in the same way as before (Massey 2005). I've been away from home for ten years, a visitor to the house my Mom painted pink one summer in the small town in Western New York. As I return, now as a doctoral student, I wonder about my attachment to this place that I so desperately wanted (needed) to leave. My compass of becoming daughter has become not just one of womanhood in academia, but who I am as a woman with my family as I become an academic. How do I talk to my sisters about the theories I'm reading and writing about? To my Dad about my work leading workshops to teach students how to dialogue about difficult topics? How do I return home and hold onto my becoming daughter in a way that embraces my mother without discarding my family, leaving my family behind?

Returns

As I have navigated the journey toward a Ph.D., I've returned to this narrative, of hometown-diagnosis-City-death-Alabama again and again. Writing has become a way of re-encountering my mother, of becoming woman/daughter through my scholarship, building compasses from her memory. I've found myself writing more and more about my Mom, about the moments and memories and encounters of her. I've found myself flipping through the pages of a scrapbook to find a picture, suddenly remembered as I wrote the final paper for my narrative inquiry class, Mom in front of Monet's water lilies at the Museum of Modern Art (MoMA) the first time that we visited Pratt. I've been pulled from the couch while reading Braidotti's (2013) *The Posthuman* to fix to words the memory that came rushing back about the morning Dad called me at college to tell me Mom had died in the night. In the process of writing and remembering, I've returned to art and artful methods to explore these becomings of womanhood/daughterhood. Collaging, painting, sewing along with writing have become a way of remembering—or perhaps more specifically, of not forgetting. Braidotti (2013) writes on the imperceptibility of death that, "what we humans truly yearn for is to disappear by merging into this generative flow of becoming, the precondition for which is loss, disappearance, and disruption of the atomized and individual self" (136). Through these artful methods, I find myself entwining with my mother, becoming her, becoming daughter as I build multiple compasses to chart maps of becoming woman in academia.

As I write and create, my compass of becoming daughter has again shifted. Writing and creating have become a way of indexing and embodying my mother, re-memories, re-creating her through my becoming woman (becoming daughter). At the same time, this becoming woman/daughter has become a disruption of myself as bounded and individual, an awareness of my connections and co-implications with others. I think about my becoming daughter/scholar as co-implicated with my family, my sisters as becoming daughters, my Dad as becoming mother in her absence. As my writing and creating index my mother, fix her memories in words and images through my becoming daughter, I find myself asking, what responsibility do I have to my family, to the stories that I tell, to their becomings? How do I tell the story of my mother, holding in tension her story as one that is shared with—at the same time as it is known vastly differently by my sisters and my father? Hers is not just my story to tell. This has become more important as my sisters make their own journeys, their own stories of leaving, to Denver and to New Orleans, and my Dad zigzags across the country to follow us.

> *Amelia*: you don't have a responsibility to anybody but the three of us [for how you talk about Mom]

These tensions have become even more visible as I write this chapter, sending drafts to my sisters asking, *are you okay with me sharing this?* Am I representing you, our story—Mom—in a way that you feel comfortable with? Because to write this story is to write my family, to write things that we don't say to each other, feelings and memories we never talk about (except whispered between us late at night after others have gone to bed, or those moments when her absence seems so heavy that it overcomes us, and it bubbles up…*if only your mother were here…*). To write about becoming daughter could mean to become a prodigal daughter. A daughter who shares too much, who shames the family by opening the Pandora's box of our pain and past. So, I've found myself through this chapter in spaces I haven't been before, talking with my sisters on the phone about Mom, calling my Dad, saying *so I've been invited to write this chapter…* Writing this narrative, then, has been an unexpected return, another compass, a becoming daughter unto itself, a way of remaking, re-creating connections of becoming daughter (and sister).

The compass of my ethical responsibility to "The Family" as Amelia refers to it, capital letters evident in her voice, has become increasingly significant not just in my relations with my family, but as I venture in(to) the landscape of academia. Braidotti (2006) writes that "*we* are in *this* together" (119). *This* refers to the tangled and complicated relations of the here-and-now, a present that *we* (human, more-than-human, nonhuman bodies) can only navigate the present successfully if we continually choose to practice an ethical awareness and embody care toward each other. As a scholar, then, my ethical accountability to "The Family" extends beyond my sisters and Dad to the students I work with in my research on belonging and place in higher education, the ways I (re)present their voices and produce them in academic spaces and discourses. It encompasses the doing of my research as well as what I do with it, an ethical imperative to recognize my co-implicated becomings with others, a recognition that the small and everyday practices matter (Ulmer 2017). As a developing scholar, this ethic means that I envision myself in the world of academia seeking opportunities to rupture and resist small and simple stories of place and belonging that often guide our practice in higher education and student affairs, instead exploring the possibilities for tellings and (re)presentations that embrace complication and nuance.

To return to Dorothy Allison (1995): "Two or three things I know for sure and one of them is that if we are not beautiful to each other, we cannot know beauty in any form" (86). When I think of the woman I want to become, of the women my sisters will become/are becoming, beauty, an ethic of care and responsibility to each other, as intertwined with the notion of becoming daughter, and with my mother. Beauty through possibility and connections is what this zigzagging journey across geography and memory has produced for me. It is this value, of my entangled and co-implicated relation with others that forms the compass guiding me as I complete my doctoral coursework and (even as I write this chapter) my comprehensive exams. I still think, sometimes, the difficult and heart-wrenching question; (*if your mother was here*) and sometimes it's with a sadness that wells up and fills my throat, makes it difficult to breathe. But it is also, often, accompanied by a still sureness, knowing that she is still here as I become daughter/woman, that she is part of the compasses I'm building.

References

Allison, Dorothy. 1995. *Two or Three Things I Know for Sure*. New York: Penguin Group.
Braidotti, Rosi. 2006. *Transpositions: On Nomadic Ethics*. Malden: Polity Press.
———. 2011. *Nomadic Subjects: Embodiment and Sexual Difference in Contemporary Feminist Theory*. 2nd ed. New York: Columbia University Press.
———. 2013. *The Posthuman*. Malden: Polity Press.
Butler, Judith. 1990. *Gender Trouble*. New York: Routledge.

Deleuze, Gilles, and Feliz Guattari. 1987. *A Thousand Plateaus: Capitalism and Schizophrenia*. Translated by Brian Massumi. Minneapolis: University of Minnesota Press.

Massey, Doreen. 2005. *For Space*. London: Sage.

Steedman, Carolyn Kay. 2010. *Landscape for a Good Woman: A Story of Two Lives*. New Brunswick: Rutgers University Press.

Ulmer, Jasmine B. 2017. "Writing Slow Ontology." *Qualitative Inquiry* 23, no. 3 (April): 201–211.

CHAPTER 4

The Undecided Narratives of Becoming-Mother, Becoming-Ph.D.

Kelly W. Guyotte

Annabel Crabb famously noted, "The obligation for working mothers is a very precise one: the feeling that one ought to work as if one did not have children, while raising one's children as if one did not have a job" (2015, 11). The tension between mother and academic invoked anxieties and many questions as I stumbled through my first years as a doctoral student. I found myself considering if and when I might enter into both motherhood and the academy—these were decisions I did not take lightly. To be sure, there was research involved as I gathered all the information I needed to make up my mind (perhaps it is no surprise that I now find myself positioned at a university as a researcher/research methodologist…). For me, research is not just seeking data and answers to my questions; it also involves an attunement to my body, my intuition. This form of research is equally important, though is often dismissed when we prioritize the dualistic thinking that separates mind and body—a stance too common in the academy (e.g., Snowber 2011; Spry 2001). Those who know me well might call me indecisive, but it was with careful deliberation that I decided to become a mother and decided what I would do with my Ph.D.

K. W. Guyotte (✉)
University of Alabama, Tuscaloosa, AL, USA

© The Author(s) 2018
S. A. Shelton et al. (eds.), *Feminism and Intersectionality in Academia*,
https://doi.org/10.1007/978-3-319-90590-7_4

There is a compelling concept in the philosophies I read, the notion of *becoming*. While it has been taken up often, with a variety of intents, I use becoming in this chapter as a way to make sense of my experiences as a woman/mother in the academy. Becoming is described by feminist scholar Rosi Braidotti (2011b) as a positive process that opens individuals to new possibilities. It is not simply a movement from one point to another, but a breaking away from previously travelled paths, traditions, and norms with a remapping of the self as a fluid, rather than static subject. In other words, Braidotti calls becoming a zigzagging that cuts across our encounters and experiences as we explore ourselves in relation to others. It does not suggest that we "are," but that we "become." We are always in relation and in-process.

In what follows, I share my narratives of becoming that are both chronological and disruptive of the typical progression of time. As I write, recalling my experiences toward and in the academy, the memories do not appear in my mind in strict temporal order—they enmesh and are layered with conversations and experiences that came later. The past is contextualized by present reflections and understandings. To make this layering and disruption visible, the italicized vignettes inserted below work against the linearity of time. The vignettes begin with the voices of colleagues and friends and then shift to my own tellings of poignant events—all of which have affected my becoming as a mother in the academy. Braidotti (2011b) calls female memories countermemories, as they focus and move differently than the recollections and narratives prioritized in a masculine, phallogocentric culture. The countermemory "destabilizes the sanctity of the past and the authority of experience" (236), resisting dominant representations, or metanarratives, of the female subject. In other words, it honors the nonlinear and fluid memories of the female subject and also centers the response of the body. In my writing, I embrace the complexity of feminine countermemory by putting my experiences in relation to one another, across time, while also embracing the embodiment and enfleshment of these experiences. In other words, I attend to how I remember my body responding and how I came to sense those responses in my own flesh. The flutters of anxiety, the tensions in my chest, the warmth of love. In an institution that often neglects both the body and the unique experiences of women, here, I place value on the body and attempt to make visible my experiences as a woman who is both becoming-mother and becoming-Ph.D.

Motherhood

In my younger and more naïve years, I assertively spoke about my desire to be finished having children by the time I was thirty. After all, this was normative in my parents' generation and the only frame of reference I carried. As I entered my twenties, my resolute stance wavered as I began to question whether or not I even wanted children. Through babysitting, then teaching high school, I felt uneasy entertaining the notion of bringing a child, whom I was wholly responsible for, into the world. I knew the chaos firsthand, I saw the "problem" children, I witnessed their pains. I comforted them and sometimes carried their burdens home with me. It was difficult, to be sure, and I was unsure if I was up to the challenge of motherhood. However, a few years into a teaching career, I found myself sitting in a gynecologist's office after an exam. I had been experiencing pelvic pain that I casually mentioned to my general practitioner. He referred me to a specialist and, weeks later, I shifted uncomfortably in the chair as my eyes rested on the thin film of dust on her desk. She walked in briskly, with her white lab coat trailing, as if struggling to keep pace. Shutting the door and taking the seat opposite of me, she told me she felt fairly certain of my condition, though it could only be confirmed through surgery, and then she shared with me several treatment options. "You should know. There is a decent chance of this affecting your fertility…"

In that moment, I watched the female empowerment that I had proudly carried for all those years dissipate into the dust before me. I thought it was *my* decision to have a child, mine and my partner's. Until I experienced problems conceiving, there was no way of knowing whether or not I would be affected by fertility issues. Digesting our conversation, I felt angry. As women, often the one unique given we have in our male-centered culture is the ability to facilitate procreation—to carry a child, to raise and nurture. Women have babies. Whether fair or not, whether it was always explicitly communicated, this was the message that had been embedded in my mind since I was a child. This message might have also been the reason why I questioned my very desire to have children—the stubborn side of me did not appreciate being told what *I* was (what *women* were) expected to do. I realized that if I did not have children, I wanted it to be *my* decision, not due to a problem with my reproductive system—a failure of my body. The ensuing emotions were complex, and I struggled to make sense of this new reality over the coming years. "The only way to know if it will affect you," she had explained, "is to try to get pregnant. But, you might want to do that sooner rather than later."

> *She looked at me with eyebrows raised so high I thought they might slip off her forehead.*
> *"You have a daughter?"*
> *"Yes, a 2-year old" I answered.*
> *"Well, I waited until after I got tenure. That's what a lot of women do..."*

Four years later, in my thirties and one year into my doctoral program, I was gleefully pregnant. It was surreal to watch the shape of my body shift over spring semester, and the nervous energy that came with telling my advisor and committee members I was pregnant was for naught. Somewhat surprisingly, I felt supported. While the financial timing was not ideal, the academic timing worked perfectly—I was finishing required coursework during my second year and my due date fell in early July, giving me around five weeks of "maternity leave" before the fall semester began. (Little did I know that my daughter would make an early appearance, giving me two more weeks than anticipated.) Fall semester was an important milestone as it was when I was co-teaching a course in which I would generate data for my dissertation. In preparation, the other instructor and I met weekly to plan the course, and I balanced my research assistantship and my own coursework as my belly grew and the weather warmed. In my last possible week of pregnancy travel, I jetted off to a conference with my advisor to give my first research presentation. A year later a woman who attended our presentation came up to me and introduced herself. "I remember you from last year! I remember how pregnant you looked and how calm and confident you were when you presented!" I choked a laugh. I had been so nervous, I was sure even the baby was shaking.

In the middle of the night, in the middle of summer, the baby decided it was time. Jolted from the lulls of pre-slumber, I rolled from the bed and dashed into the bathroom, returning a few minutes later to share the news with my groggy spouse. We threw our final toiletries into packed bags that had been patiently waiting and sped toward the hospital. The pain grew with intensity and in duration, and I have no conception of when night turned to day; however, at 3:26 p.m. on Father's Day, I met her differently. Until this point, I had only known this being from the kicks and movements that caused undulations in my belly.

I knew its schedule, when it liked to rest, when it was active. I knew when it got the hiccups...often. The embodiment of pregnancy was unlike anything I had experienced—a connective and life-giving force running through our bodies, mutually enacting. As women, we are taught to listen to our bodies and, usually, this listening is to whispers. During pregnancy, the frequency changed and I heard what it said whether I wanted to or not. My body talked loudly, shouting, through its transformations and movements.

> *His tone was matter-of-fact as he leaned back in his seat, scanning the faces of the young faculty in the room.*
> *"If you have kids, there are times you just have to shut the door and ignore the cries. I remember many-a-time when I was working on a paper or had a deadline and I did just that. Close the door. It's just part of it if you want to get tenure and be successful in the academy."*

The shouting continued as she made her way into the sterile room and I heard her voice for the first time. She was here. I let my doctoral studies slip to the periphery as I navigated the revolving door of visitors, the subsequent postpartum physical and emotional changes, and the moments of frustration and joy. There was much I was enduring as my body healed and as her body became acclimated to this new space outside the womb. I felt a level of sleep deprivation I had never experienced before (see also Hick, this volume) while I/we learned how to nurse—our stubborn personalities clashing as I urged and coerced, as she tried but did not. Through a haze, I remember reading an e-mail from my advisor telling me that our manuscript for a journal special issue was due in a few weeks. Wanting to be supportive, she took the lead on organizing and adding content to the paper, leaving me with a rather short, though pressing, task list. Everyone tells new parents, myself included, "sleep when the baby sleeps." From very early on, I adopted a new mantra. *Work* while the baby sleeps.

Motherhood/Work

This moment of seeking balance between work and mothering feels significant as I look back; it was the beginning of what would become my new normal. After the manuscript, I shifted attention to my dissertation prospectus and to weekly course preparations. Moving between mom and student happened as *she* moved from awake to asleep, and when my husband and I would shift parental responsibilities. Even as we tried to make it "equal," it was my body that provided the nutrients she needed and, therefore, it was my time/body that was often invested in her daily activities. While some women have confessed to me their dislike (and even disdain) for breastfeeding, I loved every minute of it. I am sure this came from the six weeks of struggle at the beginning—my stubbornness to give up led to an appreciation for the sheer ability to engage in this act of sustenance-giving. An overcoming of another potential failure of my body. I loved it, too, because it reminds me of what Adrienne Rich (1986) says: "Motherhood is earned, first through an intense physical rite of passage—pregnancy and childbirth—and then through learning to nurture, which does not come by instinct" (12). To be sure, for us, nursing was not instinctual. However, it was through these encounters that I first felt I earned the title of *Mom*.

Because of nursing, I had to protect my body during the times we were away from each other. Two afternoons per week, I fed her in the living room of her caretaker's home, drove to campus, and then pumped again before class in an office shared by adjunct instructors. I had a system, and a sign that I put on the door. The assiduous hum of the pump faded in and out of consciousness as I multitasked, reading or prepping for class that afternoon. Coincidentally, there was a mother taking the course I was teaching who had a child just a few weeks older than my own. We came to share the space and, henceforth, connected through our parental/academic struggles and successes.

> *"So, is she in preschool full-time?"*
> *"Yesss..."*
> *"Oh, I just didn't know if you worked every day."*
> *"Well, I'm an assistant professor. It's a full-time job..."*

The rest of my doctoral program became a whirlwind of writing, additional coursework (to fulfill the requirements of a research certificate), mothering, research assistantships, meetings, analyzing, nursing, and, and, and... It was during this time that I began to see the roles that were once more clearly demarcated in my life become effectively blurred. It was messy, best described by Braidotti (2011b) when she discusses the feminist subject as a nomad, inhabiting multiple time zones. I was multiple subjects in multiple time zones—coexisting in simultaneity—as I navigated the spaces of becoming-mother, becoming-Ph.D.

There was never a question of whether or not I would finish my dissertation; however, my timeline became compressed as my advisor left the institution for a new position the spring I would defend my dissertation. My graduation date was pushed forward three months. Thus, writing became more urgent, and we transitioned to a third morning of childcare each week so I could make more substantial strides in my data analysis. During this time, I remember working in the bedroom with tear-stained cheeks as I listened to my partner unsuccessfully try to calm our daughter. I also remember the flexibility of my schedule as she and I would pack up and go to our weekly play group and then laugh with the other mothers through the awkwardness of infant-held lunches at neighborhood restaurants. My body shifted between the tensions of work and very different tensions when mothering. The freedom to move through such affective time zones gave me balance and kept me sane.

Motherhood/Work/Undecided

The productiveness of these time zones shifted during this final year of my doctoral program, just after my daughter celebrated her first birthday. Present enfolded with the future, and I experienced a stark awakening upon realizing that I was unsure of what I wanted after graduation. I loved research. I loved being a mom. It was then that I considered nontraditional options in addition to the assumed direction of a Ph.D., which entailed attaining a tenure-track position (see also Richardson, this volume). I strongly entertained the possibility of a part-time position as a researcher at my Ph.D. institution and searched the job postings at a nearby undergraduate institution. There was something appealing about staying around my support group, around family, and my partner and I wondered if we could sacrifice pay for this security. Looking back, I wonder how many Ph.D. fathers consider this trajectory. To keep my options open, I began applying for tenure- track positions, sometimes thousands of miles away. There was also something alluring about entering academe as an assistant professor, challenging my thinking with new lines of research, and starting anew in a new place. Multiple time zones, indeed.

With such competing desires, I struggled with questions of what I would "give up" if I prioritized being a mom and what I would "give up" if I prioritized being an academic. I had entered college as a 19-year-old undergraduate with an "Undecided" major. Now, fourteen years later with a doctoral robe hanging in my closet, it seemed the designation still fit.

> *She clung to my legs with as much strength as her 2-year old arms could muster. "MOMMMMY!" she screamed. "NOOOOO!"*
> *I looked at her teacher with pleading eyes as she helped wedge a gap big enough for me to slip through. The last thing I saw through the tears that started pooling were her arms reaching for me as I stepped out of the Dutch door and closed the bottom portion behind me. Most days I would pause in the hall until she was calm, peek in and see her contently sitting in her teacher's lap, feeling reassured that all was well. Today, it was too hard. Today, the tears came too fast and the emotions with too much intensity. I kept my head down as I exited and stumbled into the parking lot, slinking into the driver's seat as my body heaved sobs.*

I knew that, eventually, a decision would have to be made. And just weeks shy of her second birthday, the orange tractor trailer pulled in front of our home—I had accepted a tenure-track position teaching research four hours away, in another state (and indeed, a new time zone). The three of us watched as the movers packed our belongings into boxes, efficiently, though clearly disconnected from their material significance. Our home began to look like an empty house and, though memories lingered, the only room that I felt intensely emotional about was my daughter's. It had once been an office/spare bedroom, and we had transformed it by painting it the most serene pale blue-green—almost turquoise, but softer. My mother had sewn the curtains for the window from fabric I picked, my husband had converted an old pine dresser from our favorite antique shop into a sleek white statement piece, and an artwork I made from decorative paper and acrylic paint hung on her wall. I still remember where every piece of furniture and every accent was, because I put it there. The only time I cried was taking my almost-two-year-old into her empty room one final time. The space was powerful, and my body responded to the enfolding of time, objects, memories, and becoming-mother.

Becoming-Multiple

And so I decided to pursue life on the tenure track. However, I had to force myself not to think about it as a prioritization of one thing over another. It was too painful and unproductive to see it in this way.

4 THE UNDECIDED NARRATIVES OF BECOMING-MOTHER, BECOMING-PH.D. 45

As French philosophers Gilles Deleuze and Félix Guattari discuss, it is a movement away from an either/or binary thinking that is so prevalent in a masculine culture (Braidotti 2011b), and a movement toward the complexity of *and, and, and*. Shifting from rigidity to suppleness, shifting to a becoming-mother that also encompasses the life of a Ph.D. Perhaps it might work. We had the summer to adjust to our new town, making our rental home as comfortable as possible while my spouse searched for a job.

Ever looming that summer, the new academic year carried potential but also dread. August marked my official start as an assistant professor, yet it also meant that my daughter would be starting preschool full-time and our time together would be cut, dramatically. Being a research methodologist often entails working with graduate students, many of whom are employed during the day and, therefore, take courses in the evenings. Thus, my teaching schedule kept me on campus one evening a week in the fall semester and two evenings in the spring, late enough to miss our afternoon play time, dinner, and our bedtime routine. I began to feel guilty about being away. Feelings of guilt that, perhaps, I was prioritizing my career over family continued to creep back and I, with frustration, tried swatting them away just like I might an aggressive fly. I am not one to subscribe to the notion of mom-guilt because it singularizes our experiences. It signifies that mom-guilt is "a" static thing that all moms know and feel. Rather, I think all parents (regardless of gender) experience guilt differently and at different times. For me, this guilt reared its head often as I traversed my first year.

> *We rest in the darkness befalling her room, me sitting at the edge of her bed, and she laying, sprawled on top of her covers.*
> *"Mommy?" Her lilting 4-year old voice disrupts the silence and rings through the room. "Yes, sweetie?"*
> *"I wish you didn't have to teach at night."*
> *We pause as pain swells through my chest, warming my face, and tears pierce and collect in my eyes. Thankful for the concealing veil of dusk, I whisper back, as it is all I can muster,*
> *"Me, too." I tell her I love her to the moon and back, kiss her forehead, and leave, collecting myself as I walk down the hall.*

During this year, I came to create new lines of movement that carried me through my days both on and off campus. There were no boundaries separating home life and work life, it was all just *life*. I quickly realized the job of a (new) tenure-track academic is not relegated to the hours of 9:00 to 5:00; it often functions in the in-between spaces that I had started to discover as a Ph.D. student. And, just like I did during my daughter's very first month of life, whenever she slept, I worked. I would work when she took her afternoon nap and for an hour or so right after we put her to bed at night. I would often spend my Saturday or Sunday afternoons reading for class the upcoming week. When I could, I would steal away for a few minutes to check my e-mail or send a quick response to a pressing request. At the same time, and more importantly, I tried to soak up every second with my growing girl. When I was home in the afternoons and on the weekends, we went on walks, visited playgrounds, read book after book after book, made art, and explored the blossoming creativity of her imagination. I watched her face/body change from baby-round to slimming-toddler, and I came to laugh at the silly personality that was emerging. *Life* was busy.

Life *is* busy. Through navigating the perils and possibilities of academia, many people have told me, "I don't know how you did/do it!" It makes me utterly uncomfortable to think that I am doing something extraordinary. Like most (all, really), I just do what needs to be done. In the words of television personality Tim Gunn, I "make it work." However, I find myself looking to other colleagues—without children, with three and four children, balancing lives that look much more strenuous than my own—and I think the very same thing. *How do they do it?!* As I have come to encounter my own feelings of indecisiveness, guilt, and the fear that I won't be successful—all accompanying this foray into motherhood/Ph.D.—I have realized that it is not productive to hold others in comparison. In all honesty, I struggle with this daily. It always looks like someone is doing more—reading more, publishing more, getting more awards, even being a better parent. We, especially women, in this world of academia are inhabiting multiple subjectivities and multiple time zones, and we are all in the unrelentingly vibrant process of just making it/*life* work.

"What are you doing?"
The chalk in her hand slid smoothly and with great purpose as she moved it across the chalkboard easel in the corner of the room.
"Teaching qual-itative re-search." Her 3-year old voice piped as she furrowed her brow.
"Where do you teach?"

"At the Univer-sity of Ala-bama."
My heart exploded into a million little pieces right there in her playroom.

CODA

In narratives, the coda signals a conclusion, a shift back to the present. Here, I do this literally. It is August 8, 2017, and I am sitting in my office after dropping my daughter off for her first day of Kindergarten. Nervous worry about the act of leaving her at a new school, *big kid* school, caused anxious dreams to wash over me last night as I tossed my body in and out of consciousness. At 7:38 a.m., we pulled up to her school in a sheet of torrential rain and I paused in the driver's seat, suggesting we wait to see if the rain would let up. "Nooooooo," she moaned, "I'm ready to go in." So, we did.

She was eager, thrilled even, as I attempted to snap one last picture of her in front of her classroom door. I waited for the tears (either hers or mine) and the clenching leg-hug she had perfected over the years when I had to leave her against her will. Instead, she traipsed into her classroom without as much as a glance backward. "Have a wonderful day, sweetie!" I called loudly after her. "I love you!" She turned and muttered something quick like "Okay. Bye, Mommy!" and proceeded to talk to her teacher about where to put her backpack and lunchbox. Shocked, I stood in the hallway for a few moments watching her, still processing and not sure of what to do next. Adrienne Rich explains, "All human life on the planet is born of woman. The one unifying, incontrovertible experience shared by all women and men is that months-long period we spent unfolding inside a woman's body" (1986, 11). Five years, one month, and twenty-one and a half days since she was born of my body, I had to let her go. Decidedly, *she* was ready.

In unpacking my "undecided" narratives of motherhood and academia, it has not been my intention to write only for those who are mothers or expect to be; instead, I strive to write through complexity and difference to show another perspective of the academic experience. As we know, there is no singular experience for women inside or outside the academy. Braidotti (2011a) asserts this in explaining that sexual difference varies across gender lines, within gender lines, and even within the self. These differences can also be expanded to consider other intersecting identities, including my own as a cisgender, heterosexual, white woman (pronouns: she/her/hers). To be sure, we/women are a motley crew.

Thus, the experiences I have shared in these narratives may or may not be exceptional or even unique, but they are what *I* have come to live. I share these things because we/women need spaces to normalize discourses on womanhood and motherhood in academe, and to make visible the challenges/successes that permeate our movements as we navigate various becomings. Rather than focus our conversations on teaching, research, and service, we have much to learn and offer if we also open ourselves to the entanglements of life as it exceeds the bounds of institutional spaces. This, for me, echoes the philosophical leanings that underlie my own scholarly work—life as an assemblage of complex, multifarious, entwining, inseparable people/places/things whose boundaries encroach and blur. And so I end with a gentle nudge. Let us open ourselves up to share our experiences in academe as they plug into all the other facets of our lives, let us listen to our bodies and our flesh, and let us create more spaces for our stories, memories, and countermemories to be shared…and to actually pause to hear them—listening to all the whispers and the shouts.

REFERENCES

Braidotti, Rosi. 2011a. *Nomadic Subjects: Embodiment and Sexual Difference in Contemporary Feminist Theory.* New York: Columbia University Press.

———. 2011b. *Nomadic Theory: The Portable Rosi Braidotti.* New York: Columbia University Press.

Crabb, Annabel. 2015. *The Wife Drought.* North Sydney: Penguin Random House Australia.

Rich, Adrienne. 1986. *Of Woman Born: Motherhood as Experience and Institution.* New York: W. W. Norton and Company.

Snowber, Celeste. 2011. "Let the Body Out: A Love Letter to the Academy from the BODY." In *Epistemologies of Ignorance in Education*, edited by Erik Malewski and Nathalia Jaramillo, 187–198. Charlotte: IAP Information Age Publishing.

Spry, T. 2001. "Performing Autoethnography: An Embodied Methodological Praxis." *Qualitative Inquiry* 7, no. 6 (December): 706–732.

CHAPTER 5

Showing Up

Sarah R. Hick

"She didn't even show up for the last class!" That's the course evaluation comment that sticks with me from Spring 2010. Like I just decided not to come. Like class was just something I could show up for or not, depending on what tickled my fancy that day. Like maybe I was sitting by the pool with a drink. Like I was thinking, "Eh, whatev! They're just leading their final lessons anyway—they'll be fine! Pour me another lemon drop!"

Where was I? I was at the hospital with my wife. She had already been on bed rest at home for four weeks because of cervical shortening. I missed class the day that diagnosis was made. She was an emotional wreck, of course, and so was I. This day, the last day of my class, she was admitted to the hospital antepartum unit. So, yes, when I found that out, an hour before class, I asked a colleague if he'd stand in for me and video record my students' teaching sessions, then I left for the hospital.

I graded my students' unit plans and read their clinical journals in my wife's hospital room, unsure if we would become parents or not, unsure what our future would look like if we did not. My wife is an obstetrician herself, and I doubted that she could continue on in that profession if we

S. R. Hick (✉)
Hamline University, St. Paul, MN, USA

© The Author(s) 2018
S. A. Shelton et al. (eds.), *Feminism and Intersectionality in Academia*,
https://doi.org/10.1007/978-3-319-90590-7_5

lost this pregnancy. I wondered if she'd ever be "her" again if we lost this pregnancy. I wondered if we could still be "we."

"She didn't even come to class." You're right. I didn't. There were more important things that I needed to attend to.

Getting There

The ironic thing about the comment from my student is that just a few years before, that comment could have come from me. Before having kids, I was one of those people for whom "DINK" (double income, no kids) was not just an acronym, but an appropriate descriptor—or, rather, insult. I regularly found myself thinking, "I don't care that you have kids, there are readings and assignments to be done. Do them when they're in bed if you need to!" and "You need to leave work to pick up your kids? This is your JOB! Figure it out and get a sitter or something!" I pooh-poohed people who claimed they couldn't work past a certain time because they had to meet with their son's teacher or attend their daughter's piano recital. I inwardly rolled my eyes at colleagues who had limits on work time. "You're not really committed to your job," I'd silently think and judge. "What MATTERS is changing the K-12 experience for kids, not just your precious jewels. SEE THE BIGGER PICTURE!" What I said out loud to colleagues and students didn't use all caps or exclamation points—or the rude, judgy words—but what I was thinking did.

Part of my complete lack of compassion or understanding for the parent role was that I simply had no interest in having kids. I was never one of those little girls who imagined herself as a mom or liked to play with baby dolls or even dress the cat. I imagined myself as a baseball player or a firefighter or a doctor or a teacher—I imagined myself as a professional adult, not as a parent.

Once I became an adult, I actively did not want kids. I wasn't just "meh" about them; I thought it was a terrible idea and wanted no part of it. I'm enough of an environmentalist that not only do I pick up other people's bottles from rest stops and cart them home to a recycling bin, but I also know that children—especially middle to upper-middle class kids in the USA—have a VERY negative effect on the environment. The only reasons to intentionally have children, I reasoned to the high school environmental science classes I was teaching back then, were either arrogant or selfish.

How then, did this complete DINK, guilty of untold numbers of silent anti-parent rampages, became a parent? I can explain it only this way: Living in a relationship that cartoonists represent with hearts sailing out of their characters' eyes makes lots of things change. Rational and calculating as my partner and I both are, the decision to have kids wasn't one led by our frontal lobes. Nor, of course, are we the sort of couple who can get pregnant through the throes of passion. Highly emotional as the decision was, it was one that withstood four years of various appointments, sperm hunts, strategies, attempts, failures, donors, and legal documentation until finally, there they were, tiny, screaming, and pink.

Getting Through, Getting By

Shortly after the twins' arrival—and for a good long while after that—I wondered if having kids was really a very good decision. A friend of ours said to me as we commiserated about parenting twins, "What were we thinking? We've ruined our lives!" It did, in fact, seem that way. Before kids, my life was a balance of relentless pursuits of professional goals and fun with my wife. A colleague of mine and I were working hard at our lives' mission to change how science teaching—and more importantly, science learning—is done. We were creating a nonprofit, building a Web platform, writing curricula, and figuring out how to finance our start-up. I worked tirelessly into the night and still had plenty of time for fun and relaxation with my partner. I did research, I taught, I graded, I wrote, and I served on committees; my partner and I snuggled and did crosswords; we canoed, we hiked, we walked the dogs, and we went on vacations to Utah and Belize and Costa Rica.

Now with newborn preemie twins at home, our sun-dappled babbling brook of professional and personal life became a flooded maelstrom. A love-drenched maelstrom, but a flooded maelstrom nonetheless. If I could trace it to one source, it would be this: We didn't sleep (see also Guyotte, this volume). At all. Before the kids were born, we had read a book about one couple's struggle with having twin babies. We laughed at their recountings of various approaches to sleeping every night: One night the husband takes both kids and the wife sleeps all night, another night they take shifts with both, and then, they split the kids up and each take one. "For the love of God, pick the one that works best!" we laughed. And then, we had twins and realized, "Oh. NONE of those things work. We're jerks."

We, too, tried all sorts of different sleeping configurations and schedules and on-duty arrangements. From co-sleeping to shifts to alternating nights, we didn't find a sleep solution that worked; we just ran out of ideas. So, for most of the first six months, we took turns sleeping on the floor with one kid one night, the other the next night, waking with our assigned twin to do feedings. I gained weight as I treated myself to a snack each time they had one, forgetting that their bodies were supposed to double in size in a few months and mine was not. On the good days, I slept three to four hours—not all together, but in 15–20 minute segments strung across most of the 24 hours of the day. Lack of sleep was a cruel and progressive form of torture. It robbed me, incrementally, of my higher brain functions, eroding all the things that made me who I am— my rationality, my cognition, and my emotional control. I was left mainly with my autonomous and motor functions intact.

The sleep crisis at home couldn't help but breach the banks and flow out into my professional life. Surprisingly, it wasn't my failing cognitive skills that I noticed first; they apparently weren't up to the task of being able to notice their own demise. It was my emotional control that was the canary in the coal mine. One morning a few months after my children were born, I had a meeting with two professors I had never met: the chair of the chemistry department and one of her colleagues. I began crying as soon as I left my garage. I wasn't sad; I was just so tired that my brain signals misfired and flipped the "cry" switch to "on." I cried all the way to campus, cried from the car to the building, cried going into the bathroom, cried on the way out of the bathroom, cried all the way to the meeting room, and cried in the meeting room. Unless I'm menstruating or watching a particularly heartfelt advertisement for greeting cards, I'm not a crier. I might get emotionally worked up, but I could easily shift gears and turn off the tears when needed. Not this time. I was able to sputter out, "I'm sorry. I just...I'm not sleeping. And, I'm... crazy." They looked a little bewildered. I'm a little bewildered now wondering why I didn't cancel or postpone the meeting. All I can come up with is either (1) I didn't have the cognitive wherewithal to do that or (2) I was well aware that any other day would have been just as bad.

I was fortunate that, due to flexibility in how parental leave is taken at my university, I was able to teach only one course the fall just after my kids were born. But even one course was a monstrously difficult task without the benefit of my usual neural functions. Anyone looking at a graph of my course evaluation scores over time would see what appears to be the Marianas Trench located over the fall of 2010. I can't blame my students. They deserved more. I did my best, but nobody was happy. Nobody except, I guess, at times, those two adorable pooping machines at home who loved nothing more than to snuggle on my chest as I slept on the couch after work, mouth agape.

Sleep crept back into our lives slowly over the twins' first three years. We went from being woken up four times a night to three, then two, then one. Only being woken up once a night seemed like a gift for a few weeks, but in my early 40s, and after a couple years of terrible sleep, being woken up once a night was still preventing my body from restoring itself. I was drawing from reserves faster than they could be replenished.

While lack of sleep slowly but relentlessly chipped away at all my skills and stability and personality, virulent viral and bacterial infections launched short-term assaults. At least once a year, I would be besieged by something that snuck into our home on my children's little warm, moist bodies. The twins would get serially sick for a day with a low fever; I would be laid up for a week with a 103-degree fever and vomiting or eruptive coughing or sores all over my throat. I'd miss more than a week each year, spend two more weeks battling back to health, and be hopelessly behind the remainder of the term.

It was clear that having kids had a serious negative impact on my work: lack of sleep and the world of microbiology were teaming up to ruin me as a professor.

As it turns out, being a professor isn't the only thing that is hard when you have small children. Parenting small children is hard when you have small children. As a friend said, "It's not that parenting is that *hard*, it's just that you have to do it *all the time*." My unmarried, non-parent buddy from graduate school was shocked to hear me say that parenting was by far the hardest thing I'd ever done in my life. "Harder than getting the thesis written?" he asked, innocently. "Listen," I told him, "if difficulty was plotted on a graph over the time of my adult life, my high school teaching time would be pretty high, graduate school would be far below that, and my parenting years would require the zigzaggy break in the y axis and *still* make the line look like it's on an exponential growth track." I went from running my brain at full power at work and then relaxing with hobbies and my partner in the intervening hours, to running my brain at full power at work and then having to run it at full power for the rest of the day and night on my kids. On little sleep. At 40.

If I were employed in the role of "Parent" as my full-time, 40-hours-a-week, 1.0 FTE job, I'm fairly confident that I could handle situations with my twins with the grace and skill expected of a master child-rearer. I could have had a break from them to do fun stuff, let my brain unwind, distance myself from their needs and issues, and even choose to spend some off-work hours researching child development. I could have, I like to believe, thought creatively about how to engage them and how to respond to their needs and complaints with the agility and humor that would lead them to be charming, sensitive, and kind children and responsible, self-actualized, innovative, relationship-savvy adults. But with little sleep and another full-time job as a professor, I did not and do not rock this parenting thing. I'm not a bad parent: I've seen bad parenting, and I'm not doing that. But I am pretty sure, almost every day, that there are better ways to respond to and interact with my kids that I might be able to muster if I were able to approach the role with sleep and distance.

Also hard when you're a parent? Being a wife. Before trying to get pregnant, my wife and I had the sort of relationship you just can't believe anyone really has—all flowers and bliss and amazingness, the only occasional grousey words or looks occurring when one of us was pre-menstrual. We had each entered the marriage with a tremendous sense of comfort with who we were, what we needed, and how to communicate about both. But now, with one-eighth of the usual sleep and four times the usual demands on us—including the creeping suspicion that we were in for a very long, hard road—we discovered parts of ourselves which were wildly uncomfortable. Rather than looking into a mirror of our own behaviors or emotions and thinking, "Awesome!" as we had before, we were more likely to think, "What the…?" or, more likely, "AAAAAAAAIIIIIIIIIIIIIIIIEEEEEEEEEEEEE!!!!!!!!!" We had similar reactions to seeing the newly revealed parts of each other. We were often frustrated and sad, wanting the other version of our wife or our self back, the one who was almost always available and upbeat and confident and balanced and patient. We now used up most of our positive energy where it was needed to keep our jobs and tend to our adorable but helpless babies, leaving little for each other. And, of course, there was no time or place for snuggling.

The final difficulty now that I had kids was simply maintaining *me*. I had been an athlete and a reader and a crossword doer and a traveler. With kids, I had no time for working out or reading, no alertness for puzzles, no ability to travel with the babies, and no ability to leave my wife or the kids behind. What had I been reduced to? Who was I without my impressive resting heart rate, my completed Sunday crossword, and my hiking trips in the mountains?

I decided that I wasn't much of anything, just one more overtired mom doing a mediocre job of raising a couple kids while holding down a job and trying to maintain both a relationship and some sense of self.

I wasn't comfortable with that.

Things were going to need to change. I was probably one of them.

First, I had to get more productive at work. Once I had twins, it became clear that nothing (NOTHING!) work-y could get done around my kids. It also became clear that I had assumed that I *would* be able to work with children around. Where did I get that ridiculous idea? Ah, yes, one of my older colleagues told stories of all the times he had brought his toddler twins to school, sealing them into a playpen of overturned tables to happily chatter and build with blocks as he met with students or finished his dissertation. I also realized that because I had viewed having dogs as good training for having kids, I figured that I could grade with the kids around just like I could with the dogs. As it turns out, kids are a little different. And, too, my twins are a little different than my colleague's. Whether because of my age or their temperament or my temperament, I found that I was incapable of higher cognitive functioning while my kids were around me. I could attend to email, clean, do other low-level tasks, but planning, grading, and writing needed to be done alone.

I realized that any frittering away of time at work meant work would be left undone since I couldn't do it once I got home. I knuckled down, adjusted my settings, and found myself able to be wildly efficient in my office, running copies, planning ahead, firing off emails, and making phone calls. It was impressive and somewhat alarming (as in—my GOD I used to waste a lot of time!) how much I could get done when there were two screaming children and no sleep waiting for me at home.

That sort of adjustment was fairly easy. The harder adjustments were the internal ones, the ones that guided my self-talk and my identity.

I came to the realization that perhaps many driven, successful, professional, type-A moms come to: I was unfit to parent. I was used to setting a goal, working hard, and reaching the goal. I was used to the product of my effort being success. I was used to navigating through systems and around personalities in order to get things done. I was used to gold stars and A pluses and accolades. And, well, that shit just doesn't happen as a parent. Babies, toddlers, and—perhaps—children of all ages are unbridled by the confines of rational thought that had ruled the rest of my life up until now. My intellect and argumentation skills could not convince them that they should either get their flailing, infant hands to quit knocking the pacifier out of their mouth or quit depending on it for sleep. Their needs were not able to be timed and balanced with the other pressing tasks of the day. The moments when they had explosive poop that wound up in their hair and when they put fistfuls of dog food in their mouth could not simply be penciled in between yoga and the weekly department meeting. And that inability to reason, to schedule, to control, to expect fairness left me mad—in both senses of the word.

To continue on each day, I had to first recognize that *failure to be perfect* (at professor-ing, at parenting, at wife-ing, and me-ing) was not the same thing as *Failure*. For a type-A perfectionist, that lesson was a dirty, exhausting, shoulder-dislocating wrestling match of wills that left me face down and limp. It meant admitting how much I valued my life and others' lives based on a threshold of productivity and charm that wasn't reasonable or even possible. It made me explore where those expectations came from and how they might have both helped and harmed me along the way. I had to stop thinking of what I was doing as "failure" or even "mediocrity." I had to think of it as "okay." For a perfectionist who has almost always been able to get what she wants through hard work, for someone who turned her very few "C" grades into hilarious stories of teacher ineptitude, this "okay" neighborhood is a scary, uncomfortable place. It has norms and a culture that are foreign to me. There is no travel guide, just a lot of dark, unnamed streets with raccoons skittering around and branches hanging low.

Once I accepted "okay" as a substitute for "failure," I had to get comfortable with being okay. I had to get comfortable with choosing at every moment which things to be okay at—Wife? Parent? Professor? Colleague? Daughter? Me?—while I focused on being a bit better at something else. Choosing what to be okay at in the moment—choosing what to "let go"—is still, in reality, being in control, but that is as close as I can get to letting go of the reins.

As I wrestled with this "failure" issue and imagined trying to be happy with "okay"ness, I realized that my wife and I were paying our nanny exactly my annual take-home salary. I was, in fact, working full-time to pay someone to raise my kids. Well. That sucks.

I struggled for a few years, every day, with the decision of whether to continue to work, to quit, or to take a leave of absence. Perhaps due to the difficulty of making good decisions on little sleep, I decided—on a daily basis—to not make a decision in my current state. Not that day. I just kept showing up at work. As I waffled between wanting to cut out this one part of life that I was "failing" or "being okay" at (professoring) so that I could at least spend more time with my rapidly growing children, I was able to recognize a couple key points. One, our nannies—each of them, in turn—were good for our kids. They brought freshness and interest and energy and new relationships and ideas to our kids' lives that I could not. Two, I am simply not cut out for stay-at-home parenting. For starters, I'd become a lunatic not being able to talk to other adults. And by "talk to other adults," I mean "talk to other adults about things beyond the topics I normally engage in when in the presence of my children: my children, my parenting, and my sleep patterns." Also, I'd be bored. Not the good kind of bored: the haunting, soul-crushing sort of bored. All I'd be able to see would be the possible professional contributions that I imagine I could have made to the world (overstated as they may be) slipping through the sieve of time. Finally, days with twin little ones are loooooooooooooooong. Every day was like the movie *Groundhog Day* (Rubin and Ramis 1993), where I'd wake up and everything looked exactly the same, and I'd need to keep doing the same things. Except there was no "right" way to do it that got me past that day. I just kept reliving it. I love my kids with all of my heart and my might, but I realized that in order to love them, I also needed space from them. So when they got to age three, and they were headed to half-day pre-school, and I was still going to my professor gig each day, I felt comfort and relief for not having stepped away from my job. Not making a decision had been the right thing to do.

It has never been lost on me that, hard as parenting and working and being a wife were, we had life so much easier than most new parents. We were healthy, living in a safe neighborhood, employed. We had health insurance, a knowledge of how systems work, and the power to make our voices heard. We were financially well-off with an excellent support system of family and friends. To feel like I was failing and flailing when I had every advantage behind me was incredibly humbling. Here, I had thought I was so competent and successful when, in fact, I had really just been riding a wave of privilege with little in the way of real challenges.

Getting Better

Now that our kids are entering first grade, sleep has returned to our home, and our kids don't require four adult hands to keep on top of their survival needs. My in-office productivity has dropped, and work sneaks into some evenings and weekends. "Work" doesn't look like just me being in the office or teaching; it looks like me on the family chair with the dog at my feet, typing away at an article while the kids do daring feats on the play set. It looks like me alternating writing a syllabus with planning construction of a backyard zip line. It looks like me rushing from camp drop-off to the nearest coffee shop to grade like my hair's on fire until their camp gets out at noon and we can spend the afternoon together at the pool. It looks like starting class while my kids eat their snack in the room next door and wait for Mommy to pick them up. There is integration and flow and overlap where I never thought there was any possible.

Seven years in, I can see that the challenge of raising kids has made me a more whole, more honest, more forgiving, more self-reflective person. After seven years, it has become clear that I need to do more than just grit my teeth and be a good host to serious introspection: I need to build it a comfortable guest room, find ways to try to enjoy its company, and invite friends over to meet it. I am not working on getting past my introspection; I'm working on digging in and learning. As a result, I am more attuned to other people's needs and more comfortable being honest about what I can do, what I struggle with, and how I cope—right or wrong—when I'm not meeting my own expectations. At the same time, I'm much more sensitive to the needs and pressures of the people around me in my life. I see us all as imperfect beings, negotiating our way through life, trying to be the best we can while trying not to fight too hard with our imperfections.

Seven years in, I can also confidently claim that I have a deeper relationship with my wife. Over the years, we have learned to talk more about our individual struggles and anxieties, hold up a mirror (always metaphorical!) to each other when needed, and choose to work through rather than soldier through our tough spots. We are working on looking longer and softer at each other and at our own individual reflections. Looking for a long time allows us to really see, accept, and focus on details of who we are. Looking "softer" rather than harder allows us to temper our frustrations by thinking—whether about ourselves or each other—"I love her. She is brilliant. She is reasonable. She is trying so hard."

Seven years in, I can also see that having kids has allowed me to become a better professor. Sure, I have less time to devote to planning and providing feedback, but my kids make me more aware of my students' time, their need to be with their families, and their need to socialize and do fun things besides study. I don't want my own kids to be robots, trained by school to do school things; I want them to have exciting learning adventures and have relationships that help them grow; I want us as a family to have time for just us, when we want it; and I want school to be important but not paramount. And now I teach that way. I also teach *people* now instead of students—people who are imperfect but trying. People who are sons and daughters, who have families, who were once little and vulnerable and slobbery and deeply loved. I also teach people who were once little and vulnerable and slobbery and then got hurt and now help and love. My students are learning more, doing more, and enjoying class more because, as strong an advocate as I was for student voice and meeting students where they were, I only had my pre-mom understanding of that to go by. My "mom" understanding of what that means allows me to show up as a professor in a so-much-more-human way. At the same time, I get the sense from course evaluations and class dynamics that when I make my identity as a mom and wife more visible—through stories, pictures, and child-care hand-offs—my students engage more with me and with the course. Perhaps seeing me as more than just a professor allows them to humanize me and, thus, be more receptive to the learning challenges I give them.

Getting to Class

When I think back to my student who was so incensed that I'd missed our last class period to be at the hospital with my wife, I know that that sort of comment would never pop up on a course evaluation now. I had always prided myself on establishing excellent rapport with students and on building a community in the classroom, but I realize now that I had not been bringing my whole person to the classroom or seeing or welcoming my students' whole selves. After struggling to regain a balance in my new life with kids, I have become more comfortable with myself, more aware and honest about my shortcomings and limits, and abler to be open and honest with my classes. They know me well, they have a relationship with me, and they trust me. I'm not just a professor in the classroom; I'm imperfect, working-on-stuff, honest, comfortable-with-my-discomfort *me*. My student was right in a way that they had not meant: I hadn't been truly showing up as *me* all term. Now, I do.

REFERENCE

Rubin, Danny, and Harold Ramis (Writers). 1993. *Groundhog Day*. Directed by Harold Ramis. Los Angeles, CA: Columbia Pictures. Motion Picture.

CHAPTER 6

Superwoman Goes Camping: The On-Going Quest to Right-Size My Life

Sharon I. Radd

Every summer for years, my husband and I have taken our kids camping. Initially, when we had preschoolers, we bought a pop-up camper and stayed relatively close to home. As our kids got older, we longed to travel west to experience the beauty and adventure of the mountains but knew that hauling the camper would be unnecessarily arduous. Believing that a good long road trip builds closeness and lifelong memories, we decided to store our camper and experiment with the freedom and possibilities of tent camping.

Our first tent camping adventure in 2010 took us to Yellowstone and the Grand Canyon. Our trip began in Yellowstone National Park with thirty-five degree nights in the tent in the mountains where we all donned long underwear, hats, and mittens to stay warm while sleeping. A few days later, we ate lunch by and went swimming in a lake at the base of *The* Grand Teton. Our impromptu drive through, and overnight stay in, a seven-mile-long canyon along a rushing river was a great lead-up to several days in the Grand Canyon. All in all, it was truly a trip to remember. Ten days after starting out, we pulled back into our

S. I. Radd (✉)
St. Catherine University, St. Paul, MN, USA

© The Author(s) 2018
S. A. Shelton et al. (Eds.), *Feminism and Intersectionality in Academia*,
https://doi.org/10.1007/978-3-319-90590-7_6

driveway and unloaded the car, ready to sell the camper without looking back, and excited to plan our next adventure.

That's the backdrop against which we took off for Montana in July 2011. Our ultimate destination was Glacier National Park. In addition, my oldest son, then seventeen, was looking at colleges and interested in the mountains, so we planned our drive to include stops at Montana State in Bozeman and the University of Montana in Missoula.

The trip was remarkable in new ways, different from the year before. Our first night in Montana, we drove forty-five minutes off the highway along a dirt road and into the mountains to reach a National Forest campground. Upon arrival, we found that we were literally the only people there, and the grass hadn't been mowed in weeks. Still, we were able to locate a camping spot far enough from the swollen river to feel safe but to be close enough to hear it and feel like we were waterside. We woke at midnight to a full moon shining so bright and unimpeded that it was as if someone had switched on an overhead light in our tent.

Over the next two days, we continued farther west across Montana, taking in campus visits and spending a very enjoyable two nights in another National Forest campground situated on a fairly large lake, in preparation for moving on to Glacier National Park.

We had planned our entrance into Glacier from the west side of the park carefully, as without a reservation, we needed to arrive early in the day in order to secure a decent camping spot. We were excited to set up in a campground right on Lake McDonald, a glacial lake near the west entrance. Our time in that majestic land was incredible. We went swimming, horseback riding, and white water rafting, and we boated in our inflatable kayaks several times.

Our last day in the park, we were enjoying ourselves so much that we waited to leave our campsite until the final check-out time at three in the afternoon, with new campers swarming around to seize our site the moment it was free. Our plan was to drive from our campground through the park to the east side, a seventy-five-minute drive, then travel on to Great Falls where we would rent a hotel room for the night. Our drive through the park, however, quickly expanded to almost four hours, as we stopped to "shower" in one of the roadside mountain waterfalls, to take photos as the traffic crawled up the mountain, and to hike in the snow at the Logan Pass Visitor Center. Leaving the east side of the park well after seven at night, we watched the sunset as we headed south to Great Falls, and I picked out a hotel for us via my Blackberry as we neared the city in the dark.

The next day, we departed Great Falls after breakfast with the intention to drive along Highway 2 until it joined with Interstate 94. Our goal was to reach Bismarck, North Dakota, an eight-hour drive, in time for dinner and swimming at our yet-to-be-booked hotel. The drive across Montana was amazing. The land was more expansive than I had ever imagined, and the vistas unlike anything we'd seen before. Somewhere along the way, we stopped for gas and happened to meet another family returning home to Minnesota from Glacier. All along the highway, we passed each other back and forth, until they exited at Roosevelt National Park in western North Dakota; even from the highway, that park beckons adventurous travelers with its aesthetic splendor. Still, we continued on our drive, and I remember being grateful that my kids were older than theirs and that we could pack more car time into one day.

Simultaneously, as we neared North Dakota, I decided that it was time to book a hotel room for us for the night. I pulled out my Blackberry and whenever I could get a signal, I searched for a hotel room for us in Bismarck, which is smack-dab in the middle of the otherwise rural state. To my surprise, I could not find one! Not easily deterred, I continued to repeat my search, again and again. Again and again, no room! As anxiety and negative self-talk began to creep in, I shared my concern with my husband and began my apologies.

Late in the afternoon, as planned, we arrived in Bismarck and decided to visit some hotels—surely somewhere, someone must have a room. After stopping at three or four hotels, we learned that there were two conventions in the city, and that, as *the* city where the state's two interstates intersected, *everyone* plans to stay in Bismarck. Apparently wise travelers book their rooms early.

Though I felt foolish and somewhat panicked, the rest of my family handled the situation quite well. We decided we should not take the time for a sit-down dinner, and grabbing take-out, we hit the road again. Once again, I began searching my Blackberry for available rooms, now east of Bismarck. One here, one there, all eerily reminiscent of a dirty, musty room we'd had one night when my kids were babies. We kept on driving. Though no one was complaining, I continued my apologies: "This is my fault. I should have booked this room yesterday. Heck, I could have booked it days, weeks ago. This is my fault. I'm so sorry." I praised my kids for their patience and flexibility, and thanked my husband for continuing to be the unshakeable rock that he always is.

Still, my negative self-talk continued. In-between thoughts about how I had utterly failed my family, I invited others' judgments into my head. In particular, I frequently thought of how this never would have happened to my administrative assistant, who was usually extremely frustrated with me because I failed to plan in advance and to manage timelines in the orderly, detailed, and controlled way she did. I saw this particular situation as incontrovertible evidence that, as I had always suspected deep down inside, I was fundamentally and irrevocably flawed in the most existential of ways.

Shortly after ten at night, having been on the road since before nine in the morning, I finally booked a room in western Minnesota, a full four hours from Bismarck, and ninety minutes further down the road than we were at the time. Around midnight, we pulled into our otherwise nice-looking hotel, surprised to find three police cars parked near the front entrance.

Career as Camping

As I reflect on these travels, the highs and the lows, I realize that they provide a remarkably accurate metaphor for the very experiences and reflections I have had navigating my career and family life.

The trip has already been so full. My career as an academic is a second-career that I launched at the late age of forty-eight. At the time, I had already had a full and rewarding twenty-three years in K-12, most of them as an administrator, and then one year as an independent consultant and adjunct professor. I decided to leave K-12 because, although I was making a generous income and had attained a cabinet-level position, I concluded that there was a steep, steep cost to the high salary that I was earning, and that along with me, my entire family was paying for it. My oldest son was graduating from high school, my beloved mentor (and dissertation chair) was about to leave his high-ranking faculty position in deference to his ALS-induced declining capacity to work, and more significantly, I knew that the time to raise my two younger children was passing me by while I was away at work for what seemed like *all the time*.

From my early days in K-12 in the metaphorical pup tent, and the middle years in a pop-up camper, the later years of being an administrator mirrored a luxurious RV. These large, endlessly equipped vehicles promise to take you anywhere that you want to go and contain everything you need for travel, including Internet, television, comfortable sleeping accommodations, showers and toilets, and small but fully operable kitchens. Still, while loaded with amenities, they also come with many restrictions. I've often wondered as I pass one on the highway how the occupants get around once they get to their destination. If they are towing a vehicle and hauling bicycles, I think of how burdensome it is to carry all of that gear a long distance, and how careful one must be to maneuver so much girth to avoid damage to vehicle, property, or worse, person. And then there's the cost to the pocketbook and to the environment for fueling so much mass. Though my administrator-life RV was certainly abundant in many ways, I ultimately felt overwhelmingly constricted, realizing that while money can buy so many things, it cannot buy time or relationships.

As I contemplated leaving K-12, I realized that throughout my career I had longed to be in a faculty position. I wanted to teach, conduct research, write, and importantly, work from home. So, with my partner's full support and knowing that a local position was unlikely, I launched an extensive, nationwide search. However, through campus visits and some deep soul-searching, I came to two important realizations: First, though my spouse was willing to relocate and the idea was enticing, we would be giving up so much of what we knew and loved (our metro area, our faith community, our neighbors, my husband's job) for a serious pay-cut and an employer, a work environment, and a set of colleagues that may or may not have been healthy and positive. In short, most of our life was really outstanding, so why disrupt it? Further, almost everything that I wanted professionally was in reach, without leaving our home or community. Teaching? I could continue to do that in my existing position as an adjunct at my alma mater. Working from home and a flexible schedule? The emerging work that I had as an independent consultant and my adjunct role allowed me that. Research and writing? My affiliation with my alma mater and my flexible schedule would offer me the space to do this, even if self-funded.

With enough savings to pay the mortgage for a year, one consulting contract in hand, and the promise of several adjunct courses, I left K-12 and became self-employed. I was immediately lightened, and the feeling of no longer being "owned" by an employer and restricted by their rules was incredible. Like selling the RV and hopping into a small SUV with only a tent, sleeping bag, and cooking gear in the back, I was only limited by my imagination and my budget as to what I could do and where I would go. I honestly thought that I would remain an independent contractor for the rest of my working years.

As such, my move into a full-time faculty position came as a surprise. When the opportunity to join a faculty on a full-time basis arose, without the need to relocate my family, I hesitated at first, but as the hiring process unfolded, I fell in love with my future colleagues. When the job was offered at less than half of my school administrator salary, I was able to negotiate a slight increase and made sure to negotiate the latitude to continue my consulting work. Having calculated that I would make enough money to meet my financial commitments to my family, my intuition directed me to proceed, and I wholeheartedly said, "yes."

I joined the faculty of St. Catherine University in Fall 2013 as an assistant professor in the Masters of Arts in Organizational Leadership program, fourteen months after leaving K-12. I was thrilled and excited about this move, and felt like I'd "arrived." St. Kate's is a teaching-centered, highly regarded regional university with a college for women at its core. The colleagues I fell in love with at my interview have proven to be as supportive, ethical, and accomplished as I first suspected. Like anywhere and anyone else, the university is not a utopia; human beings coming together to do work is always messy, complicated, and prone to conflict. Still, the faculty and administration are committed to living out the core values of the institution, even if we all are imperfect and diverse in the ways that we do so. Importantly, my "productivity" can take many forms and still count; both beautifully and painfully, I can choose anything from a good solid tent to a giant, luxurious RV and be on track for tenure.

Moreover, the university is truly "women-centered." Founded by the Sisters of St. Joseph of Carondelet (CSJs), a fierce, bold, courageous, and ambitious group of women by anyone's standards, the campus *feels* different from other universities in the most embodied way, due to its strong commitment to remaining women-centered. This reality is hard to describe but profoundly important to my story.

Does Superwoman Own a Tent or Drive an RV?

When someone says "Superwoman," I don't automatically picture the CSJs, nor do I picture myself. Instead, I'm immediately transported to the jingle from a perfume commercial that played on the television when I was growing up. The commercial featured a tall, thin-but-curvy, attractive woman in a white button-down shirt, black skirt, with perfectly styled long, flowing blonde hair singing, "I can bring home the bacon, serve it up in a pan, and never let you forget you're a man." In other words, *real* women were supposed to be successful money-making professionals, skilled homemakers, and talented lovers who made sure that they bolstered rather than threatened their husband's "manhood," all while smelling fabulously sexy. While it may seem startling and iconic in its sexism, heteronormativity, and gender rigidity, these messages were commonplace and pervasive, and permeated my mind about how things "should" be.

These narratives were accompanied by powerful messages in my family of origin. Importantly, the males were centered and prioritized, even when they were insensitive and abusive. This gendered centering was insidious but masked in valuing their professional pursuits. As someone who innately wants to experience her own life and accomplish her own pursuits, living in the space around these men meant that I had to figure out how to make my interests happen on my own. Combined with the dominant narratives of the time, the ultimate messages that I absorbed were that men are more interesting and important, and allowed to harm others without repercussions, while women must do well to please men so as to avoid those repercussions. Though I witnessed how work and accomplishments could be important sources of fulfillment and status, I was also taught that no matter what I achieved, I would never, could never, be or do "enough." I came to constantly assess whether my actions and my self were pleasing or displeasing others, and far too often used these notions to guide my behavior and decisions. To deal with the ongoing disappointment that comes with persistently denying my inner voice, I found peace by remembering, "If not this time, another time."

From my work related to critical theory and adult learning, I know these types of narratives powerfully shape a person's foundational understandings of the "right" way to be and to do things. These narratives live in our unconscious and subconscious minds and manifest in our self-talk, the ongoing internal chatter that is often repeated in part or whole in our spoken words. Importantly, they show up in our actions as they shape and constrict our behavior. As we grow and experience life, if we are capable and willing, our individual desires and perspectives evolve and enter into a complicated internal struggle with these narratives. It's surprising how often the dominant discourse and the narratives from our early experiences overtake our individual desires, perspectives, and values with as much ease as a full-size RV can run right over a pup tent. Still, this struggle is also a place where we can see the opportunity for liberation.

In my life, my evolving desires and perspectives have prompted cycles of complicated internal negotiations between what both dominant and family narratives taught me about what I *should* do, how I *should* be, what I could expect, and who I am within the larger world. For me, the move to leave my K-12 career after successfully climbing the ladder was one particularly significant negotiation. The dominant narrative told me that I had reached a pinnacle, and if I were just a good enough time/work/family/life manager, I could (and should) make it work until what would then be my generously- funded retirement. In contrast, my inner voice, my professional dreams, my values, and my health all whimpered that they would wither away if I continued to try the impossible. When I finally faced the prospect of giving up both my big salary and my lofty professional title, I had to face the decision to choose my own liberation in a way that entirely opposed the dominant narrative. In the end, the decision to end my administrative career was not only an act of survival, but also an act of submission. I did not realize that my surrender was actually the beginning of a deliverance.

Similarly, I did not realize that working in a woman-centered environment would have such a profound impact on me. The time I've spent in this context has silently and powerfully released so much of my internalized oppression related to the sexism and male patriarchy that is insidious in US society. One of the greatest blessings has been to let go of the dream to be Superwoman in the world's (or my family's, or my colleagues') eyes, and to work to identify and then live out what truly brings me joy and peace. Though my younger self, in K-12, was driven by ego and ambition to be Superwoman, to have and do it all in ways that brought recognition and admiration, my over-fifty, second-career, more-liberated self knows that inherent to being Superwoman is a pursuit of perfection that is nothing but a destructive and oppressive lie.

I am absolutely certain that doing meaningful work that contributes to improving our world will be enough of a professional legacy for me. Like switching from a pop-up camper to a tent, moving to academia via a women-centered institution has given me a bit less professional and economic security but a great deal more freedom and flexibility, and has allowed me to stretch my wings, dream bigger, travel farther.

Because of this, in a basic but beautiful way, I can have anything that I want. In contrast to many other settings, I can prioritize my family and do meaningful work that interests me. I can have a flexible schedule and work from home. I'm usually able to teach the courses that interest me most, and am absolutely able to pursue the research and writing projects that I choose. I am often offered opportunities for additional projects and work in the field, many that are paid, and all of which are interesting and important. My family is supportive and flexibly accommodates my work demands. By rejecting the dominant narrative about my career, I have access to a much better life.

Every Day, Another Opportunity to Fuel the RV or Enjoy the Tent

Nevertheless, while becoming an academic at this stage in both my personal and my professional life has been a liberating experience on the one hand, on the other it consistently brings me face-to-face with the fundamental primordial issues of who and how I am. Because I now have the privilege to pursue this work that I love, my desire to do meaningful work can be met one hundred times over. My days are *filled* with options for how I spend my time and what work I will do. It is so exhilarating to view all the opportunities that are right in front of me and to feel the excitement of the possibility. At the same time, I consistently struggle, at the deepest levels, to accurately assess both the opportunity and the cost of each, and to feel and say no to the ones that seem to offer so much, yet will ultimately cost me more. Whether it's money, the opportunity to work and connect with people I enjoy and admire, or the opportunity to learn, grow, and meaningfully contribute, it's easy to forget that I cannot do it all, nor should I try. I am wise enough to know that time, money, energy, and attention really are finite resources, often competing with one another; that every yes actually requires a no to something else. Still, though in my head I have chosen the tent, I live with the ongoing challenge to decide wisely from among many desirable choices so as to properly love the people with whom I travel.

I wish that solving this struggle could be as easy as selling the camper and buying a tent was. Instead, it is as if there is still an RV in the garage, tempting me to forgo the slowness of cooking by the fire for the convenience of the camper's kitchen, suggesting every day that having and doing it all will mean I don't have to miss out on *anything*. While I absolutely know that's not true, it's so very easy to forget. While the opportunity to create the right-sized life that I crave exists around me at all times, I too often find myself in the metaphorical car, riding down the highway, without a hotel room in sight, having packed so much in that I didn't plan for the next stop. Internally, I beat myself up in the very same way I did in the real car on that real night when we had to drive for so many hours past our intended destination before we found a room for the night. I think things like, "Why did I...?" "Why didn't I...?" "If only I had..." "Why can't I ever..." Even further, I often find myself believing that what I judge to be poor planning means I'm without the prospect of a suitably good outcome, as if one hasn't already occurred and another won't come soon enough. As if planning properly guarantees a good outcome. I know better than that.

Part of my own journey to maturity has been letting go of the dominant narrative that I should strive for everything to happen perfectly, or to come off without a glitch, or most important, that a life well lived doesn't involve trade-offs. Everyone I know who has truly faced the totality of our world and lives comes to realize life and people are far more imperfect than we can imagine. In reality, we can have a perfectly planned, spectacularly fun camping trip and on the way home, learn that our house burned down while we were away, and we are faced with a "Now what?" of the most frightening and painful kind. The pursuit of the most spectacular career, the perfect people with whom to have relationships, and the most amazing experiences—that is, the belief that owning the biggest and best RV will guarantee happiness—will always leave us coming up short, in more ways than we can imagine. Part of being a feeling human is that our hearts get broken and our spirits are disappointed over and over and over again. Then hopefully, we dream and love each other, our work and the ways we fill our days more and again.

I've realized that the "fundamental flaw" of so many of my days has been to spend too much time and energy believing that I am fundamentally and irrevocably flawed and in need of fixing. Working in a women-centered environment has helped me learn that I am just like everyone else in that I'm utterly and uniquely imperfect, and my life will be as well. We are in the tent together, in all our imperfection. The challenges we face, even the horrors, can walk peaceably together with beauty if we prioritize our humanity and our relationships. We can trust that the most promising way through anything is to be kind to one another and simply do our best, even given the possibilities and limitations of our human condition.

I realize that dusk is approaching. Though "if not this time, maybe next time" has helped me cope with disappointment and brought me a lot of peace throughout my life, I'm acutely aware that time is in fact quite finite. More than I ever realized, the truth is, "if not this time, maybe never." The idea that I might "get through" my pre-tenure years at this intense pace and then slow down is not viable if I actually want to be meaningfully involved in raising my children and maintain my health so that I have the hope of being around for their adulthood. My two younger kids will be just about graduated from high school by the time I go up for tenure, their entire childhood marked by "not now, Mommy has to work" if I don't make the space to be present now. My over-fifty body means I only have so many nights of not getting enough sleep before my mind and spirit are compromised. In search of the most comfortable if-not-distant hotel, I often forget that I have everything that I need in the car, this very moment, to stop and set up camp, have a nutritious meal, and rest well for the night with the people I love the most. My greatest challenge, the most important thing I can do, is to become far more clear and intentional about what I must do, and what I need never do.

Embracing the Tent

About a year ago, the memory of the long drive across North Dakota came up on my Facebook feed. Notably, it didn't show my negative self-talk, nor the panic or failure I felt. Instead, it was a photo of the incredible full, orange moon that greeted us as we drove into Minnesota just after eleven that night and still had forty-five minutes of driving to reach our hotel. I was reminded of the surprise we had when we walked into our room at midnight to find they had booked us into a suite, and what a great time my kids had swimming in the hotel pool in the morning because, with only had a few hours left to drive to get back to our home in Minneapolis, we had the time to pause and enjoy the moment. The police cars turned out to be nothing, and the time in the hotel turned out to be wonderful. Moreover, it prepared us to problem solve rather than panic when, five years later, we showed up to our Airbnb rental in Amsterdam at eight at night, with no car or phone, just two kids and our suitcases, to find out the apartment we had rented did not actually exist. Then, as in almost every less-than-perfect situation, though even a monetary deposit didn't guarantee that our plan would materialize, we found that there are multiple paths to a satisfying way of enjoying our days. They all involve being present in the moment and traveling lightly.

In the last year or so, I have taken a clearer stand in responding to the challenges my students face as they experience competing demands on their time and attention. Strengthened by the women-centered context in which I work and reflecting my own struggles with making similar choices, I take an active role in offering them an important framing for their decision making. I now challenge them to consider what can wait and what can't wait, to recognize when they'll have a chance for a do-over and when they won't. Having a baby? Take the semester off. Your mother is dying? Go be with her. This course? It will be here next semester. The vacation you take every year? Schedule it around your classes.

Every day, I have the same opportunity to make the same type of decision between what is most important that day, what can wait, and what need never happen at all. Every day, I am tasked to choose the tent that I know is right, while often offered the RV that promises freedom and possibility but actually means burden.

Beautifully, painfully—full of both the liberation and the responsibility that the Sisters of St. Joseph of Carondelet envisioned—it really is up to me.

PART II

The Less Traveled and Less Valued Pathways: Examining the Devaluation of Women's Contributions to the Academy

CHAPTER 7

There and Back and There Again: Notes on a Professional Journey

Cheryl R. Richardson

During my first year of graduate school at Stanford University, a prominent scholar told me that all of her students find tenure-track positions at Research-1 institutions. It was 1992. I have never forgotten those terrifying words. This was what was expected of me—to follow a straight academic path to a research intensive university.

I was young and easily shaken. I thought that I must pursue a research-based academic career. Looking back at that time, I realize that I struggled with following this trail because I was unsure of what it meant to live a life of the mind. This led to a few stops and restarts of graduate study but ultimately, an understanding that the activism that motivated my graduate study could drive me in any direction I chose. I thus pursued work in and around academia, always animated by my commitment to seeking justice for Black people. While my path has emphasized issues of professionalism, feminism, international economic development, teaching, and learning, I sustained a professional direction by tying myself to issues of racial equity.

C. R. Richardson (✉)
University of Chicago, Chicago, IL, USA

© The Author(s) 2018
S. A. Shelton et al. (eds.), *Feminism and Intersectionality in Academia*,
https://doi.org/10.1007/978-3-319-90590-7_7

Beginning of the Journey

I could not have predicted my path when I started college in 1987. I followed my curiosities and passions, which led to a series of adventures that now tell a story. And the story helps me to maintain a sense of myself.

I studied African and African American social histories as an undergraduate at the University of California, Los Angeles (UCLA). It was the first time that I heard stories about and voices of people from my African American community and from the larger African diaspora. I learned a great deal about oppression and resistance and vowed to be a part of Black liberation. My parents—first generation university graduates—did not understand what I might do with a degree in history. They thought that I should pursue business or law. I couldn't understand how to motivate my own life by pursuing someone else's profits, so I excluded business. I was curious about law and engaged in a summer internship at the public defender's office. Most of the associates in that office were very overworked and unhappy, which turned me away from that pursuit. I thus persisted in history with no clear post-graduation course.

I won a summer fellowship to work on a history professor's research on C. L. R. James. I read primary documents, took copious notes, and tried to understand how to do a literature review. I found the topic of study very cerebral but inspiring. I was enthralled by reading the words and thoughts of a Black intellectual who connected the impetus of the Haitian revolution to revolutionary ideas and not as a reaction to extreme oppression. This intellectually driven thesis was new to me, as I had primarily studied opposition as a reaction to material strife.

During my senior year, I met a graduate student who helped me think of ways to apply my passion for seeking justice for Black people. He, a student in the school of education, helped me to understand how research and theory shaped the policies that gravely impacted the treatment of Black children in schools; he introduced me to a study on the connection between academic tracking and race. I was sold and applied to doctoral programs in education.

Charting a Path

I started a doctoral program in education at Stanford University within a year of graduating from UCLA. I focused on the history of education and was paired with scholars who emphasized social justice. I soaked up my advisor David Tyack's theses on spiralized reform. I also relished every philosopher that Ron Glass introduced me to—Michael Apple, Henry Giroux, and Paulo Freire. I was riding a fantastic intellectual highway but unfortunately had no sense of which off-ramp I might take toward my own study.

I was encouraged to investigate the experience of African American families during the Great Depression. I was curious about Black Panther activities in schools but was told that it was too contemporary. I looked at changing perceptions of unwed Black and white teenage mothers. I felt directionless, but my internal compass continued to guide me toward understanding some aspect of education focused on people like me: African American and committed to learning.

I took a leave of absence from my doctoral studies to earn a teaching credential. My advisor rightly advised me to seek some classroom teaching experience, which might hone my research interests. I taught history and English as a Second Language in a local high school. I also advised the Black Student Union and became immersed in a small, well-established African American community.

Diversions, Timing, and Detours

Just before deciding to teach, I met, courted, and married a Kenyan man. He pursued a different degree and planned to apply his graduate work to fixing problems in his community in Western Kenya. I planned to continue to work in California. But once we decided to marry, we had to think of ways to compromise or at least to agree to compromise whenever necessary.

For a while, the relative progress of our respective graduate work seemed to guide our situation. He was three years ahead of me in graduate study, more certain of the scope of his research and obligated to return to a university position in Kenya. When we celebrated his graduation and our first child on the same day, it made "sense" for him to return to Kenya to fulfill his obligation and for me to remain in California, where I could continue working toward my career goals. Importantly, my teaching position provided necessary health insurance and chances for better educational opportunities for our child. He left for Kenya when our son was three months old.

The loneliness and stress of being a young, single parent were more than I could bear, and I joined him within two years. I extended the leave of absence from graduate school that began when I started teaching.

Over the next eight years, we moved to different parts of Europe and East Africa, making decisions that re-configured his career trajectory from one focused on academic research to being a global civil servant. I enjoyed the adventure, had two more children, and volunteered and worked in schools when I could. I also carried the nagging weight of my incomplete degree.

The weight of my unfinished doctorate made my journey difficult. My devoted partner and I were responsible for three lives, and I could neither imagine abandoning them nor dragging them to California for me to complete my studies. I felt it was best that I continue to figure out ways to fit my career interests around our movements, which followed my husband's career.

While moving around in the expatriate world, I was known as a "trailing spouse" (see also Tondreau, this volume) and often could not legally work in the local economy. I therefore sought new opportunities to apply my research educational skills to find work. I created a nonprofit organization that promoted higher education in Uganda with another trailing spouse. I created curriculum for domestic violence prevention in Botswana. I also served on strategic planning committees for international schools.

My pattern of making my professional path fit around the work of my husband was similar to that of my mother. She shifted her work as a nurse educator from one university to another while my father climbed a corporate ladder that required us to move from one American state to another. She stopped pursuing her Ph.D. when he was asked to move from a position in Michigan to one in California. She never became a tenured faculty member but found a great deal of professional fulfillment from being a clinical educator.

However, my husband, who—like my parents—could see me being a powerful educational reformer, cajoled and encouraged me to find a way to complete my doctoral work. My husband's model for educational achievement was based on seeing long periods of separation between his parents. His mother and father had spent seven years apart while his father completed two degrees in India. His mother went alone to study at Berea College in Kentucky when one of her children was still nursing. His example was very different from mine. He thus could see a way forward for us that involved my returning to complete my doctoral work in the USA while he remained in Kenya.

We found a way, largely following my husband's direction.

I considered what I valued, switched dissertation advisors, and returned to graduate school with renewed questions about the professional lives of women educators. My inquiry changed because I wanted to grasp my own experience. And, given my location at the time, I focused on women in Kenya. I found a way to limit my separation from my husband by making sure my research was conducted where we lived. This change in my research focus meant that my professional aim shifted away from explaining and easing episodes of African American marginalization. Instead, I targeted women teachers in an attempt to understand the strange juxtaposition of their power in shaping the future and their sidelined status in society.

Starting ten years before Kenya achieved independence from England, my dissertation narrated fifteen women's understandings of their roles as women, professional educators and nation builders. The research subjects explained their roles in forming and maintaining an independent, post-colonial country in a way that harkened back to my work on C. L. R. James. I argued that they, similar to James, were driven by principles. In this case, values about professional work, women's roles in families, and indigenous national leadership drove their decisions. At the same time, I explained how their choices must be understood in the context of a nation that offered very few professional opportunities for educated women.

Their stories gave me solace. Like them, I charted a path that was buffered by current opportunities, family needs, and external expectations.

I curved, twisted, and finally plowed my way through my Ph.D., earning a teaching credential and two master's degrees, teaching high school, and having three children along the way. Each educational, career, and family decision was negotiated with my husband. While he completed his Ph.D. in our second year of marriage, I finished in our eighth.

Charting a Professional Life

I was relieved and extremely proud to have completed my doctorate. Although I had a clearer view of my journey, I was unsure of where to go next. I made a fortuitous connection to ideas around professionalism and found work at the Carnegie Foundation for the Advancement of Teaching's Preparation for the Professions project.

As a junior member of a stellar group of scholars, I studied how schools of law, engineering, theology, business, and education teach ethics. We considered how ethical behavior appeared among each professional group and traced the distinct ways that it was presented in classes. We investigated syllabi, interviewed faculty, and plowed through large student outcome data sets. We explored different methods of planning, mentoring, and teaching and the impacts of these on the ways that emerging professionals thought about their ethical commitments. We then promoted various best practices for university departments, faculty, and cocurricular units to follow.

I also became connected to a scholarship of teaching and learning (SoTL) project that was similarly predicated on the power of careful thought, reflection, and assessment to make change in college classrooms. I worked with university faculty who wanted their students to think and act differently after engaging in specific activities and materials.

I moved to another university, doing similar SoTL work. One memorable English professor wanted to investigate how reading a contemporary text about a murder trial might impact students' engagement and understanding of the idea of heroism. This white woman professor included the book *Monster*, a novel about a young African American boy on trial. She tried to trace her students' considerations of various paths to heroism by carefully analyzing their essays' word choices, as students were required to use html to show their thinking by linking specific passages to relevant Web sites.

I latched on to that professor and her cohort. There was another who worked with students to understand Plato's dialogues by rewriting them using contemporary English. He found that most of his students did so by appropriating African American slang. He was excited about students' abilities to make connections across time. I was intrigued about how the mostly white students used words whose origins they probably did not understand. I helped the professor explore his questions and kept mine to myself.

This was a very generative time in my life. As I observed how faculty helped students connect specific, classical ideas to their contemporary worlds, I tested ways to help faculty connect ideas about the difference to their classrooms.

In 2002, I led my first diversity-oriented faculty development workshop. Many faculty at the time were concerned about their lack of knowledge on how to engage their students of color. With little experience, an incredible amount of preparation, and following the lead of a few pioneers, I attempted to help by focusing on changes in content. Using examples from the two specific professors described above, I emphasized adding questions and texts that allowed experiences of people of color to emerge. Following a somewhat curving path, I returned to my initial position of working on specific ways to improve the experiences of Black students.

As my experience in faculty development and diversity started to grow, my husband's work dictated another overseas move for us and another chance for me to remake myself. We thus relocated to Kampala, Uganda, where I wrote about African higher education and started a nonprofit organization.

Mapping a Career

My husband and I continued to spend time living separately and together. He lived overseas, furthering his career in international development, and I continued to focus on improving the lives of Black people while living with and without him.

After living in Uganda for two years, I returned with our children to the USA hoping to advance my own career. I served as an administrator of Stanford University's African and African American Studies Program. I used the position to advocate for the value of studying and valuing Black experiences. The program was very focused on the salience of race in the USA. My work with Kenyan teachers and experience as an African American in East Africa and Europe provided me a view of the African diaspora that was not as race-based. I instead saw forms of oppression and sources of strength that were founded in culturally specific conceptions of gender, wealth, and birthplace. Based on this natural merger of my intellectual work and personal experience, I tried to help students complement their studies of race with other ways of understanding the lives of people from various parts of the African diaspora. This diverse view broadened the perspectives of many African American students who had a natural understanding of race. It also embraced the Caribbean and African students who did not. I worked with assorted centers, deans, and schools to develop this direction and sustain the interdisciplinary program. I also connected with many students as an advisor and confidante.

I thoroughly enjoyed this position and would have loved to have remained there. However, I again lived as a single parent. My husband had moved to Italy and offered as much support as he could from afar. It was not enough, and it was not fair to our children. So, I joined him.

Living in Rome, I struggled to help my Black children adjust to a closed Roman community. Not only were we non-Roman, we were Black. Like many foreigners, our interaction with Italians was largely as tourists. Although we joined a local tennis club, went to every children's party we could, and sat on the beach with hundreds of others, we did so alone. We existed in a bubble in public spaces. Heartbreakingly, my six-year-old daughter learned that her color was not appreciated one day on the playground when another child refused to share lip gloss with my girl. While I strived to help her and my sons adjust to overt exclusion in a language and a context that I did not fully understand, I also tried to continue to mark a professional trail.

Without a work permit, I could not work at English-speaking universities. Therefore, I used my research abilities to gain a short-term consultancy. Over the course of six months, I helped to write a grant that focused on addressing the nutritional needs of stunted children south of the equator. I learned about the physical needs of youth and the long-term impact of poor nutrition on learning. I also saw how policies that emphasized the growth of cash crops, women's lack of access to property, and inappropriate understandings of culture exacerbated incidences of hunger. I provided help with background research, editing, and the perspective of a potential educated donor. I also assisted a foundation that wanted to open schools in sub-Saharan Africa. The foundation solicited bankers, who wanted to invest in schools and were tasked with writing proposals to earn matched funds. I helped the bankers develop appropriate plans for schools.

Our nomadic lifestyle did not bode well for our children, especially when they started high school. Although they attended schools with American-based curricula, they experienced gaps in specific subjects like math. They also had the disheartening experience of having to re-demonstrate their intelligence, sports ability, and friendliness in a new school every two years. My husband and I thus enrolled them in boarding schools by the time they were in ninth grade. We honored the uniqueness of each child, resulting in their attending residential schools in three different places on two continents. While they adjusted to these environments and my husband earned most of our living income, I leapt from family weekends to boarders' weekends, while officially working as a consultant. My flexible time allowed me to physically be present for our children, while also giving me a chance to support my mother as she took care of my dying father.

After helping my mother begin to adjust to being a widow and making sure my children were settled, I entered full-time work again as a professional developer in higher education. The timing seemed right, and I was thrilled to return to working with faculty again in a way that combined my love of teaching and social change. While addressing teaching and learning for all undergraduates, I found ways to emphasize the needs of Black, brown, low-income, and cognitively challenged children in American university classrooms. My husband continued to work in East Africa and Europe as a consultant. I was alone most of the time, but his time was flexible, and he could visit me frequently and work from my base. We saw each other at least every six weeks. After one stressful year of him trying to juggle three commitments at one time (as consultants often must do), he pursued a regular, salaried position. This put an abrupt stop to our visits, and the strain of living apart became intolerable. I decided to move to where he lived in Italy because his income and benefits supported our dispersed family. While based in Europe, I continued to be connected to equity, teaching, and learning through professional societies and by mentoring new faculty developers.

Looking Back on My Journey

The idea of "career" helps me to organize the direction of my work and gives it meaning. I relish the idea that I have a career in educational equity, and I find comfort in feeling like an overarching ethos guides my decisions. In reality, the requirements of my family and the opportunities of an international life buttress and constrain my decisions.

Initially, biology meant that I needed to remain close to our children. One significant impact was that my husband's career was able to flourish in ways mine could not because he could easily move for work. His advanced stage in graduate school and career also released him before me. He thus climbed international development ladders and made increasing amounts of money. So, as the years passed, his career continued to be in the forefront, as it supported the lifestyle that we wanted for our family. It provided for stable boarding schools while we moved every one to two years. I worked around this reality.

At the same time, my life was greatly enriched by international travel. I learned different ways of seeing oppression and of understanding the relative significance of race and gender. My experiences working to understand teachers in Kenya, students in Uganda, malnourished children, and self-focused Italians provided various tributaries that helped direct my path toward improving classroom experiences for various students in American university classrooms.

I work in the academic world and hold staff positions that do not garner as much respect or benefits as those given to tenure-track professors. Nevertheless, my work is extremely valuable because it benefits a population of African American children, whom I sought to serve at the start of my journey. My professional journey merged with my personal path, making new, unexpected routes that brought me back to a more deeply understood and expanded starting place. Over time, my conception of how and whom I assist has expanded and I have rewritten my map, adjusted my compass, and continue to head in fulfilling directions.

CHAPTER 8

A Woman's Worth: Valuing Self, Risk, and (Re)vision

Tanetha Jamay Grosland

I have been immersed in the field of education for fifteen years, seven of which have been in academia. I have experienced an unquestionably unique journey of risk and (re)vision, learning the importance of staying true to myself personally and professionally. I've definitely traveled a unique professional pathway, and regardless of how it is deemed by those who more conventionally "stay in their lane" professionally, my journey has proven to be immensely valuable many times over. Because my pathway is and will not be exactly the same as other female academics (particularly in my field), I know it's important to *allow* myself to be true to myself.

Currently, I'm an assistant professor in education at a public urban research university with a specialty in urban education leadership; my research concerns leadership experiences in urban contexts. I am particularly interested in the role of affect concerning social ("controversial") issues. I'm extremely satisfied in my current position at my institution, as I have been with all my career opportunities, but my journey has been one of constant *risk* and cycles of *(re)visioning* myself.

T. J. Grosland (✉)
University of South Florida, Tampa, FL, USA

My professional path to and in education is not "linear" or intentional per se—it may even be unorthodox—but it is borne from my emotionally driven, (un)conscious desires. For example, prior to becoming an educator, I was a successful political scientist working for members of Congress. There is a plethora of women who, like myself, have unique professional stories; these women run the *risk* of being overlooked or not given substantial professional status due to their "unorthodox" work histories. This undervaluing is related to systemic oppression, too many superficial accolades (like a head nod, a pat on the back, or a "good job"), but too little action to disrupt inequity. Yet, many women realize such oppression exists while continuing to commit their professional lives to their purposes, all the while placing self-care at the center of everything, i.e., "no one will value you unless you value yourself." Self-care is especially important for women who identify with multiple, traditionally marginalized identities and/or are raised in the context of such a community. It is in all my uniqueness that my academic journey sometimes feels like a bumpy pathway. But I hold on white-knuckled and enjoy the ride.

Here I share more details about my curvy—yet *perfect*—professional story through a lens of narrative inquiry. I chose this approach because I wanted to focus on my own experiences, emotions, thoughts, reflections, interpretations, and events as a story (Chase 2005; Clandinin and Connelly 2004; Clandinin and Rosiek 2007). Using my own narrative, I do not suggest narrow solutions to complex issues related to sexism, gender identity, and women in academia; instead, I emphasize an understanding of the politics of gender in women's contributions to the academy (see Elbaz-Luwisch 1997). Writing this story, I continue to learn how sexism and gender oppression have obscured my own participation in an oppressive system, and therefore I continually re-emphasize my need for self-care (Clandinin and Rosiek 2007). My approach to writing my narrative as a single case may be seen as a "radical challenge" to the academy (Elbaz-Luwisch 1997). Nevertheless, throughout this professional story, I reflect and share my context and location (*place*), my transitions and changes (*temporality*), and my relationships and dispositions with myself and others involved (*sociality*) (Clandinin and Raymond 2006). Although sometimes emotionally experiencing self-doubt and self-inspiration, in this story I've made an earnest attempt to treat my own experiences, reality, and perceptions as truth. I've also constantly allowed myself, through regular reminders, relaxation, meditation, and forgiveness, to see my story as a constant act of creativity and as something very unique; therefore, I did not question the factuality of my own story (see Chase 2005). My professional story is one of value and no regrets.

R*ISK* AND (T*RANS*)F*ORMATION*

My career path started when I was an inquisitive and underchallenged student in a highly diverse public high school located in an urban area (dense metropolitan area, city proper). I did not like high school much—actually, I hated it; I was not engaged, and therefore my grades were not stellar. I did not do well on the American College Testing (ACT) because I went into the testing room with the perspective that it was "just another *stupid* hoop that I have to jump through." Regardless of my unimpressive grades and terrible ACT scores, I always asked questions, loved to investigate society, and went on to successfully graduate with a diploma. Although my academic shortcomings are sometimes embarrassing, I'm proud that I graduated and fostered critical thinking skills.

I went on to college as the first (on both sides) of my family to earn a university degree. I knew nothing about college—I didn't even know that it costs money!—I just knew that I had to go; otherwise, as my mother told me, I would remain in project low-income housing. Therefore, I was determined, not only because I thought college would be more interesting than high school, but because I wanted the opportunity to expand my sociocultural contexts and socioeconomic options.

After I completed an associate's degree at my local community college, I packed a duffle bag—being sure to remember all the warm clothes my Illinois grandmother, who had traveled the Great Migration, sent me. Then, as a way to escape my local context and expand my perspective, I jumped on an Amtrak train and traveled thousands of miles to the University of Minnesota. My cousin met me at the train station in Saint Paul, where the weather was finally beginning to warm after recently dropping to a near-record-setting −32 °F. Yes, this was balmy.

While completing my degree in political science, I went on to practice my craft on Capitol Hill, working for a US Senator from Minnesota (Rodney "Rod" Grams). Here I was involved in general staff operations, constituent relations, and press relations. I went back to Minnesota to continue my political science career for a US Representative for

Saint Paul's 4th Congressional District (Bruce Vento) and worked in general office operations and on press relations. I loved working in politics, but I wanted an advanced degree; initially I thought I'd apply for law school, but instead, after talking with Representative Vento and friends in education, decided to earn a Master's in Elementary Education and Middle School Social Studies. I realize my shift from political science to education was sudden and *risky*, but I welcomed the *risk*.

Fourth-Grade Excitement

Leaving my successful career as a political scientist and going into education was exciting, and the transition was smooth. My husband (at the time) accepted a position to teach elementary school in the Chicagoland city of Elgin, Illinois. So, after I finished my degree and earned my Minnesota teaching license, I joined him in Illinois. After substitute teaching for a few months and obtaining my Illinois license, I was offered an elementary position in Elgin (public school district U-46).

I was exceedingly happy teaching elementary students, but, due to budget cuts, everyone in the district who was not tenured (i.e., all those with zero to four years of employment) were "pink slipped." Luckily, a teacher in my school put me in touch with a Twin Cities area principal. Since both my partner and I needed jobs, we talked to the principal about the available positions in his school district. Shortly thereafter, we interviewed and received offers; we happily returned to Minnesota where I taught at Oakdale Elementary in North Saint Paul, while my partner taught at a different school in the district.

As an urban fourth-grade teacher in a highly diverse school located in a first-ring suburb/inner ring city near Saint Paul, I was genuinely comfortable. It was there, with the support of the administration, that I was able to practice my love of teaching social topics through a lens of multicultural education. I was awarded internal grants and external international travel awards, specifically a Fulbright Memorial Fund award to study in Japan and a Transatlantic Outreach Program award to study in Germany. I then became a Teacher on Special Assignment position as an Integration Equity Coach for my school district. After settling into this position, I knew that it was time to go back and get my Ph.D. due to being granted flexible leave. I had long dreamed about a Ph.D. in political science, but I knew a Ph.D. in education was more practical because I had settled into that field.

I thus enrolled in a Ph.D. program at the University of Minnesota in Curriculum and Instruction, with a concentration in Culture and Teaching. This program had a focus on teacher leadership and teacher development, as well as multiculturalism, justice, and equity, so it was a perfect marriage for what I was doing in my special district job, i.e., developing leaders who were committed to multiculturalism and equity. My immediate school district supervisor was generously supportive. She was the Integration Equity Coordinator, as well as the coordinator of our team of coaches, and too was committed to cultural competence, justice, integration, and equity. However, after a few years, she vacated this position and the district hired a new coordinator. It was a truly scary time for all of the coaches because, although a pleasant person, the new coordinator had a different vision for integration and equity. I was afraid of this change and had fears for the future, due to warning signs that I had noticed in his practices, such as withdrawing from previous integration agreements with neighboring districts and hiring new personnel with different approaches and philosophies about adult learning—approaches that did not involve instructional coaching. My fears were confirmed. Soon after he came on board, all of the coaches in integration and equity, including myself, were either reassigned to classroom teaching positions or retired.

I was tenured in my district and therefore was offered a fourth-grade position at a wonderful elementary school that served typically underserved students, led by a visionary principal. I loved the idea of working at this school, and I loved my district; but I could not work full-time as an elementary teacher and continue to pursue my doctorate full-time. At this point, I was about half-way to Ph.D. completion. I chose my Ph.D. studies over my elementary teaching career and resigned from my district. In my mind, it was a messy resignation because I wanted my situation to remain how it had been. I was confused and in a whirl of emotions—on the one hand happy to continue my studies, on the other hand remorseful about the departure. I resented the new coordinator because I felt that he was more committed to the idea of diversity than to empowering teachers and students to be more self-efficacious on integration and equity in their own communities. Notwithstanding my bad feelings, I went on to continue my studies as a full-time student and held two assistantships to help pay for them. In the end, my departure from the school district was a gift, because it allowed me more financial freedom.

In My Clinic

As I was finishing my doctorate, I became active on the job market. I knew I would experience significant changes because, in lieu of elementary or middle school public teaching, I wanted to seek employment in higher education. I was offered a position at the University of Florida as Clinical Assistant Professor-in-Residence in Teacher Leadership at the College of Education, School of Teaching and Learning with the Lastinger Center. I was uncertain about accepting this position because it was a year-to-year contract, and it hinged on public school partnerships. Based on my experience working in Minnesota, I knew that these relationships could be fickle. Regardless of my reservations, I accepted the position.

I was extremely happy because I loved working with staff and students in schools and had familial ties to Florida. Furthermore, the position allowed to me to utilize my coaching skills and all that I'd learned in my doctoral program. It was a remarkably exciting job! Service in the field through the partnership was considered the major criteria of success in this position; researching one's field-based "clinic" earned one internal accolades. As part of my work, I taught courses and collaborated with educators in some of the most underserved schools in a Florida school district. I made the conscious decision to actively publish in peer-reviewed academic journals because I enjoy the challenge of writing. My publications were noted in my evaluation, but were not valued in this clinical position; this was no surprise to me because, again, it was made clear that I was to focus on my service to the "clinic," regardless of whether I published or wrote about it. Although risky, I simply chose to continue to write with the goal of publishing in peer-reviewed journals, because I was hoping that it would help me in future roles; and, I enjoyed it! More importantly, I was staying true to what I loved, regardless of the presumed import to others in the academy.

I was successful in all aspects of my career as a clinical assistant professor, and received high marks. I was engaged in helping leadership teams throughout the district develop professional development plans. I worked with graduate students in our partnership schools to help them develop an inquiry stance about their work and execute their own action research projects. Upon completion of their program, I presented and published with students about using inquiry as a tool for equity (Grosland et al. 2014). I taught classes all year long to teacher-leaders throughout Florida on topics like teacher leadership, action research, differentiated instruction, and cultural responsiveness. But sadly, less than a year after I started, the partnership started to unhinge, eventually dissolving due to matters too expansive to address in this chapter. It was heartbreaking to watch it unfold in a political explosion and create massive change for so many who were involved. Although I ultimately stayed in the position for two years, I was back on the job market only a year after starting the job.

My World as a Teaching Academic

Of course, it was inevitable that I was to experience professional change, because my position ended. In the face of this, I reminded myself to be open to all possibilities. After conducting a nationwide search, I was fortunate to be offered a faculty position at Morgan State University, an urban, historically Black university in Baltimore, Maryland. I was a tad trepidatious because, although I'm a risk-taker, change has always been scary for me. Nevertheless, I quickly accepted the appointment, because working in an historically Black university was an amazing opportunity. With this enthusiasm, I happily went to work as an Assistant Professor in Urban Education Leadership.

In this position, teaching was the primary criterion by which I would be evaluated, and I was overwhelmingly successful. My colleagues and students were amazing. I taught some dynamic classes, chaired and sat on a plethora of dissertation committees, and participated in service-oriented work in partnership with the Baltimore City Public Schools. Although not a key determinant of success, I continued my passion of publishing several articles in high-impact education journals.

I was comfortable and successful at Morgan State University, but my personal life was changing. My over 15-year relationship with my then-husband deteriorated. During this extremely confusing time for me (and us), I tried to express my emotions without having them overwhelm me [this was a skill I learned during the dissertation process (Grosland 2010)]. Yet, I was deeply emotional and became sick, contracting walking pneumonia (unaware of it for days—a problematic situation for an asthmatic), breaking out into hives for the first time ever, and experiencing my first (and hopefully only) anxiety attack. Due to the shifting of our personal goals and views on life, it was at that point our marriage ended. It was difficult, but the ending of our marriage changed my whole perspective and made me a better person. I have continued on my path to be truer to who I am and to come more into congruence with my purpose—personally and professionally.

I continued to live and work in Baltimore and eventually went on to meet a wonderful new partner. I was/am happy. However, over time my mother's health became a concern, and I went to Tampa to visit her more. Though I didn't have any of the previous symptoms, my health too started to change in different ways. My doctor told me to settle down and that moving, or other major life changes, were probably not good for me.

But change is inevitable. My partner was offered a new job as a vice president of a construction company, located in the Orlando, Florida area. I stayed in Maryland because my home and job were there, but the stress of a long-distance relationship and my mother's changing health took emotional, health, and financial tolls on me. Eventually, I chose to leave my tenure-track position at Morgan State University to relocate for family reasons (see also Davila and Aviles, this volume). Academia waits for no one, so it was a *risky* move, but I had to do it for my own health and well-being. It was an emotional departure for me. I didn't know what the future would hold career-wise or if I would choose to remain in academia. Perhaps I should have learned by this point that changing jobs in academia was not something I preferred, but in reflection I was—and am—living out a larger narrative for many working women: we sacrifice and risk our careers in the name of family and caretaking, and through these actions, we come to know the complexities of our worth.

Regardless of this narrative, and the larger issues related to the marginalization of working women, I was thrust back onto the job market. I knew that it didn't matter that I had been successful in every measurable way in all of my K-12 and higher education positions. Higher education and the professoriate are fickle, so I was open to any and everything.

The (Un)Familiar: The Not New of Newness

Even though I was "prepared" for a change, I could never be really prepared enough until it *actually* happened. Truth of the matter was that I had engaged in several types of faculty positions that I could imagine having. I was proud of my accomplishments. I enthusiastically and rigorously searched job postings and networked in as many ways as my introversion could perceive. I met some amazing people along the way.

I conducted a mostly regional job search that resulted in a position at the University of South Florida as Assistant Professor in Educational Leadership. I was ecstatic! I was fortunate that my search did not result in a full geographic change. The competition for academic positions is fierce, and I know many women academics who have had to uproot themselves or their families (see also Tondreau, Guyotte, and Richardson, this volume) in order to stay active as faculty or to advance in their careers. This sort of risk, combined with persistent gender inequity, adds additional stress for women, so reducing this stress was important for me (as well as for my "stop moving" doctor).

My enthusiasm is also part and parcel of the unexpected changes that come with a new context. At the time of this writing, I've been in a faculty tenure-track position at my research-intensive institution for less than a year. I'm living in an area of the country that I'm familiar with, and in a line of work that is similar to previous roles. In my current position, I'm not new to the academic work (e.g., high-impact publishing, chairing dissertations, teaching, and conference presentations) but I *am* new to my institution. Within every higher education institution I've worked, I've found similarities, but I also recognize that each has unique expectations; therefore, beginning anew I'm in (re)vision. Be it new classes or a different emphasis on teaching, research, or service, this feeling of both *unfamiliar and new*, and *familiar and not new* sometimes feels like a conundrum. But, guess what? I'm profoundly excited to be the not/new colleague again.

Unwieldy but Highly Valued and Traveled

I know well some of the choices I've made felt like sacrifices at the time, but I have no regrets. Throughout my professional life, I have always had positive experiences and, most importantly, have gotten to know myself better as a woman and as an academic. I've learned not to compare myself to other people, to do quality work, and to be open to all possibilities. I would say my career lessons are applicable to all aspects of life, but I offer these especially for women who come from traditionally marginalized backgrounds and to our allies.

As for me, I'm planning to take my doctor's advice to slow down my rate of change, though that's hard because everything in the universe changes. However, I have accepted my own pace of change and that I am a risk-taker who often goes against the grain—so who knows what the future holds? Change is usually good, and starting something new is good. I've found it to be a way to (re)invent myself. I think that I realize this more when I steadfastly fulfill the aspects of my life that are not related to academia. I'm excited to learn, accomplish goals, and experience the newness in my current academic position, but mostly I'm looking forward to learning something new about myself.

References

Chase, Susan E. 2005. "Narrative Inquiry: Multiple Lenses, Approaches, Voices." In *The SAGE Handbook of Qualitative Research*, edited by Norman K. Denzin and Yvonna S. Lincoln, 651–681. Thousand Oaks: Sage.

Clandinin, D. Jean, and F. Michael Connelly. 2004. *Narrative Inquiry: Experience and Story in Qualitative Research*. San Francisco: Jossey-Bass.

Clandinin, D. Jean, and Heather Raymond. 2006. "Note on Narrating Disability." *Equity & Excellence in Education: University of Massachusetts School of Education Journal* 39 (2): 101–104.

Clandinin, D. Jean, and Jerry Rosiek. 2007. "Mapping a Landscape of Narrative Inquiry: Borderland Spaces and Tensions." In *Handbook of Narrative Inquiry: Mapping a Methodology*, 35–76. Thousand Oaks: Sage.

Elbaz-Luwisch, Freema. 1997. "Narrative Research: Political Issues and Implications," *Teaching and Teacher Education* 13, no. 1 (January): 75–83.

Grosland, Tanetha J. 2010. "'We Better Learn Something'—Antiracist Pedagogy in Graduate School." PhD dissertation, University of Minnesota, Twin Cities.

Grosland, Tanetha J., Venus McGhee, and Holly Brody. 2014. "Asking Hard Questions: Engaging Equity and Inquiry for Professional Development." *Scholar-Practitioner Quarterly* 7 (4): 416–428.

CHAPTER 9

The Ancestral Double Dutch: From Cotton Myths to Future Dreams

Stephanie P. Jones

ON MY WAY BACK

Black women scholars are always in the act of (re)living. We live our own lives while simultaneously reaching out to others through their stories. These stories float toward us as we are the users and hearers of their words.

Sharpe (2016) charts this voyage of "living in the wake" as a method that suggests "sitting with, a gathering, and a tracking of phenomena" (13) that impacts the lives of Black people across the diaspora. In some ways, each Black academic can chronicle how their own research sits in the wake of both the past and the present.

My very own livelihood as a professor is through the offspring of racialized trauma—memories that leave permanent traces of that history in the brain (Van der Kolk 2015). In grade school, my teacher planned a lesson about slavery that included each student receiving and picking their own cotton plant. That teacher didn't know picking cotton was already in my blood. Blood as in carrying the invisible scars of my

S. P. Jones (✉)
Grinnell College, Grinnell, IA, USA

© The Author(s) 2018
S. A. Shelton et al. (eds.), *Feminism and Intersectionality in Academia*,
https://doi.org/10.1007/978-3-319-90590-7_9

mother's mama, and bloody in terms of the currency that history still accepts from Black women's bodies.

I have been mapping my own way back to myself (and to that teacher).

Sharpe (2016) has written a note of truth in that we all might be "trying to articulate a method of encountering a past that is not past" (13).

Cotton Myths

Gather.
Pinch.
Yank.
Bleed.

Gather. Pinch. Yank. Bleed.

At first, I used two hands.
I didn't know how to reach my fingers around the ball without slicing the tips of my fingers open. I didn't want to bleed.
I ain't want my fingers to be ugly.
I pushed back the thorny sides and pulled the white center away from the edges.
It was stubborn and didn't want to be picked.
It wanted to stay there and be. In the wind.

My mama had one plant in each hand, her elbows bending straight up to heaven.

She put her hand over that white ball and it disappeared.
Like when the preacher laid hands on folks on Sunday.
That cotton—and those bodies moved so quickly with screams of hallelujah, and cries of the promised land.
When the sun went down, the weight of the bag was the only proof that counted.

One hand. Other hand. One hand. Other hand. Make the cotton disappear.

Gather, pinch, yank, bleed.

That day, my teacher tried to teach a lesson. She tried to teach from her imagination.

As a Black teacher educator, I think about her willingness and probable excitement in teaching about slavery. I wonder if she was excited to teach the lesson that day. Did she plan out how she was going to introduce cotton to her students? What about who picked the cotton versus who watched others pick cotton?

But, for a Black child, she triggered the part of my genes that slavery never forgot.

Survival

Slavery and academia are spaces in which we were never meant to survive. And some of us didn't. But those of us who are still here, we try to use our dreams, create and follow maps left for us from the past. We do this to persist here.

One of those maps left from the past is the erasure of the space between I and we. My storytelling begins with "I, me, and my," but the personal always becomes the collective. So, the use of "we" in a story about myself means a recognition of shared experiences of Blackness and womanhood both in and outside educational spaces.

The "we" that I write here is the same "we" that was sung in our battle cries for freedom and transcendence. The use of "we" is a two-letter map that shows that I am taking my sisters along with me by validating their stories as wisdom and knowledge.

Returning to Sharpe's (2016) notion of living in the wake also means that there is blurred concept of time as a linear concept. Because our past is so integrated into our daily lives, including the memories of those who lived before us, we move back and forth between the collective "we" of our narratives and the "I" from which we speak to the world.

Mapping

To travel without a map, to travel without a way. They did, long ago. That misdirection became the way.
   Dionne Brand, *A Map to the Door of No Return* (2001)

Where am I going?

Traversing academia in brown skin means this question is tattooed on our vitas, branded in our psyche through and through, by inquisitive eyes and ears that don't understand why I work so much. How do I explain (without explaining) where I'm going so that you won't follow me? When Brand (2001) talks about misdirection becoming the way, Black women academics shoulder the responsibility of navigating a world where the instructions are written in a secret "tenure" code of nuances and ambiguity. Following, in this sense, is a predatory action—following and watching us without support, not citing the work we have already published, and consuming our minds and bodies while hiding the evidence.

What if the only map I have doesn't guarantee that I will get to the place I desire?

Dionne Brand (2001) reminds me that maps are a "spiritual location," of our "deeply buried" intentions (1). My intention here is to survive. And that means there is no clear, unobstructed map to that place. So, we create maps, filled with our dreams and other's imaginations so that we can remember.

Even in this format, in a series of titled notes, I am retracing the map of Mother Brand, whose work moves toward a destination of a Black woman consciousness. I write to her, in between the shelves and office hours, by duplicating the small treasure maps that she has left for me in the water and in between the words.

I take up other sisters as my lineage: bell hooks, Dionne Brand, Patricia Hill-Collins, Christina Sharpe, and others. Their work is where I can rest. Their work offers succor, a balm to academia's fascination with preserving the fresh wounds of devaluing, of questioning, and of unrequited labor. The fresh wounds as a graduate student, forcing us to sit through discussions that theorize why Black students are so "different," to the reopened gash of academia where candidates who applied for your job tell you their reason for not accepting it—even though it was only offered to me.

Dreaming of Darkness

I wanted this little brown girl to grow up dreaming the dark and its powerful blackness as a magic space she need never fear or dread.
                                        bell hooks, *Sisters of The Yam* (1993)

I wished that I would have known that there was a difference between imagination and dreaming. Imagination has always pushed me backwards in time—thinking of things that were said or should have been said. But dreaming was the future, for thinking about possibility. I could move in between and around different worlds and times. If I had known about dreaming in the dark—that the dark might possibly be as bell hooks (1993) described it to be—magical and void of fear or concern—maybe I could have talked myself into what was doable.

What imagination looks like for me as a Black woman academic is an ancestral double dutch, tapping lightly on each foot between the past and the present, jumping over and under swinging and stinging ropes. I fall backwards into their stories, stories of aggressions, stories of disrespect and assumed incompetence, and stories of mentoring as unrecognized labor. Academia can be that dark place, eating its young, Black and talented through adjunct positions, voluntary but actually required diversity service, refusal to cite our work while also making plans to steal it.

What would my life look like if I spent it dreaming rather than imagining?

I'm trying to remember the things that I have forgotten over time. I used to know a "powerful blackness" (hooks 1993, 59) where we write for our own recovery, for our magical selves, where we know our wisdom is knowledge. I imagine talking to my Mother Scholars as if they were here with me, and hoping that I am a product of their dreaming come true.

REFERENCES

Brand, Dionne. 2001. *A Map to the Door of No Return: Notes to Belonging*. China: Doubleday Canada.
hooks, bell. 1993. *Sisters of the Yam: Black Women and Self-recovery*. Boston: South End Press.
Sharpe, Christina. 2016. *In the Wake: On Blackness and Being*. Durham: Duke University Press.
Van der Kolk, Bessel A. 2015. *The Body Keeps the Score: Brain, Mind, and Body in the Healing of Trauma*. New York: Penguin Books.

PART III

The Importance of Intersectionality: Exploring the Diversities of Women in the Academy

CHAPTER 10

Honest and Uncomfortable: A Loving Look at My Exclusive Campus

Lisa M. Dembouski

JUST ONE SMALL THING

I wasn't there to hear it, though I have been told the story. At a faculty meeting the spring of my hire, our then-Provost reportedly crowed, "The tenure track faculty searches are going very well! We already have acceptance letters from one faculty of color *and* one faculty with disabilities!"

The latter, presumably, is me. Eleven full-time, tenure-track faculties were hired that spring. I don't know if anyone else in the group has a dis/ability, or whether they had disclosed one during the search process. I know that I did, though, because I *usually* must disclose in order to explain things like the hearing assistive technologies I use.

The Provost's pleasure was probably authentic, and I imagine him grinning broadly, surveying the room, waiting expectantly for celebratory applause; no one I asked remembers if anybody clapped. This was the same Provost who, in response to my request that he enforce microphone use at faculty meetings, would, at the start of those meetings, say, "And let's all remember to use the microphones... you know...

L. M. Dembouski (✉)
Gustavus Adolphus College, St. Peter, MN, USA

so that the people who can't..." (*makes flapping hand gestures near his ear*). He is not the Provost now, though I'm pretty sure I had nothing to do with that.

Since his departure, I've enjoyed a different approach from our interim Provost who, on three different occasions, has invited me to show my fellow faculty members how to correctly and most effectively use the microphones during our meetings. "Be Beyoncé," I initially advised, thinking an alliterative catchphrase would make it easier to remember. "Speak powerfully, project, and hold the mics like this." I modeled and demonstrated the differences in sound quality between effective and ineffective microphone use, all with just a touch of campy theatricality. My colleagues applauded after the second demonstration, which surprised me; I felt understood and accepted, validated even. Their applause also felt like an acknowledgment of support: *yes, people, for the love of god, use the damn mics*. In the end, compliance with microphone use during faculty meetings that academic year was, generously, around sixty percent.

This autumn, the interim Provost again invited me to address the faculty about mic use and, in response to the compliance problem, encouraged me to "be more hard-hitting" than before. Thus, I began,

> Friends *(dramatic pause)*...
> My colleagues *(more pausing)*...
> I have a dream *(I had their full attention now)*...
> I dream of 100% inclusive faculty meetings *(room responds with enthusiastic applause. I wait, happily, then continue with my spiel)*...
> ...In closing, if we cannot make our meetings fully inclusive for everyone, my question for you is this *(one more dramatic pause for effect)*: 'Why not?'"

This left the large room silent for half a beat, then, as I returned to my seat, people applauded again, but in an awkward and uncertain way, which made me wonder if I had hit them *too* hard. I recalled that fragile, fine line between arguing for equity and killing one's chances thereof; it pisses me off.

Anyway, that day everyone used the microphone, but compliance has already slipped backward to, maybe, seventy-five percent inclusive mic use at our meetings, and we're not even at winter break yet.

Despite this equity tango of two steps forward, three steps back, I will concede that we have made progress; there is no awkward hand flapping, for example. However, we're still not inclusive and, frequently, compliance is openly resisted. To illustrate: Once a faculty member, who happened to be next to me, stood up and started to speak; he was stopped and redirected toward a microphone. In response he bellowed,

"Oh, *c'mon*! You all honestly mean to tell me you can't hear me when I talk without it?" Red-faced and furious at his presumption, his hearing privilege, I hiss-growled at him,

"*Y-E-S!*" He looked down to see who had just challenged him, realized it was me, and, recognizing what he had done, muttered, "My apologies." He used the microphone. If I had been across the room, I would have missed that entire exchange. He also may not have yielded to the mic without my blistering glare helping him to decide.

It's a modest request, not that big a deal: Appropriately use a microphone when you speak at the faculty meetings. Simple. The room is large, the acoustics are poor, there are a lot of us in there, and it makes an important difference for equitable access to spoken/auditory information, no matter what kind of hearing you have. Reasonable. The fact that such a request has to be pointed out as reasonable is another part of the problem, though, another indication of how *not* inclusive we are. If I have to justify one small thing like this, how would it work when I—or anyone—needed more complex adaptations?

Truthfully, to *completely*—and most equitably—access faculty (and other) meetings, I would utilize far more complicated and expensive accommodations, like the ones offered for free to me as a student and adjunct instructor at my previous institution. But here, I lay low, try not to ask for too much, not cost a lot, not stand out, accepting the less-than-optimal, just as so many of my dis/abled faculty colleagues, particularly my dis/abled *women* faculty colleagues, do (Albanesi and Nusbaum 2017; Svyantek 2017). Therefore, you'd think my request, being so minor, would not be a problem. Yet *it very clearly is*. Something beyond me is so deeply entrenched that regular reminders at the start of each faculty meeting, three microphone demonstrations, and two Deans running around bringing mics to people on the floor have been insufficient to garner compliance or fully effect positive change. I suspect the problem is this: exclusion borne of ableism. A variety of definitions for "ableism" exist; theorizing this topic has been evolving over time. It is a complex and multilayered concept that requires thoughtful consideration and openness to explore effectively. I personally align with the descriptions of ableism provided by Evans et al. (2017, 1–4). Essentially, in an ableist environment, able-bodiedness is the assumed—and desired—standard.

In this chapter, I will explain ways that I see ableism functioning on my campus. I will also contend that it is past time that we change our exclusive ways and will suggest actions to begin our individual and institutional paths toward dis/ability inclusion. (Nomenclature note: I understand the ongoing academic conversations about how or when to use words like "disability" or "disabled" or "impaired," and I acknowledge merit in every viewpoint. I personally prefer the use of the slash—"dis/ability"—that Anderson and Merrell (2001) discuss. To me, the slash represents *the range* of ability; that we are all, always, at some point on a spectrum of more or less ability, depending on the situation and what we are expected to do.)

Me, Briefly

To provide you with a bit of context, so that you know where I'm coming from when I say the things that I do about dis/ability, I offer "my elevator speech"—the most abbreviated version I've got—of mine: I'm pretty much deaf.

Elevator speech for taller buildings: the medical term for me is late-deafened. I was hearing until my mid-twenties when I was diagnosed with Ménière's disease; I rapidly lost most of my hearing over a few years' time shortly thereafter. Going from a hearing person to a Deaf without my devices, and Hard of Hearing one with them (DHH) one has definitely presented the most challenges for me, since hearing is the norm in most places, had been all I had known, and I needed time to adapt. There are other Ménière's characteristics that affect me, too, but that I don't write as much about. For example, I experience constant tinnitus and regular inner ear pressure akin to flying in an airplane; these can reach unholy levels when the barometric pressure is falling. Ménière's is an inner ear disease, so I also have quite poor balance, and I frequently walk tipsily and/or trip, even when I am stone sober. I also continue to experience occasional bouts of dizziness, though nothing as bad as what I had before the (two) surgeries that alleviated most of that vertigo. Ménière's kind of sucks.

Anyway, now in my early fifties, I call myself DHH. I use a high-powered hearing aid and an FM microphone when I am in the hearing public. I use other supports such as captioning, amplification systems, or sign language interpreters whenever they are provided, too. The devices are for my left ear, which sustains a moderate-to-profound hearing loss depending on the Hz/frequency; my right ear has no useable hearing and is deaf no matter what I do.

One thing I want you to know about my assistive devices: While they *help*, they do not give me perfect hearing; far from it. I still spend an extraordinary amount of effort and energy listening, searching for visual cues (including whatever speechreading I can manage, which is harder than it looks), and mentally filling in the blanks when I miss words or key content, which happens, well, always. What hearing people do effortlessly and without thinking actually consumes a great deal of my cognitive and physical reserves every day. So, behaviors like correctly using the microphones at faculty meetings really freakin' matter to me.

As for the rest of me, I am many things, same as you. I partake of several rewarding interests, enjoy fulfilling relationships, and relish my comfortable and restorative home life. I am white, European American, middle class, heterosexual, and cisgender, features that exemplify ways that I am also very "able," very high on the privilege continuum. It is important to me that I am known as a whole person. For example, I am not *only* my "DHHness," a term I prefer to "hearing loss" because it carries no judgment and does not value hearing over not hearing. We are all so much more than a singular self, and I am no different. We are our intersections. That said, I also believe each of us can take up the mantle of our chosen activism, social justice issues that we want to spotlight and change, and one of mine is dis/ability equity, so here I am.

My Work

I love my job.

I am an Assistant Professor of Education at a nationally ranked, faith-based, residential, liberal arts college in the US Upper Midwest. My institution is recognized as highly selective and emphasizes excellence for students and all campus members, including faculty. I love this community and feel grateful to be a part of it.

The current academic year is my fourth here; if all goes well, I will earn tenure in spring of 2020. I am the newest faculty hire in my department and in the lowermost percentile of seniority at the college overall;

the top person has been here since 1971. Therefore, tenure does not feel particularly safe or reassuring for me. It is unlikely our department will grow larger, and "last in, first out" is still the law of the academic land. I feel pressure to prove myself, to be essential, while simultaneously appearing independent and unneedy: A reality I imagine is familiar to many of my untenured sisters in academia. I also know my efforts at non-needy essentialness could be futile if my department is downsized.

As I mentioned, I am a professor of education. To help my mom understand my job, I explain that "I teach people to be teachers." I instruct an array of courses mandated by the state teaching board, supervise students during various licensure preparations, advise education majors, and in 2020 will lead a school-based January-term study-away course that I developed (to the Caribbean—don't hate). Opportunities here, for students *and* faculty, are wide-ranging, very liberal arts-y, and attractive on multiple levels. As a liberal arts college graduate myself, I find our diverse offerings both familiar and tremendously appealing.

My scholarly work is equally varied, typically qualitative and narrative, exploring topics of teacher preparation and induction, equity and inclusion, and, increasingly, dis/ability, including my own (i.e., Dembouski 2018). This chapter you're reading is a perfect example of the scholarship I most enjoy: honest, transparent, investigative, and purposeful, with an eye toward socially just change. It feels both liberating and terrifying to research and write this personally. I love adding my voice to so many academic conversations, and I am joyous when people respond positively to my contributions, especially when I write about dis/ability. I also worry incessantly about my scholarly activity and feel anxious when my marginalized selves—particularly the DHH, female ones—are ignored or considered inconsequential within the realm of academic thought and effort. Such minimizing of my scholarship, by someone in a position of power over me, has already happened in my short time on this campus. That incident, naturally, exacerbated my fears, but also fuels my resolve to continue.

My service and committee work are intentionally more focused than my teaching or scholarship. I initially chose them because of my personal interests and continue with them primarily because I see a niche on this campus that needs filling: We have too few people who understand dis/ability topics. So, I serve on committees that address issues of diversity, equity, and inclusion. I also participate in shorter, one-off service opportunities toward a more inclusive campus, like teach-ins and panel events. I have pursued grant dollars that would improve accessibility for students, staff, and visitors here. Access and inclusion are things that matter to me. I love and care about this college community, too. I am therefore willing to contribute my service time and efforts toward achieving greater equity on campus.

Because here's the uncomfortable truth: My college *sucks* when it comes to inclusion. There. I said it. I named the elephant in our institutional room. Specifically, and until very recently, dis/ability accessibility and inclusion were glaringly absent from *every* place I looked for them on this campus, and the invisibility bothered me. As an easy example: Until I arrived on campus in 2014, there were no automatic door openers for the building that housed the Education and Nursing departments. The entrances had been that way—inaccessible and out of ADA compliance—since the building was added in 1998. For context, the ADA, or Americans with Disabilities Act, was first enacted as federal law eight years earlier, in 1990, and was amended in 2008, primarily to help people out with things like how to *define* the dis/abilities protected by the law. Imagine this: accessibility rights were not guaranteed for dis/abled people in the USA *until 1990*, implementation did not happen immediately upon the signing of the law, eight years later buildings that did not meet ADA standards were still being added to college campuses, and 18 years after *that* there continued to be so much "confusion" that more attention to the law was required. *I can't even.*

Back to my easy example: People used that building every day, and no one did anything about the inaccessible doors until I got there sixteen years later (and *twenty-four* years after the ADA was passed) to squawk about it. It's clear that able-bodied people have dominated this campus for decades, so much so that *there is pushback and persistent noncompliance about using microphones at faculty meetings*, for god's sake. Ableism—particularly hegemonic, internalized ableism—is the norm here on my campus and, quite likely, on your campuses, too.

Getting Woke

I recognize dis/ability equity will take some doing to achieve. Accessible entrances and compliant microphone use are just two small examples of the inclusion work we have yet to do on my campus. I do not mean to sound judgmental or to condemn anyone here; as I hope I've made clear, I love this community and these people. I only want to highlight that we, myself included, are far from "woke" (as my students say), even among those of us I consider more "woke," more knowledgeable and aware, than others.

For instance, last summer two colleagues who were looking for suggestions approached me. One coordinates student accessibility services on campus, and the other teaches a world language. Both were looking for input to make the language course more accessible for a hard of hearing student. First, how great is that? I would definitely write both their names in the "more aware" column of people at my institution. I was eager to work with them because I was so pleased—I felt *grateful*—that they cared, that they wanted to make a difference for one of My People, this DHH student I have never met.

I also suspect my colleagues contacted me because they had their doubts about this student's ability to succeed in a world language course: How could a person with a hearing loss learn when so much of language can be tonal, involving nuanced aural elements that might be challenging to discern? What about the fact that a great deal of homework relies on listening to audio recordings? I wanted them to know these needn't be barriers to success, that I knew a Deaf person who had successfully taken French *and* Spanish classes, for example. To their credit, neither person outright said the hard of hearing student didn't belong in the course, but I think they were wary; I know both were motivated to support the student however they could.

At one point during our conversations, we were discussing those accommodation letters that originate from the Accessibility Services Office, the ones that essentially "out" a student and their dis/ability and identify the accommodations that they should be provided, like test-taking in alternative settings or more time to complete assignments (though such letters rarely tell instructors *how* to provide these, which is problematic in other ways). Feeling frustrated, like I was not getting through to my colleagues, I decided it was time for another uncomfortable truth.

> One thing you should know: we—and I'll presume to speak for many of us here—we hate those letters. They scare the hell out of the people who receive them, they do not permit us to disclose our dis/abilities on our own terms, and they feel so extreme, like we're going begging for what will put us on the same level as our peers. They do not represent 'an unfair advantage,' as many people wrongly assume, they instead represent actions toward equity. But the way the letters are usually worded, they're more

like patronizingly patting us on the head while saying, 'Oh, here, please do these things for the poor little student who can't.' Infuriating. So disempowering.

This was probably really offensive to the woman who spends a lot of her day writing and sending those letters and, from the look on her face, it was. Still, amazingly, she did not get defensive, nor did she minimize or dismiss what I'd said. Instead, she listened and allowed me to elaborate. I detailed the various ways I'd had professors react to those letters, none of them positive. I talked about the privacy theft inherent in the letters, and how that makes me feel equal parts misrepresented, exposed, incensed, and raw. I shared how I'd taken over sending my own letters during grad school, to reclaim my power and autonomy, curtail potential misunderstanding, and invite dialogue with my professors.

Meanwhile, my world languages colleague was just listening as I explained all this, when suddenly she blurted, "RIGHT! I mean, *right*?! What IF there wasn't any need for accommodation or accessibility request letters *because my classroom already was accessible?!*"

Boom.

Right there I knew she got it, that she understood what I have been preaching all along: If inclusion were the law of the land, accessibility would simply *be there*. No one would have to go begging for it. No one would be singled out. No one would have to feel vulnerable: *What will they think about me if they know I am X? What if they tell me "no," or refuse this thing I need? What if they feel sorry for me, or see me as incapable now?*

Best of all, no one will have to disclose if they don't want to. Though I am confident that, if we had a more inclusive campus, people *would* disclose, because they would know it was safe to do so, safe to be wholly ourselves. This vicious cycle of silence and anonymity also means we don't listen to and learn from the very people who can teach us how to be more inclusive in the first place. On a safe and inclusive campus, the Deans wouldn't have to run around the faculty meeting jamming microphones under my colleagues' noses, *and* I wouldn't have to plead my case for mic use in the first place; it would simply be acknowledged as necessary for equitable access and everyone would unquestioningly comply. We're not there yet, but we could be, and you could be, too. I offer suggestions for how in the remainder of this chapter.

Inclusion: "Easy" as 1–2–3

Safety

As I hinted earlier, safety is essential to dis/ability inclusion. Beyond the obvious requirements that all campus community members have their physical safety needs met, our intellectual and emotional safety must also be ensured, and should be equally "obvious" as essential for a healthy and inclusive community. These kinds of safeties mean people can speak their truths—and honestly represent themselves—without fear. We will not have to worry about job security, or how others will treat us. We will not question whether we belong or can contribute positively to our campus. We will feel not only accepted for who we are, but *valued* as unique and welcomed community members who enhance the quality and diversity of who we are as a whole.

Achieving safety means we must be willing to be uncomfortable, invite honesty and transparency, must listen to, and really *hear* what others tell us. Like my Accessibility Services colleague had to do when I raged on a key activity of her job description. We must also be trustworthy with what we're told and honor any follow through we might promise. When people feel safe on campus, those of us who have something to say, such as a dis/ability to disclose, can also speak to what works best for us in terms of access and accommodation. Like compliant mic use at meetings. Expect to be surprised, by the way, at how do-able most accommodations really are.

Also, while I would never call out dis/abled people and say, "Here. You've got a willing audience, so now disclose," I will gently suggest that the more that we reveal about ourselves and our needs, the better able-bodied people will know how to accommodate us. They cannot read our minds and often have *no idea* what to do until we explicitly tell them. This can be awkward and wearisome, yes, but is also necessary. For multiple reasons, including the ways Western culture trains women to express our needs, I personally have been mildly benign when I have introduced myself and my accessibility preferences, but have felt emboldened just in the writing of this chapter to change my timidity. I am practicing being direct about what I'm asking for and why it matters. Which is still scary, but will be less so the safer our campuses become.

It's on All of Us

The president of my college recently hired a faculty colleague to serve as her "Special Assistant for Diversity, Equity, and Inclusion (DEI)." I think this direct and public action originating from our institution's leader is wonderful, because it makes a powerful statement about the value of inclusion and its place on our campus. The new Special Assistant is also more "woke" in terms of how she defines "diversity," and I am delighted to report dis/ability is on her DEI radar. I simultaneously feel trepidation, because it is possible that a high-profile faculty member wearing this new administrative hat could translate to the rest of us forgetting that inclusion is *everyone's* responsibility. Dis/ability must be a part of everything done on our campus. We all must be willing to learn more about inclusion topics and to implement inclusive practices in what we do every day. It also means we must not rely on the marginalized or minoritized members of various groups on campus to do all the work, or to be the "ambassadors" and represent for their groups and/or their dis/abilities. Instead, we all learn, contribute, and care about equity, and we all make daily efforts toward inclusive ends.

Once in my service committee work here, and before the DEI Special Assistant's hire, I asked why dis/ability was not already a part of our focus regarding diversity, equity, and inclusion. The answer, delivered by a Black man who was then the committee's leader, was, "We'll get there, we'll get there, but first we must address this other thing" (which was racial equity). No one in the room said another word, nor did anyone appear to question his reply. Internally, I felt a blizzard of responses, depending on which aspect of me was feeling it. As a DHH person, I felt stunned and silenced, and my identity as a dis/abled person was swiftly and publicly deemed unimportant for our group's work. That no one contested our leader's answer made me feel alone, unsupported, and wishing I wasn't already "out" as a person with a dis/ability. As a white woman, I felt powerless to refute this Black man's statement. I had no intention of being the race-majority asshat who displaces the importance of racial equity. Nor do I ever *want* to displace racial equity as essential to a healthy campus; I felt frustrated that if I challenged his reply, I would be misunderstood in these ways. I also felt indignation and resentment, because I could not disagree with his answer more. Rather, I believe we can, *and should*, address topics of diversity, equity, and inclusion simultaneously. Such concerns will vary across campuses, and even on the same campus will change over time. But I do not agree that we must exclude some groups in the interest of supporting others; I am certain this work can happen concurrently.

I recognize this "it's on us all" suggestion toward inclusion will be challenging. We'll need strong, effective, and ongoing professional development with support from campus leaders. We'll need time, and to talk with each other. We'll likewise need to be generous and recognize that, similar to the continuum of ability, there is also a range for those who are more and less inclusive: Some people simply have more practice and are more skilled at inclusion, than others. But all of us are developing, we all are learning. The work need not be excessive, nor does it require a ton of extra time to do well. It simply takes intention and an open heart. The point is not perfection, it's growth.

A Willingness to Change

I agree with my coworker who recently wrote that, while our campus is welcoming, we are not inclusive:

> Many of our under-represented colleagues are tolerated—but not included...inclusion means our communities will change, which we tend to forget. We tend to be welcoming as long as the person joining us will be "like us." Yet, the "us" is often a small homogenous group with privilege. (Cooper 2017, para. 9)

What Cooper writes has been precisely my experience here. Most important in her message is the part about change. It seems so obvious, yet it is also so quickly forgotten: If we want things to be different, we must change the ways that we do them. How that change plays out will depend on who you are and what your campus community is already like.

On my campus, what I see as most critical for change are, (a) a willingness to work together as allies, which includes being vulnerable, making mistakes, apologizing and moving on, and, (b) more devotion to *mindfulness*, attentiveness toward inclusion that is not rooted in able-bodied ways of being; we need to think in differently abled ways. Such "inclusive mindfulness" is precisely what my world languages faculty colleague attempted for her DHH student this year. I was curious to hear how that student's story ended, so contacted my colleague to find out. She reports he did great all year, earning A grades in both of his language courses. She mentioned he spent more time than the hearing students on the audio/listening homework, and that this served him well, offered him some advantages. She also volunteered this: She is convinced that the various pedagogical steps she took to create an inclusive classroom made her a better teacher overall.

My analogy for this third "how to be more inclusive" suggestion may seem strange, but bear with me: It's like my cooking spices. All my life, I thought spices were supposed to be stored "up high," in cabinets mounted above the countertops. Other than those countertop spice racks that revolve (and that I have always considered decorative rather than functional), I have only ever known spices to be kept in upper cabinets. Two years ago, I moved to a new home with a "tall" kitchen, and I, following the spice-storage pathways I always have, unpacked my spices into an upper cabinet. Which, at five feet tall, I have been struggling to reach on tiptoe ever since. It finally occurred to me *last week*: This is just not working. I either can't reach what I want, I tip half the rest of them over trying to get the one I need, going for a step stool every time I want oregano irritates me, these spices just ... Hey! *I can move them*! It no longer matters that I have always ever known spices to be stored up high; they just are not accessible to me this way. The old ways did not work. I moved the spices and changed the makeup of my kitchen from there on out. Et voilà. It's a silly metaphor, but an apt one: This small, easy change has made a big difference. All it took was for me to notice there was a problem, consider another way of being that I had never really known, and then decide to act.

...

As I mentioned before, I know I am not solely my DHHness. While dis/ability equity and inclusion are essential to my professional (and personal) productivity and well-being, they are not all I am. We are so diverse, and our intersectionalities show up in so many ways. None of them are more important or essential than others; all of them matter.

At the same time, some of those intersections, those unique parts of who we are, must occasionally be spotlighted, given air play, allowed to instruct in ways that enhance the health and wellness of our profession and communities. Ableism-based exclusion is too often the norm, the way of things in our society and on our campuses, and this must change. Although I shouldn't have to point it out, I'll do so anyway: Inclusion benefits everyone. If you have used automatic door openers to get into your building when your hands were full, if you appreciate curb cuts and elevators when you're pushing a cart or stroller, if you've used inclusive pedagogies and realized that, as a result, you're now a better teacher, then you have benefitted from inclusion, too. Facets of inclusion and the "easy" ways to become more so will vary depending on who you are and where you're starting as a community. The end point, though, is the same: inclusion must be as much a part of our institutional DNA as anything else. "Inclusive" must be who we *are*, not something "we do." Thank you for the ways you'll make it so on your campuses. I'll keep working on mine.

REFERENCES

Albanesi, Heather, and Emily A. Nusbaum. 2017. "Encountering Institutional Barriers and Resistance: Disability Discomfort on One Campus." In *Disability as Diversity in Higher Education: Policies and Practices to Enhance Student Success*, edited by Eunyoung Kim and Katherine C. Aquino, 185–199. New York: Routledge.

Americans with Disabilities Act, Pub. L. No. 101–336, §2, 104 Stat. 328 (1990).

Anderson, Myrdene, and Floyd Merrell. 2001. "End Notes: Semiotically Digesting Dis/Ability." In *Semiotics and Dis/Ability: Interrogating Categories of Difference*, edited by Linda J. Rogers and Beth Blue Swadener, 267–272. Albany: State University of New York Press.

Cooper, Thia. 2017. "The Edit Opinion Piece: What Does Liberty Look Like Now?" *Edit Magazine*, Summer. http://www.ed.ac.uk/edit-magazine/editions/issue-4/liberty-look-like-now.

Dembouski, Lisa M. 2018. "The Instructor Is Partially Deaf: Hard of Hearing Professing in Higher Education." In *International Perspectives on Teaching with Disability: Overcoming Obstacles and Enriching Lives*, edited by Michael S. Jeffress. New York: Routledge Press.

Evans, Nancy J., Ellen M. Broido, Kirsten R. Brown, and Autumn K. Wilke. 2017. *Disability in Higher Education: A Social Justice Approach*. San Francisco: Jossey-Bass.

Svyantek, Martina. 2017. "'Differing Abilities' and Hula-Hooping Bears: Disability Activism on Campus." Paper Presented at the International Conference of Disability Studies in Education, Minneapolis, MN, June 2017.

CHAPTER 11

Afro-Puerto Rican Primas: Identity, Pedagogy, and Solidarity

Erica R. Davila and Ann M. Aviles

SITUATING OUR HERSTORY

As we sat around our grandmother's dining room table making paper flowers for our uncle's wedding with our aunts and female cousins, the conversation focused on marriage. The message was clear: It was our responsibility to keep a happy home by being "good" women who could cook and clean in order to find and keep a good man. "One day we'll be making flowers for your wedding," was the comment directed at the young girls sitting at the table by the adult women. We were about eight and nine years old at the time, and already, we were being told and shown that our worth as women was directly connected to our relationship with men. The irony of this message was subtle at the time. Thirty something years later, the contradiction is even more pronounced.

Our familial dynamics reflect a strong presence of matriarchy; our mothers/aunts and grandmothers were integral to our upbringing, household decisions, and overall care, supporting each other through

E. R. Davila (✉)
Lewis University, Romeoville, IL, USA

A. M. Aviles
University of Delaware, Newark, DE, USA

© The Author(s) 2018
S. A. Shelton et al. (eds.), *Feminism and Intersectionality in Academia*,
https://doi.org/10.1007/978-3-319-90590-7_11

experiences with interpersonal violence, housing instability, financial instability, and health/mental health calamities. Although we had such strong female influences in our family, the women in our family were socialized within a patriarchal context, so our own socialization as Puerto Rican women is nuanced. While women in our family were integral to ensuring the family stayed together by demonstrating a lot of love and power in their familial positions, they also exhibited a subordinate role by catering to the men of the family in many ways. These actions, while not intentional, worked to reproduce gender dynamics by constantly conveying messages centering our and their worth around male approval.

As first cousins who both found our way into higher education, we have the advantage of sharing many entangled lived experiences based on our familial connections and the concurrent development of our scholarly identities. In this chapter, we highlight some of these shared experiences in an attempt to examine our identity development and how our Afro-Puerto Rican identities intersect and mingle as scholars embedded in institutional spaces. These narratives are not meant to be chronological, but instead provide highlights of our experiences that reflect significant aspects of our development and subsequent approach to navigating our respective institutions and various spaces imbued with social constructs of gender and race. We both completed our studies close to home, staying in Illinois for the duration of our college careers. Our decision in staying local reflects the limited institutional guidance from our high schools (we both attended Chicago Public Schools K-12), our lack of navigational capital (Yosso 2005) within institutions of higher education, and our family's financial limitations to pay out-of-state tuition. Further, as girls/women, we were encouraged to stay close to home/live at home while attending school, reflective of a racialized/gendered experience—in many Latinx families, girls are expected to remain tied to their households to assist with household responsibilities and often do not move out until marriage.

Our experiences were (and are) embedded in institutional spaces, especially schools that did not value our understanding of family. For example, as women in academia without children of our own, many colleagues question our other familial relationships, like caring for other children within and outside of our families, or even caring for our parents. I (Erica) recall when I had to make the hard decision to leave a tenured position to care for my mother (see also Grosland, this volume). One of my colleagues (who was above me in rank) directly questioned my plan to leave my position and move across the country, wondering why I could not simply hire someone to care for her, although each culture and even family unit has their own understanding of the responsibility to care for parents and family in general. As Puerto Rican women raised in a matriarchal family, we see the necessity for children to care for their parents as being as natural as parents caring for their children.

It is important to note that while matriarchy is sometimes understood as the opposite of patriarchy, it is not simply the opposite. Unlike patriarchy, matriarchies do not work within hierarchy; instead, we argue it is about putting needs at the center, and in this narrative, my (Erica) mother was in need, and it was a natural response to take care of her. We believe from our lived experiences (highlighted in the narrative above) this understanding of caring for our parents is not the norm within the mainstream culture of the USA. Therefore, when we demonstrate or exhibit cultural norms instilled in us as Puerto Rican women, there are many times that we are misunderstood within institutional spaces, such as misinterpreting a faculty member's (Erica) decision to leave a position as an indicator of not valuing the position or our role as scholars/professors. As we reflect on our upbringing, we understand the contradictions inherent in our familial dynamics and choose to deliberately focus on the power of matriarchy that constantly shapes our worldview, while simultaneously working to be critical of traditional male/female identities, roles, and responsibilities.

Tides of Consciousness

"Donde esta sus pantallas?" (Where are your earrings?) my mother asked me (Ann) as I walked out the door to the gym. "I'm going to work out," I responded. She looked at me with a smirk on her face, stating, "You never know." As a young woman in my early twenties, I was not in a serious, long-term relationship, and my mother was growing concerned. She had married by eighteen and had had her first child by nineteen. In comparison, I was quickly becoming an "old maid" in her eyes. A few years later, still single and in a master's program, I made the decision to move out. My mother was confused, asking, "What did we do?" The implication was that I was moving out because my parents had done something displeasing, but in reality, having lived at home during my undergraduate studies, I just wanted to experience independence.

She didn't understand and even commented, "I assumed you wouldn't move out until you got married." The message was that girls stay home until there is a home provided by a man. I tried as best as I could to explain my intent. Reluctantly, my parents came to terms with my decision. Years later, my mother expressed that she was proud of my bravery and independence, something she would have not imagined for herself during her early twenties. Her affirmation of my moving out demonstrates the tides of consciousness many women experience as we recognize the generative nature of matriarchy within a patriarchal society.

Similar to our proactive stance that centers the power of matriarchy, which was carried to us from the *mujeres* who raised us, we have also made a conscious and deliberate decision to honor and embrace our connections to Blackness. In a society that still maintains a White/Black binary, it was clear from an early age that we were not White. Together we have a multitude of lived experiences that have informed our racial consciousness, and we are framing these experiences as a push/pull or a tide of consciousness because at moments we felt pushed away from Whiteness, and other times we were pulled toward our Blackness. For this chapter, I (Erica) want to share one narrative from my early years and one from not that long ago, during my graduate studies, demonstrating this tide. The first story is about my experience being mainstreamed in the 4th grade after being a student in a bilingual education program from K-3 and learning side-by-side with other Latinx, Spanish-speaking students and teachers. At the age of nine, I felt my world shift, and it was a moment that has stayed with me my whole life. For the first time, I felt like an outsider, not just new to the space but feeling inadequate. The students who were not enrolled in bilingual program (mostly White) teased me for my accent, made fun of my mom's classroom/school presence (which quickly declined), and laughed at the way I dressed. And while I never had a teacher tease me, they did correct my English enough to make me feel incompetent. For the first time, I had to reflect on what made me different and less than; it was clear to me that my cultural identity as Puerto Rican was not accepted. Fortunately, my family (especially my mom) instilled a strong sense of Puerto Rican pride in me, although this self-respect was not easy for me to navigate; the school did not value this identity and sent me a clear message that being Puerto Rican meant that I was not White. While my African American peers and teachers did not make me feel less than or tease me, nevertheless I felt different.

Reflecting on these early experiences in my (Erica's) transition to the English mainstreamed classroom, now I am also entangling an experience that I had in my late twenties in graduate school. By this time, I had reflected a lot on my identity but was still trying to understand and articulate my connections to Blackness as a Puerto Rican. I was in an educational foundations master's level course with students from various departments, and one of my classmates asked me about what I was studying. I mentioned that I was in the Educational Policy Studies Department and was studying the Puerto Rican student experience in Chicago; she responded that my department was really good at not only studying affirmative action, but also successful at applying it. It was clear that this was a direct response to me being a student of color and could be categorized as a microaggression; the underlying message was that students like me were only there to fill a quota. And I recall consciously choosing to align myself with my peers of color for protection and love. While these narratives are quite distinct, both are examples of being pushed and pulled into racial consciousness. Recognizing these ebbs and flows will continue, we choose to embrace our Blackness in the White/Black binary that pervades the USA as we are clear that the power and strength that guide our work are rooted in us embodying our Afro-Puerto Rican identities.

We claim and assert our identities as Afro-Puerto Ricans to respect and re-center our connections to the African Diaspora. Our political ideology reflects that of community organizer and political commentator Rosa Clemente (2017), who in a recent response to the events in Charlottesville, VA, stated,

> Now is the time for us as a [Latinx] people to understand that **as long as anti-Blackness exists within our communities, we have a responsibility to fight anti-Blackness and the system of white supremacy by any means necessary.** It is up to all of us to push back against the race to whiteness. (para. 21, bold in original)

Clemente (2017) believes we must "align ourselves unapologetically with our Blackness" (para. 11). Our shared understandings compel us to assert our Afro-Puerto Rican identities as a conscious and deliberate coalition-building strategy to further create and support anti-oppressive and liberatory spaces within schools and communities. The shared histories of Black and Brown communities set the stage for our work and pedagogical practices. As Critical Race scholars, we work to develop solidarity and coalitions among scholars of color in the academy while seeking to continue to create and support collaborative, liberatory spaces. Our scholarship seeks to contribute to the evolving significance of race and its intersections with gender in the context of higher education.

Our perspectives are not meant to ignore anti-Black rhetoric and sentiment (e.g., Colorism) in Latinx communities, as many Puerto Ricans (and other Latinxs) resist identification with Blackness; we believe this opposition is deeply rooted in ideologies of White supremacy and colonialism. Conversely, many African Americans do not perceive Latinxs as racially Black, contributing to racial/ethnic dichotomies that serve to divide rather than unite. This is not to place blame on any particular community; we highlight these complexities to educate, dispel and nuance racial binaries in the hopes of creating understanding, connection, and solidarity among our respective communities.

Reflections Remain in Broken Mirrors

Walking into the large ballroom to attend the breakfast meeting, we felt nervous excitement stirring in our stomachs. At this point in our educational trajectories, we had both entered Ph.D. programs in education policy (Erica at the University of Illinois-Urbana Champaign and Ann at the University of Illinois-Chicago) and were both recipients of the Diversifying Faculty in Illinois (DFI) fellowship. As recipients, one of the "perks" of being a fellow was attending an annual conference for graduate students of color also pursuing their graduate degrees. The room buzzed with a mix of folks greeting one another. Some seemed to know each other, exchanging hugs and warm greetings, while others meeting for the first time introduced themselves as they found seats at the many tables arranged throughout the room. It was a wondrous sea of Black and Brown university faculty, staff, and students. During the morning breakfast, we heard from faculty of color who encouraged us to address issues of critical importance to our lived experiences, families, and communities. They also impressed upon us the importance of solidarity among Black and Brown communities, creating a safe space in which to advance our scholarship, and importantly expanded our professional and personal sociopolitical consciousness, emphasizing the commonalities and connections (e.g., African diasporic communities) among students and faculty of color in higher education.

After breakfast, we engaged in a full day of workshops and networking. Attending the sessions illuminated for us the flawed "objective" approaches to research, and exposed us to theoretical frameworks such as Critical Race Theory and methodologies such as autoethnography, that affirmed our ancestral ways of being, knowing, and doing (see also Jones, this volume). Throughout the day, we had the opportunity to interact with DFI faculty who provided critical care, guidance, and mentoring, contributing to a network of current and aspiring faculty of color in a variety of academic fields. At the end of the day, a few students arranged an informal small gathering. Even in this more informal setting, we were overwhelmed by the amazing energy created by being in the presence of our Black and Brown *gente*. We discussed our families, school experiences, music, movies, and other topics for a few hours before we headed back to our hotel rooms to prepare for another day of learning from faculty, staff, and students who sought to increase our navigational and institutional capital. This experience and the subsequent conferences, programming, and support provided by our involvement with DFI created lasting collaborations, friendships, and allyship for us—academic collaborations and friendships that we continue to cultivate and nurture some fifteen years later. DFI also provided a model of mentorship that resists traditional exploitation of graduate student labor (often stratified along gender and racial lines) and is instead rooted in communal, loving relationships in which we "lift as we climb." In our current faculty roles, it is our responsibility to continue traditions that we had the privilege of experiencing as graduate students.

Attending these conferences was one of our first experiences with being in a large community with scholars of color who provided critical feedback regarding our scholarship and guidance on navigating our respective institutions/doctoral programs. Moreover, these experiences solidified our rights to claim spaces in predominantly white institutions (PWIs), while simultaneously strengthening our identities as Afro-Puerto Rican scholars. Our involvement in the DFI program reminds us of our responsibility to expand upon spaces in which students of color and other underrepresented groups feel welcomed on campuses. We work to help them understand their right to critique systems of power and privilege, center their experiential knowledge as *counternarrative* (Delgado and Stefancic 2001) to what society writ large says about them, and finally develop a sociopolitical consciousness in which they are "unapologetically" Black and/or Brown. For example, in collaboration with other

DFI alumni, we have developed course assignments and an annual student community forum in which students are asked to reflect on their own experiences with education, make connections to larger social/structural issues, and conduct research to better understand social problems. Working with local community-based organizations exposes and connects students to others engaged in movement building and social justice, while providing examples and tools to address and combat social issues (e.g., racism, sexism, classism) impacting educational access and outcomes for youth of color, women, and other marginalized groups.

While programs such as DFI should not be the only approach to addressing said inequities, in the interim they can/do serve as spaces for critical analysis, coalition building, and action/advocacy across Black and Brown communities. We understand the contradictions inherent in such programs, as they can be culpable in reifying the status quo, rather than dismantling systems of White supremacist capitalist heteropatriarchy (WSCH). Although programs such as DFI create necessary spaces within institutions of higher education, they can also serve White supremacist interests—by having programs that demonstrate their "commitment to diversity" while institutions still center Whiteness and do little to address the systems, ideologies, and policies that maintain WSCH. Ideally, if inequitable systems of access to quality education, housing, healthcare, etc., ceased to exist, programs such as DFI would not be necessary to repair the "broken mirrors" that exist in academia limiting the reflections for many women and students of color; however, long-standing and continued inequities do exist, necessitating the need for programs such as DFI as we work to develop more socially just systems in relation to practices and policies for women and people of color. While critiques of programs such as DFI are warranted, we share our involvement in this program to illuminate the ways in which our engagement informed and shaped our development as critical scholars/educators.

STRUGGLE, LOVE, AND LIBERATION

After successfully completing our doctorates, we continued to be involved in community-based educational programs. As junior faculty, we both participated in a seven-day "Civil and Immigrant Rights Tour," in which we drove two vans across the Midwest and Southern USA with sixteen youth and six adults. We visited six cities (Memphis, Jackson, Selma, Atlanta, Cincinnati, and Toledo) in order to bring to life the issues and topics that were part of a six-week summer youth leadership program geared at facilitating the educational attainment and leadership capacities of Black and Brown youth in Chicago. With co-facilitators, we made a collective, conscious, and deliberate pedagogical decision to identify organizations and individuals that would expose students to our nation's historical realities of oppression, marginalization, inequity, and resistance that have and continue to shape the lived experiences of Black and Brown folks, such as The National Civil Rights Museum, Mississippi Immigrants Rights Alliance (MIRA!), the home of Medgar Evers, National Voting Rights Museum & Institute, Martin Luther King Jr. Center for Non-Violent Social Change, Human Rights Network, National Underground Railroad Freedom Center, and the Farm Labor Organizing Committee, AFL-CIO (FLOC). Exposing students to historical and current issues impacting Black and Brown communities created a better understanding of their collective histories. Throughout our trip, we made explicit connections to common threads of oppression and marginalization within and across our respective Black and Brown communities. These threads laid the foundation for student understandings and the collective action needed to address WSCH.

As junior faculty, we found this experience to be integral to our learning as facilitators, as well as for students' learning and engagement. We believe that all students, particularly students of color living in disinvested communities, can and will excel in education, particularly with culturally relevant, justice-centered approaches to teaching and learning. Further, given our positionalities as Afro-Puerto Ricans, we work to raise awareness of Black ancestry within Puerto Rican and other Latinx communities in an effort to build solidarity among Latinx and Black communities, recognizing our shared histories, struggles, and marginalization within schools and society, due to systems and structures of White supremacy.

One experience that stood out during this summer program was our visit to the Slavery and Civil War Museum, in Selma, Alabama. We were part of the leadership team, but on that hot afternoon, we felt far from being in charge. About twenty of us, youth and facilitators, were walking approximately two city blocks to our next stop on the civil rights youth leadership trip, when we begin to hear two women yelling at us to "bend down and walk faster!" The command was full of rage and berating. We quickly went into the protective role, since we had over a dozen teenagers with us, and as the adults, we were responsible for their safety. Quickly, we became the participants in a slavery simulation and felt that we should model and follow instructions (this was a planned re-enactment; therefore, we knew we were all safe). We were directed to stand against the wall as the women continued to yell out instructions regarding our stance and behavior. They began examining us—asking us to open our mouths, grabbing at us, demanding we turn around so they could get a good look at our physiques. As they began to sort us, they started letting some of us inside while others anxiously awaited outside.

As co-leaders of this simulation, we were informed that we would be "treated as slaves," but what did that really mean? Given the whitewashing of slavery most of us received in our K-12 schooling, did the students, or even we as leaders, really understand what that entailed? We, the authors, were split into separate groups, allowing us to tell the story now from both groups' perspectives as the events unfolded. One group was taken to a dark basement where they were told to yell for help, while the other part of our group was instructed to call out the names of the members in our group from whom we had been separated. We were told they would be able to hear our cries. Seven of us (two adults, five youth) began shouting for help: "Help me, Cynthia!", "Adrian, help!" The cries for assistance went on for three to five minutes.

The other group was led to a different dark room that was set up to feel as though we were in the woods, with trees and other barriers for us to navigate, while literally hearing the shouting from our missing group members. We were genuinely terrified and had to fight the fear and remind ourselves that we were in a simulation; the thoughts of what our ancestors endured overtook us. After this, we were reunited and placed into a simulated slave ship, cramming our entire group of twenty into the space.

The room was dimly lit, and once we were all on the ship, the room went completely dark. One of the simulation facilitators in a loud, exaggerated voice described our cramped conditions; she belted, "Imagine being chained to a sick or dead human being, at your feet, the ship floor covered in vomit, feces, urine, and menses. You haven't eaten for weeks…" We felt waves of grief visualizing the images she described. This simulation provided a perspective, experience, and emotions that no textbook or movie had ever ignited. The heaviness of this reality sunk in, and the intellectual and emotional weight was almost unbearable. Yet before we could begin to process these feelings and thoughts, we were moved on to the next aspect of the simulation.

The facilitators angrily and harshly transplanted us to another dark room, demanding that we "move faster!" Their demands were peppered with verbal assaults of the "n" word. Anxiety filled the room as we heard loud, painful cries coming from a woman. She yelled out, "Don't take my baby!" She continued to plead for her child between her cries of grief. What was likely thirty seconds of this woman's pleas felt like an eternity. Slowly, the room began to light up. We could now see the woman, standing in defense mode, baby clutched in her arms, continuing her crying and pleas to keep her child. The (simulated) baby was eventually snatched from her arms, despite her protective efforts. The woman fell to her knees and continued to cry out for her child. We will never forget this moment in the simulation, as her final cry was filled with so much pain, anger, and grief that even now, over six years later, we both feel chills. By this point, most of our group was either in tears or enraged.

Our simulation ended, and we sat down with our facilitators to process the events in relation to our emotions. One of the students, a Black female, was so impacted by this situation that she made the decision to never use the "n" word again. Prior to this experience, she had used it regularly because she felt the word "wasn't a big deal." This simulation provided insight into her ancestors' experiences—the impact so profound that it resulted in a paradigm shift—she would no longer use a word that stirred up so much anger, pain, and oppression. Reflecting back at that situation currently, we wonder how much of that experience was not only raced, but gendered too. What did, and does, it mean to have our children taken from us—whether it is through the historic practice of slavery, forced sterilization of Puerto Rican women, or the current child welfare system that disproportionately penalizes women of color for domestic violence situations, poverty, and unfair labor/wage practices?

We provide the above illustration to demonstrate the type of work in which we engage given our pedagogical beliefs in critical, justice-centered, education. Through this experience, students better understood their collective histories and those histories' impacts on their current realities. We recognize this work is risky, emotional, and personal, but we continue to be present in these spaces and to practice a pedagogy of love (Darder 2002). We believe that education is a tool for empowerment, liberation, and positive social change. Throughout the six-week program, we shared and cultivated this belief with youth, as we constantly asked,

"Beyond this program, how will you stay connected and involved in leadership and activism in your community and the larger world?" This is also the question we consistently ask ourselves: In what ways can our education and teaching be harnessed as a tool to dismantle the system and structure of White supremacy beyond the classroom and in the daily lives of our students, communities, and families? A few years after the program, while attending a rally on Chicago's west side advocating for "The Fight for $15" (advocacy for a living wage), we ran into one of the summer leadership students. She was enrolled in college at the University of Illinois, Chicago, and was attending the rally with a group she was a part of from campus. She shared how she has been involved in various actions/clubs since her experience with the summer leadership program and continues to work toward justice and equity through her studies and organizational involvement.

This experience is another reminder of the need to build bridges across communities, stay connected to communities of color, and root our teaching, research, and service into our equity efforts with communities; justice is the crux of our work within and beyond the academy. Many academics may (and/or have been conditioned to) view these areas as separate from one another; we view them as overlapping engagements that perpetually inform and shape one another. Our engagement with and in community informs our scholarship—what we choose to study and how we approach research; our teaching—the pedagogical choices including curriculum, assignments, and classroom dynamics; and our service—the types of activities we put energy toward, on and off campus.

Culturally Sustaining Pedagogy

We are continually traversing and negotiating contested space. WSCH is woven into the fabric of US society and its institutions; it must continually be named. Efforts to dismantle these structures are a never-ending struggle for anyone working toward educational, racial, and gender justice. Our continued presence and assertion of our identities as Afro-Puerto Rican women in higher education serve to persistently contest WSCH and anti-Blackness, simultaneously creating alternative spaces and approaches to teaching and learning that work toward transformative processes for liberatory education.

As faculty in the fields of education, human development and family sciences, we have the honor to work with many in-service teachers, pre-service teachers, school leaders, human service candidates, and community organizations. We are intentional in creating introspective spaces in our courses in which students reflect on their own identities (utilizing methods such as critical autoethnography) and positionality; understanding one's "status" when engaging educational and community spaces is necessary in order to address (and ultimately transform) the dynamics of power/privilege and marginalization/oppression occurring in these spaces. We must be honest, critical, and reflective about the ways in which our experiences and positionalities shape the dynamics of our interactions with the world, as well as the ways in which we may become complicit in perpetuating White supremacy and patriarchy. While we work to discuss these issues from a structural standpoint, it is inevitable that discussions regarding privilege, especially White, male privilege, create angst among students associated with these identities. As critical educators, it is our responsibility to push our students into a space of "discomfort" in order to facilitate transformative self-reflection, praxis, and pedagogies that are culturally sustainable (Paris 2012).

The recent events in Charlottesville, Virginia, bear witness to the pervasiveness and function of White supremacy in society. These acts of terror reflect ideologies and systems that perpetuate White supremacy and the oppression of "Other," reminding us of our responsibilities and of our human right to continue to use our platform as educators to work toward a society that is equitable and just. Continuing to build on the mentorship and work that we have been inducted into, we continually seek to create opportunities that build solidarity among Black and Brown faculty as an act of resistance and self-determination within institutions of higher education. Our collaborations thus far have led to networks and professional affiliations that provide literal and figurative space(s) to collaborate and grow through shared community. These networks provide support when we struggle with the oppressive symptoms of White supremacy and racial/gender microaggressions. The racialized and gendered dynamics of our nation necessitate organizing and resistance. We call on scholars of all ranks to face Black/Brown racial tensions and realities, build resistance and solidarity, continually working to dismantle ideologies of WSCH, while creating spaces that are affirming, inclusive, and equitable.

REFERENCES

Clemente, Rosa. 2017. "Not in Our Name: A Puerto Rican White Supremacist in Charlottesville." *rosaclemente.net*. August 17, 2017. http://rosaclemente.net/not-name-puerto-rican-white-supremacist-charlottesville/.

Darder, Antonia. 2002. *Reinventing Paulo Freire: A Pedagogy of Love*. Cambridge: Westview Press.

Delgado, Richard, and Jean Stefancic. 2001. *Critical Race Theory: An Introduction*. New York: New York University Press.

Paris, Django. 2012. "Culturally Sustaining Pedagogy: A Needed Change in Stance, Terminology, and Practice." *Educational Researcher* 41, no. 3 (April): 93–97.

Yosso, Tara. 2005. "Whose Culture Has Capital? A Critical Race Theory Discussion of Community Cultural Wealth." *Race, Ethnicity and Education* 8, no. 1 (March): 69–91.

CHAPTER 12

Lessons on Humility: White Women's Racial Allyship in Academia

Daniela Gachago

BECOMING WHITE IN SOUTH AFRICA

There are a vast number of articles currently being written around decolonisation. A quick search on The Conversation (https://theconversation.com/africa), an online platform that offers academics the opportunity to disseminate their research to the wider public, brings up hundreds of articles written since 2015 with the word decolonisation in the title—many by white authors. However, what is missing so far from the conversation is a discussion about the role of white academics in challenging the systemic inequalities so prevalent in South African higher education. What does it mean to be an "ally" in the context of decolonisation? Is there a role for us? Should there be a role? And if yes, what would such a role look like? In this chapter, I am reflecting on my own ongoing struggles as a white, middle-class female academic, deeply concerned with social justice issues, trying to find my space in the decolonial project in higher education in South Africa. I recognize that by writing about and challenging Whiteness, I am centering Whiteness while white allyship should be concerned with decentering what is usually centered.

D. Gachago (✉)
Cape Peninsula University of Technology, Cape Town, South Africa

As such, this piece is addressed primarily to a white audience although it might be of interest for people of colour as well—even if only to affirm that Whiteness should and can be challenged from within.

My family and I arrived in Cape Town in 2010. Born in Austria, I had for many years travelled around Africa, including four years spent at the University of Botswana. This is where I met my husband, who was born in Kenya. We have two mixed-race children. Before getting married, our long conversations were not about our own racial positions and the different levels of privilege these entailed. Somehow that didn't seem important, as in general we encountered openness, support and curiosity when we engaged with others. What we spoke more about was having and raising mixed-race children: about challenges they might encounter when growing up, their complex identities and their lack of a place called home. It was our firm belief that it would be up to us to create a home for them and that their rich cultural heritage would ultimately be an advantage to them, making them global citizens.

In 2010, we arrived in South Africa, where I took up a position as an academic staff developer at a large university of technology serving predominantly underprivileged students. My rose-coloured view of difference quickly changed. I realised that race—in my case, being white—mattered in a way that I had never experienced before. I signed the lease for a flat within a month of arrival; I got my bank card within a week; I suddenly had a voice in departmental meetings; I was listened to although I was often the youngest and a woman, a combination that in other contexts had presented a struggle for me to be acknowledged or recognised. I never got stopped by the police; I was never asked for my staff card when entering the library; I never experienced problems booking a table in restaurants... and the list goes on. I only noticed these things because others, who had a different skin colour, did not share these experiences. My husband started complaining that people overlooked him when they greeted me. He pointed out how people locked their car doors when he passed by. He showed me how women suddenly held their bags closer in a queue at the supermarket when he stood behind them. I was shocked and initially unconvinced. I told him not to be paranoid, implying that he had a chip on his shoulder. That is how blind I was to my own Whiteness.

I eventually realised that as a partner to a black man and as a mother to two mixed-race children, growing up in South Africa, I needed help to learn to understand this context better—to learn how to respond to my partner's experiences of racism or how to prepare my sons for this world. What I quickly learnt, however, is that it was not easy to talk about race—both in my professional and in my personal spaces I encountered mostly silence when I tried. Apartheid worked by separating people by race, culture and gender. When Apartheid was finally abolished in 1994, South Africa introduced a new ideology in the name of collective nation building: "rainbowism". Rainbowism emphasised common ground and sameness rather than a focus on difference and was meant to fight racism and discrimination, much as the phenomenon of "color blindness" in the USA (Bonilla-Silva and Embrick 2006). One of the side effects of rainbowism is that South Africa—and in particular white South Africa—is highly uncomfortable with talking about race, which in turn contributes to rendering black experience or black pain invisible while keeping white privilege in place.

Eventually, about a year and half after arriving South Africa, I decided to start an interracial dialogue group with some women I knew and who were equally frustrated by the lack of spaces to engage around race. The group, which we called "This Dialogue Thing", embraced bell hooks' (2000) principles for dialogue: meeting at somebody's house, honouring everybody's voice, creating an alternative space focusing on the lived experience of participants. We distinguished these encounters from what we experienced as theoretical, guarded, disembodied and—unfortunately—often predominantly white debates on race and reconciliation in South Africa found in academia.

Being part of this dialogue was transformative for me. I had to let go of the idea that being married to a black man, having mixed-race children and living in diverse spaces meant I was not racist. By sharing our stories of our own deep-seated racism, owning up, for example, to our own racial profiling (and if we didn't by being immediately called out on these by our black group members), we learnt to become more sensitive to it and understand racism as systemic, implicating each and every one of us. I remember one of those stories I shared: it was parent teacher evening at my children's school and my husband and I were late. The black security guard at the school gate did not want my husband to park inside the school, claiming that there were no parking slots left, while he allowed the next car in, driven by a white parent. My husband was livid and started arguing with the guard. Instead of supporting him, I felt embarrassed, got out of the car and left him there, fighting by himself, in order to try and get to the parent meeting in time. I didn't want to see that racism at that moment, didn't want to step in, torn between my responsibilities towards my children (making it in time to the parent teacher meeting) and my responsibility towards my husband (calling out racism). It helped unpack this moment with my group members, trying to understand the difficult choices we have to make at all times and trying to struggle with competing responsibilities, loyalties and needs.

What I learnt in this group impacted on my work with my students, my relationships with my colleagues and my personal life, as I became more and more aware of how white privilege plays itself out in everyday interactions. I actively sought out people of colour to work with—called in strategically by course lecturers when a white voice was needed to explain concepts such as white privilege, white fragility or whitesplaining to students. I tried to show how white defensiveness or white fragility, i.e. the inability to engage with in race conversations, is a symptom of the affective investments in social norms, which we accumulate over a lifetime, and which make it so difficult to shift our worldviews and behaviours (Ahmed 2004). DiAngelo (2011), who coined the term "white fragility", argues that white people have grown up in an "insulated environment of racial protection [which] builds white expectations for racial comfort while at the same time lowering the ability to tolerate racial stress", leading to what she refers to as "White Fragility" (54). I shared my own personal story of "becoming white" in South Africa over and over again—both in my academic work and in my personal life (Gachago 2016). I was convinced that interracial dialogue was the way forward for South Africa.

Although the dialogue allowed us to become better at talking about race, we struggled to address the intersectionality of, for example, race and gender or race and class in our group. In retrospect, I understand that gender can allow women—in particular white women—to hide behind their own oppression in relation to patriarchy, rather than addressing their own personal racism. As such as a focus on intersectionality can be a form of white fragility (DiAngelo 2011), if not checked properly. Similarly, what we also learnt is the importance of a women-only group, to establish trust and solidarity, but also to be able to focus on race, rather than be compromised by other power dynamics such as female/male hierarchies. This is why this chapter emphasises racial rather than, for example, gender or class oppression. It focuses on my role as white ally, rather than as a white female ally, as this is where I feel I learnt the most, although I see gender oppression in academia as real and important to unpack.

The Role of White Allies

About five years after I arrived in South Africa came #RhodesMustFall, in 2015, led by black students at the University of Cape Town (UCT), calling for the removal of the Cecil Rhodes statue dominating the central space of the campus and more generally raising an awareness around the lack of decolonisation of higher education locally and globally (Chaudhuri 2016). Higher education institutions all over South Africa were swept away in a storm of protests, closing down campuses for months and reigniting debates around our colonial past, the legacy of Apartheid and the deeply unsettling process of decolonising the curriculum.

I was first excited by this movement, hoping that maybe finally the moment had come, where we could widen the dialogue, using our experiences of interracial dialogue to start a conversation across difference, power and privilege at our institutions. But I soon realised that the #RhodesMustFall movement was defined as a black movement, emphasising the centrality of black voices and black pain—not necessarily calling for the kind of interracial work that I had been doing. For the first time, the concept of "White Allyship" made the rounds. The literature around allyship, whether in the context of race, gender, disability or sexuality activism, is vast—globally and locally. Opinions around the value of allyship are divided. It is widely acknowledged that allies can be useful in calling out racism or sexism, and working amongst those like them. By recognising and acknowledging their own privileges, they can help to dismantle stereotypes and provide valuable support to individuals in oppressed groups who may not have the power, status or opportunity to influence institutional and systemic change (Alandzes 2017; Alexander 2016; Dlavalku 2015; Murphy 2015).

In the context of #RhodesMustFall, white allies were asked to step back from the conversation and show silent support, using their white privilege strategically by, for example, acting as human shields and protecting their black peers from police brutality during protests and demonstrations, setting up support stations, dropping food and drinks during building occupations or raising bail money for students who had been arrested during protests (Sherriff 2015). White voices should be limited, if heard at all, to white-only spaces in which they should engage white academics in conversation and help to build support for the movement there ("Disrupting Whiteness: UCT" n.d.). For a long time, I felt paralysed, not knowing how to engage in the protests, although I in my heart supported them. I watched the movement from a safe distance, struggling to understand what my role should be. Our dialogue group also took a break during those times, as in particular our black group members felt strongly that their energies were needed elsewhere.

STEPPING BACK AND CALLING OUT

My white allyship was first tested in a discussion about decolonising the curriculum on our departmental WhatsApp group. During the height of the 2016 #FeesMustFall protests, which called for free decolonial education in South Africa, my colleagues engaged in a long conversation about the implications of another campus closure. Opinions varied widely but the conversation was polite, not allowing emotions to flare up, until a black person wrote an angry response arguing that "white liberal academics" were the worst enemies of the movement. A white colleague responded reprimanding her for her "aggressive tone"—putting forth the argument of "I understand your anger" but—for the sake of interracial conversations—asking her to use a more conciliatory approach. I saw this as "tone policing" in its worst possible form. I had stayed quiet so far but felt the need to step in at that point and said as much, including an article about the danger of such silencing (Hugs 2015). My comment was met with defensiveness but also a question by an Indian colleague whether white people should have a say in this debate at all. It felt deeply uncomfortable: stepping out and challenging Whiteness openly like that, the awkwardness of meeting my white colleagues face-to-face later, doubts about my approach (should I have had a back channel talk with the colleague about "tone policing" rather than calling her out openly?). But it was also reaffirming, as my black colleague sent me a private message later thanking me for standing up for her.

Taking the decolonising project seriously means challenging established power structures and systems in higher education. It means challenging everything academia holds dear: who teaches, the knowledges that are being taught, the teaching and learning approaches used, the spaces we teach within. It means a deep reflection on the purpose of higher education—in particular in contested spaces as South Africa. How can education transform society? Or society education? How can we create an academic space that is meaningful to our staff and our students?

How can education help address inequality? And what does that mean then for the white ally?

Rigby and Ziyad (2016) suggest: "Perhaps the only action white folks can take—barring physical disappearance—in the struggle for black liberation, for them to successfully put an end to their own Whiteness, is the absolute absolving of their places and power" (para. 19). Is that our only role? To give up power and make space for the other? What does this mean for our academic practices? What does it mean to step back and allowing others to take the lead? *Can* Whiteness ever step aside and let others lead? Recently, I worked on a presentation with a black colleague on our attempts to decolonise her course curriculum. We decided she should be the one to present. It made sense—it was her course, her students and conversations around decolonisation must be led by people of colour. Still it was not easy. As white academics, we are so used to being at the front and talking, to be leading the conversation, to be at the centre of the debate; stepping back takes strain. Keeping quiet creates strain.

But I believe there is more to it. Macedo (1993) writes about the "social construction of not seeing" (189) in the context of American education, which has been equally prevalent among white South Africans for decades. As Heleta (2017) points out, "leaders, managers, staff members, academics and well-off students often turn a blind eye to the painful lived experiences that many black students and workers go through on a daily basis" (6). Stepping back cannot mean turning away, giving up responsibility. Although this might very well be a defence or survival mechanism, a response to not feeling "wanted" as ally, being told to keep silent, or a strategy to continue navigating and negotiating deeply unjust systems, as white allies we have to start seeing, listening and calling out oppressive systems and practices.

Listening to Others

Another step then towards white allyship is to learn humility, to recognise that we *don't know*, that we might not hold the knowledge, experience and skills necessary to take South African higher education further at this moment. We may need to acknowledge that others may hold more important knowledge—first and foremost our colleagues and our students, whose lived experiences and needs should shape curricula. Pett (2015) calls for teachers to be retaught—not only new knowledge, but also new ways of engaging with students, facilitating difficult conversations, handling emotions, allowing the personal into the classroom. Within this decolonial project, there is a huge opportunity to create democratic spaces for authentic co-production of knowledge, in the Freirean sense (1970) in which lecturers and students jointly work on "unveiling the reality", understanding it critically and creating new knowledge in the process, if we allow ourselves to step back and really, actively listen (69). As Sevenhuijsen (2002) asks us to do: to retreat to make space for the other. Over the last few years, we introduced the Privilege Walk (Unsaid 2017) to our students in an attempt to start a conversation around the systemic, intersectional and complex nature of privilege. While the activity worked well to give students an embodied experience of privilege and led to fruitful conversations, it also left us unsettled. One of the main points of discomfort for us was the question "who learns and at whose cost does the learning take place?" The Privilege Walk powerfully visualises the inequality of today's society, but can be traumatising for those at the back of the grid—as our students mentioned many times. Listening to our students, we developed the activity further and asked them to come up with new statements to create a new grid, based on different societal values—statements that allowed other students to be in the front. Through this activity students set up a new social grid, a new system, a new society, one that they could feel proud of and one that affirmed them, even if just for those few minutes in class (Ngoasheng and Gachago 2017).

White People Setting Up White Spaces

There are strong voices in the decolonial debate who challenge the notion of white allyship, emphasising the danger of involving white allies in the fight against white supremacy. These arguments are framed by the belief that whites can never be separated from Whiteness and that Whiteness cannot operate in any way that does not first perpetuate white supremacy (Rigby and Ziyad 2016). The inability to step back and listen can derail the process, take centre space and thus re-centre Whiteness "[b]ecause for white people 'to do' anything means that Whiteness must be centered in a way that would perpetuate its oppressive essentiality" (Rigby and Ziyad 2016, para. 6).

This can be seen in calls for "black only" spaces, such as the recent lecture on "decolonizing the mind, securing the base" by Ngũgĩ wa Thiong'o at UCT, which was disrupted by students questioning the presence of white bodies—the enemy—in the room (Chutel 2017; Fongoqa and Maasdorp 2017). When I heard what had gone down at UCT, I was at first taken aback. How can students ask white people to leave the room? Were we not an important part of the dialogue? Of the conversation? I still struggled with the idea of not being wanted, not playing a role in a cause that I felt so deeply passionate about. It took me a while and a number of conflicts with my black colleagues, in which I caused harm and pain and abused the trust that was placed in me as white ally and friend, to understand the violence that white people can cause in mixed-race spaces (Leonardo and Porter 2010).

My dialogue members had warned me repeatedly: white people set up white spaces. What does that mean? It took me a while to fully understand the scope of this statement. Only a few weeks ago I was tasked to organise a workshop for early career researchers on supporting diverse students in higher education. Decolonising the curriculum was a core theme of the debates in the online phase before the face-to-face workshop. When it came to workshop facilitation, I reached out for recommendations on social media, and since Cape Town's facilitation scene is dominated by white women, the first names I was given by my network of friends and colleagues were all members of this group. I contacted the first person suggested, who immediately showed interest and even offered to do the facilitation pro bono because she liked the project so much. And I just accepted. I—who has presented at various occasions around the power of cross racial collaboration, about the danger of Whiteness—organised a workshop on decolonisation facilitated by a white woman and didn't see the problem. Very quickly, my black colleagues and friends stepped in and in no uncertain words demanded that I look for a person of colour to co-facilitate the process. I was floored. How could that have happened to me? I saw the deep disappointment—even anger—in my friends. Could—should—that happen to a white ally? Should I not be more careful, self-reflective, aware of these issues? Would they still see me as white ally?

Continuous Self-reflexivity

How can whites make themselves vulnerable enough to acknowledge and be open about their biases, thought and structures framed by Eurocentrism (Chaudry 2009)? Reflecting on and dismantling our biases, our own—very likely colonising—frames of thought, might be the most important thing we can do in this context. "Vulnerability, authenticity and respect—as well as imagination—are so vital in the decolonisation debate to ensure we really sink our teeth into the detail rather than bellowing at each other only about definitions" (Behari-Leak et al. 2017, para. 25). How can we achieve this? Reflecting back on my misstep when I organised a white facilitation team, I understand my friend's disappointment, her hurt. I managed to keep my white fragility at bay. I managed to listen to her and not react too defensively—although I tried to argue my case at first, citing the pro bono offer, which was quickly rejected—why hadn't I at least given people of colour a chance to do the work? She later told me that she found the pro bono argument particularly triggering as it reminded her of the recent historic silicosis court case, in which reason that was given as to why the advocates for the mine workers were all white was that they agreed to work at a reduced rate (Nontshiza and Clarke 2015). I also tried to correct my mistake by organising a diverse facilitation team. However, what I could not do was to communicate to her my deep shame and my fear of losing not just my "allyship" status, but more importantly her trust and her friendship.

Why was it so difficult to not just listen to her and argue my case, but to show her how I *felt*? To make myself really vulnerable? Buhle Zuma (2015), a lecturer in the Psychology Department at UCT, made a strong statement in a talk about violence in South Africa: *Whiteness is not able to commit suicide*. Whiteness is constructed as an absolute being or as a closed system. There is no room for doubt or change, and suffering and injustice are externalised and happen outside this system. How can we be something else other than what we constructed ourselves to be?

Heleta (2017) argues that an "involvement of white academics in the decolonisation project requires self-reflexivity, recognition of privilege, personal change and growth as well as unlearning of the old knowledge designed to subjugate and exploit the other" (6). Being a white academic ally means never allowing ourselves to be comfortable, being hyper-aware and upfront about who we are, our own intersectional subjectivities, and how this impacts on who we teach, write and do research with, who we supervise and who we invite into projects or who invites us into projects. South African academic Lis Lange (2016) describes this process of watching herself all the time beautifully:

> These are the kinds of things you learn, to watch yourself, and then you become very sensitive to your own behaviour. Sometimes I can see myself

doing what I am doing. Which is not bad all the time because then you can see yourself this close to the abyss, to just putting your feet in the wrong place, and then you correct your course. (116)

If we are lucky enough, we catch ourselves before we make mistakes, or if we can't, we might have black colleagues who trust us enough to continually challenge us and point out our own blind spots, as Alexander (2016) mentions: "Developing as an Ally is a skill that doesn't happen overnight; it comes from engaging in open conversations, asking questions, recognizing your own biases and blind spots, and stepping out of your comfort zone" (para. 5).

WHERE IS MY COOKIE?

Being a white ally in the decolonial project is a lifelong and difficult process and practice of unlearning, necessarily failing over and over again, accepting the uncertainty and complexity we have to negotiate every day, which will put us many times in highly defensive positions. Allyship is a verb, is action, is something we do, not just read and write about. It's taking risks, putting yourself on the line, asking uncomfortable questions, becoming, as Sara Ahmed (2004) termed it, a "killjoy", the one that constantly pokes and stirs, not allowing white business as usual. However, maybe most importantly, being a white ally means to be somebody who recognises, accepts, keeps working on and speaks out about their own racism. Guilt and shame should not prevent us from opening up about our own mistakes—on the contrary, as Boutte and Jackson (2014) advise, accepting one's shame and guilt can be productive: "There is no shame or guilt in what we do not know as long as we are open to learning and pursuing other possibilities. Therefore, white allies need to find ways to make peace with damage done and being done by white racism" (363). For me, this means finding a way to allow myself to feel the pain Whiteness inflicts on people of colour and at the same time feel compassion for our continued failings, our white guilt and shame. While I agree with Adichie (2013) that, "racism should never have happened and so you don't get a cookie for reducing it", I find being an ally is also highly rewarding. There is so much to learn, so much joy in doing this work, in recognising the complexity in ourselves and others, of findings ourselves in the other, in establishing deep and lasting relationships across difference.

REFERENCES

Adichie, Chimamanda Ngozi. 2013. *Americanah: A Novel*. 1st ed. New York: Alfred A. Knopf.
Ahmed, Sara. 2004. *The Cultural Politics of Emotion*. Edinburgh: Edinburgh University Press.
Alandzes, Taylor. 2017. "What It Really Means to Be an Ally." *The Radical Notion*, April 24, 2017. http://www.theradicalnotion.com/being-ally/.
Alexander, Na Shai. 2016. "A Point of View: The Importance of Allies?" *The Inclusion Solution*, September 22, 2016. http://www.theinclusionsolution.me/a-point-of-view-the-importance-of-allies/.
Behari-Leak, Kasturi, Langutani Masehela, Luyanda Marhaya, Masebala Tiabane, and Ness Merckel. 2017. "Decolonising the Curriculum: It's in the Detail, Not Just in the Definition." *The Conversation*, 1–4. March 9, 2017. https://theconversation.com/decolonising-the-curriculum-its-in-the-detail-not-just-in-the-definition-73772.
Bonilla-Silva, Eduardo, and D. G. Embrick. 2006. "Racism Without Racists: 'Killing Me Softly' with Color Blindness." In *Reinventing Critical Pedagogy*, edited by R. L. Allen and M. Pruyn, 21–34. Lanham: Rowman & Littlefield Publishers.
Boutte, Gloria S., and Tambra O. Jackson. 2014. "Advice to White Allies: Insights from Faculty of Color." *Race Ethnicity and Education* 17, no. 5 (February): 623–642.
Chaudhuri, Amit. 2016. "The Real Meaning of Rhodes Must Fall." *The Guardian*, March 16, 2016. http://www.theguardian.com/uk-news/2016/mar/16/the-real-meaning-of-rhodes-must-fall.
Chaudry, Lubna Nazir. 2009. "Forays Into the Mist." In *Voice in Qualitative Research*, edited by Alecia Youngblood Jackson and Lisa A. Mazzei, 137–164. Milton Park: Routledge.
Chutel, Lynsey. 2017. "Ngũgĩ Wa Thiong'o's Lessons for South African Students Fell on Deaf Ears." *Quartz Africa*, March 7, 2017. https://qz.com/925234/ngugi-wa-thiongos-lessons-for-south-african-students-fell-on-deaf-ears/.
DiAngelo, Robin. 2011. "White Fragility." *International Journal of Critical Pedagogy* 3 (3): 54–70.
"Disrupting Whiteness: UCT." n.d. *Facebook*. Accessed December 8, 2017. https://www.facebook.com/DisruptingWhitenessUCT/.
Dlakavu, Simamkele. 2015. "Space for White Allies in Student Uprisings?" *IOL News*, May 8, 2015. http://www.iol.co.za/news/opinion/space-for-White-allies-in-student-uprisings-1856031.
Fongoqa, Sisipho, and Lindsay Maasdorp. 2017. "Can We Trust Ngugi and Mangcu with Decolonisation?" *Black Opinion*, June 22, 2017. http://Blackopinion.co.za/2017/03/07/can-trust-ngugi-mangcu-decolonisation/.

Freire, Paulo. 1970. *Cultural Action for Freedom*. Cambridge: Harvard Educational Review.
Gachago, Daniela. 2016. "Addressing Some of the Elephants in South African Research Education: Race and Reflexivity in Postgraduate Study." In *Postgraduate Study in South Africa- Surviving and Succeeding*, edited by L. Frick, P. Mosthoane, and C. Murphy, 13–22. Stellenbosch: SUN Press.
Heleta, Savo. 2017. "Decolonisation of Higher Education: Dismantling Epistemic Violence and Eurocentrism in South Africa." *Transformation in Higher Education* 1 (1): 1–21.
Hooks, Bell. 2000. *Feminism Is for Everybody—Passionate Politics*. Cambridge: South End Press.
Hugs, Robert. 2015. "No, We Won't Calm Down—Tone Policing Is Just Another Way to Protect Privilege." *Everyday Feminism*, December 7, 2015. https://everydayfeminism.com/2015/12/tone-policing-and-privilege/.
Lange, Liz. 2016. "Transformation as an Intellectual and Ethical Project: Changing Inherited Patterns of Thought and Social Practice." In *Educational Leadership for Transformation and Social Justice: Narratives of Change in South Africa*, edited by John Ambrosio, 112–126. Abingdon: Routledge, Routledge Research in Educational Leadership.
Leonardo, Zeus, and Ronald K. Porter. 2010. "Pedagogy of Fear: Toward a Fanonian Theory of 'Safety' in Race Dialogue." *Race Ethnicity and Education* 13, no. 2 (July): 139–157.
Macedo, Donaldo P. 1993. "Literacy for Stupidification: The Pedagogy of Big Lies." *Harvard Educational Review* 6, no. 2 (July): 183–206.
Murphy, Timothy. 2015. "Ally Is Action, Not an Identity." *The Huffington Post*, December 11, 2015. https://www.huffingtonpost.com/timothy-murphy/ally-is-action-not-an-identity_b_8536518.html.
Ngoasheng, A., and D. Gachago. 2017. "Dreaming Up a New Grid: Two Lecturers' Reflections on Challenging Traditional Notions of Identity and Privilege in a South African Classroom." *Education as Change* 21 (2): 187–207.
Nontshiza, Pasika, and John Gl Clarke. 2015. "Lawyers in Black and White: Spoor vs Boqwana." *Ground Up*, October 23, 2015. https://www.groundup.org.za/article/lawyers-Black-and-White-spoor-vs-boqwana_3427/.
Pett, Sarah. 2015. "It's Time to Take the Curriculum Back from Dead White Men." *The Conversation*, May 8, 2015. https://theconversation.com/its-time-to-take-the-curriculum-back-from-dead-White-men-40268.
Rigby, Kevin, and Hari Ziyad. 2016. "White People Have No Place in Black liberation." *Racebaitr (RBR)*, March 31, 2016. http://racebaitr.com/2016/03/31/White-people-no-place-Black-liberation/#.
Sevenhuijsen, Selma. 2002. "Steps Towards an Ethic of Attention." In *Conference Proceedings of Gender, Sexuality and the Law*, Keele, England, June 2002.

Sherriff, Lucy. 2015. "White Students Form Human Shield to Protect Black #FeesMustFall Protesters From South African Police." *Huffington Post South Africa*, October 22, 2015. http://www.huffingtonpost.co.uk/2015/10/22/White-students-form-human-shield-protect-Black-protesters-south-african-police_n_8356054.html.

Unsaid. 2017. "The Privilege Walk." *UNSAID* (blog), August 9, 2017. http://www.unsaid.sg/the-privilege-walk/.

Zuma, Buhle. 2015. "Violence in the Past, Present and the Future of South Africa." Presentation at the University of Cape Town, Cape Town, South Africa, May 2015.

CHAPTER 13

Living with Three Strikes: Being a Transwoman of Color in Education

Aryah O. S. Lester

I am Black, a woman, and trans, though not necessarily in that order in every moment or every context. These are facets of my identity that I deal with in a variety of spaces all of the time. What is most challenging about these particular intersections of myself is that they are all external, all visible to others. They certainly inform who I am internally, but when I think of myself, I simply understand me to be me. I am not immediately a transwoman of color; I am just Aryah. However, my tendency to think of myself beyond these identity markers does not change others' responses to me. Others' perceptions and reactions to my very existence are everyday factors in my life. The easiest way to explain the ways that my intersectional identities matter in the day-to-day is to ask that you envision yourself walking down the street.

A. O. S. Lester (✉)
National Alliance of Transgender Advocates
(NATAL), Washington, DC, USA

Three Strikes

Imagine walking down the street while another individual—me—walks toward you from the opposite direction, from about a block away. From a full block away, you see that I am Black. And, as I learned early on in life, my skin color matters in terms of how people see me, who people see (Gray and Smakow 2015; West 2000). From even this distance, my race is Strike One. As you and I continue to approach one another, from about half a block away, you are likely able to note that I am a woman. Being perceived as female carries a new set of assumptions about who I am and how you might choose (or not) to interact with me. A Black woman: Strike Two. As we get closer to one another, I feel my anxiety begin to ratchet up. It is when we are closest that the possibility of personal danger to me is greatest, because it is likely that the closed distance between us will make it visibly clear that I am a Black transwoman. Strike Three.

I love myself and am proud to be who I am. But I recognize that my very presence is one that challenges a range of societal norms upheld by misogyny, LGBTQ+ bias, and racism and that those norms put me in constant danger by simply existing. Gradually realizing the degrees to which my very presence challenges others' notions of gender norms and race was life changing. I had always dealt with racism. It is not only prevalent in the whole of US society, but I have lived most of my life in the Southeastern USA, which remains a contemporary hotbed of racialized tensions—such as the Charlottesville, Virginia violence in August 2017.

However, I did not gain a true appreciation for the realities of misogyny until after I came out as trans. It was as if a veil had been ripped off from in front of my face as I began to confront the pervasiveness of gender roles. Being a woman made me much more aware of the ways that others and I worked to both embody and enforce gender norms on a regular basis. Even as a transwoman who does not conform fully to feminine gender norms (though others certainly do for their own reasons), I am complicit in and victimized by these social expectations of gender on a daily basis. Because I exist as one who must be constantly aware of my gender—including gender identity and expression, my racial identity, and the ways that my sexuality might be assumed by others, my understandings of the world are constantly intersectional. Gender, race, and sexuality, as well as other factors such as socioeconomic class, shape how others assess me and how I participate in society. This constant awareness of intersectionality permits me to fully appreciate the ways that ever-increasing murder rates of transwomen, and especially transwomen of color, are directly connected to the social constructs of misogyny and racism (Krell 2017; Martinez 2016). And to return to the earlier scenario, as you and I share a sidewalk, my body presumably violates a range of generally held assumptions (see also Guyotte and Niccolini, this volume) about what it means to be Black, what it means to be a woman, and what it means to be trans.

These perceived violations are the reason that, as you and I draw closer and closer to one another on the sidewalk, I become more and more anxious. I feel my heart begin to race, as my breathing becomes shallower but quicker. I place my hands flat against my thighs to dry the perspiration. I feel muscles tense, as if prepared to flee at a moment's notice. I have learned the degrees to which others understand me to be outside the lines of social norms. I have learned through discriminations. I have learned through violent encounters. I have learned through others pulling knives and guns on me. I have learned through the trauma of having my hair set on fire. What I have also learned, though, is that these violent reactions, and the more common reactions of staring and whispering, are the products of a lack of education. It is the lack of understanding and the lack of knowledge that cause people to be uncomfortable, fearful, and dangerous. It is because I have learned to comprehend both others' and my own fears that I am an educator.

My Work as an Educator

Despite this book's title and my inclusion in its contents, I am not an educator in the traditional sense. Much like my personal life, I operate on the periphery. I move in and out of educational settings, offering my experiences and knowledge to attendees and then exiting in the hope that my work has and will translate into better understandings of trans issues for those in attendance. I am the founder of Trans Miami, an advocacy group in Miami, Florida, and I have worked with a range of organizations and institutions over the years in relation to education on trans issues. I conduct workshops with government agencies, lead training sessions with major corporations, and often interact with university students in various contexts. Most often, I come to collegiate settings with an invitation extended under the framework of "social work" or the umbrella of "gender and international studies," though I have also led educational sessions for other groups, such as law schools and university residence life staff members.

When I stand in front of these various audiences, I am always nervous. Students evaluate me with intense scrutiny, while I feel near-powerless. I lack the authorities of a typical university educator; I do not assign them grades, for example, but I know that they are constantly assessing me, weighing my body against the value of the information that falls from my mouth. When I began writing this chapter, I considered what I wanted to share about what it means for me to be an educator and how my experiences might add to the diverse set of voices featured in this edited volume. Certainly, there were moments that went awry in training sessions, there were student questions that were hurtful and insensitive, and there have been instances when I've come away from teaching others with fresh, new wounds to accompany the innumerable scars that I carry from previous experiences. But, I choose instead to offer an experience that was full of hope and the best kinds of surprises.

A NARRATIVE OF TREPIDATION AND CELEBRATION

As I scanned the classroom at the University of Miami, I felt the return of the nervousness and tension that always accompany these sorts of talks. I had been invited to give a guest lecture to a group of International Studies undergraduates. I knew through both statistical probability and a quick, private assessment of the room that I was a minority in reference to every facet of my intersectional identities. There were many young White men, most or possibly all of whom were both heterosexual and cisgender. There were some young White women and a few young women of color. I literally stood apart as the featured presenter in my designated space, but my embodied identities set me apart visibly and socially, too. I was not just different because I was some sort of presumed expert on a topic; I was different because of all of the aspects of being me that draw attention from others when walking down the street. My three strikes.

Remembering to take deep breaths, I went through my presentation, trying to note throughout how the students were responding to the information. The topic of the talk was a discussion on trans issues in youth settings, with most of these students presumably planning to enter professions involving education or, more generally, young people. I saw furrowed brows, occasional nods, but no clear signs of either open hostility or acceptance. Though the question and answer (Q&A) portion of a presentation typically comes at the end, these students' questions burned from the beginning. It is the Q&A portion that is always most nerve-wracking. Because I am a practiced presenter, educator, and activist, I am well-disciplined on how to respond to a range of misinformed and problematic questions. I always try to take at least a few seconds to inwardly remind myself that there is no reason to disbelieve that even the most ignorant questions are due to exactly that: ignorance. I am an educator, and my role is to help them understand, to know. After pausing to frame such questions as simply the product of misinformation, I gently correct the problematic aspects of these inquiries and then immediately shift to providing information that will alleviate any assumptions or misunderstandings. Because I am human, these types of questions often hurt deeply, even as I offer polished and polite responses to the inquirers. At this moment, as I braced myself from the very start of the Q&A, the students' hands began to reach into the air to be called on for their questions, and the Q&A continued throughout the presentation.

This group had so many questions. So many. Not one demographic dominated the discussion, and no particular group or individual seemed silenced. It was my first clue that this group was special. As the questions continued, interspersed with my informational delivery, I realized that most of them were genuine attempts to understand, to know more. Particularly, as so many of these attendees planned to work with youth in their professional careers, their questions centered on children. Specifically, they wanted to know more about gender, gender identity, and gender expression in relation to young people. One student wanted to know, "How do kids know they're transgender when they're so young?" Another asked, "What do schools need to do when they find out a child is transgender?" I welcomed all of the questions, no matter how clumsily worded or introductory level, because all of these attendees' questions were coming from a shared desire to *know*, to *understand*, and to *support* trans issues. Specifically, the group consciously wanted to support trans children. My chest felt full, as it had in the beginning, but the anxiety had been replaced by hope. My chest felt full because my heart was.

Had the session simply ended following my presentation and their questions, I would have returned home optimistic. But this group had more gifts to give. The Q&A period transitioned into one of personal sharing and reflection. One student revealed, "I have a trans friend who recently came out, and my other friends and I think it's really important to support her." Another added, "My family member just came out as trans, and we were surprised, but we love him. I mean, why wouldn't we?" My heart, full moments before, felt light enough to soar. And then, there was one more student who wanted to share.

The student stood and addressed the group, the posture one that was visibly a contradiction of both nerves and relief. "I'm trans. I haven't told any of you before now. I've been contemplating transitioning. Sitting here today, hearing the questions that everyone asked and the ways that everyone responded to the information that was presented, I feel safe. I feel able to be me and to say who I am." The student's peers took turns congratulating and embracing their fellow student, making it clear that their community readily welcomed an individual who trusted them enough to share with them an authentic but hitherto hidden self. I was speechless. I had begun my time in this room worried about students' responses and was preparing to leave after having been energized and empowered by those responses.

Moving Forward in Education: Intersectional Educators

My very existence necessitates that I be an intersectional educator. I cannot help but to be so. My three strikes, as society often sees them, mandate that I address issues of race and of gender at all times. I address them because people see them when they see me, and I address them because they are topics about which people have questions and people need understanding. However, as I have visited various college campuses and other organizations, I have realized that often I am invited because the notion of an intersectional educator is so foreign in some spaces that they have to reach outside their own establishments to have representation and informed discussions. I become a replacement for the diversity that should already exist within these spaces. I value my invitations to speak to these groups, and the advocacy work that I do as an educator is a key component of the unseen aspects of my identity. However, education needs far more educators who actually represent intersectionality and who are actually (and intentionally) intersectional.

Certainly, there should be more conversations in education about intersectionalities, and more educators should consider the ways that they might offer intersectional understandings of various topics (e.g.,

Beck 2016; Bell 2016; Grant and Zwier 2012). I have often observed that when I am invited to speak, it is with a group that falls within a discipline that is, by its very nature, intersectional, such as international affairs or gender studies. These areas are essential to academia, and I celebrate their work, but both intersectional educators and discussions on intersectionality must exist beyond the more obvious disciplines that have to acknowledge intersectional people. The presence of intersectional educators permits representations of people less visible in society and, importantly, provides models for students of different ways of being. These educators offer students opportunities to come to terms with their own multilayered identities, while learning about others' similarly complex experiences. These students graduate and enter their respective roles in the world with both intersectional beings and understandings.

As I advocate for intersectional educators, I think that this book offers a range of examples of what it means to bring complicated experiences and multifaceted notions of identity to the academy. My own experiences are, in many respects, unique, so I do not suggest that a sudden burst of transwomen of color in higher education would be a panacea—though that degree of representation and visibility would be beautiful, I would argue. What I propose is that given the number of women in education, and the range of narratives offered in this one volume, there be a greater awareness of intersectional experiences and educational approaches. I live every day with three strikes, but I know that through those presumed (and sometimes real) liabilities, I make valuable and vital differences for those whom I educate. I would call for all of us to explore and to celebrate others' and our own intersectionalities. Our personal stories matter, and in education, they offer precious moments to address ignorance and fear while constructing communities of peace and empowerment. The role of education is to improve individuals and society, but it cannot do so without intersectional understandings and teachers.

REFERENCES

Beck, Brittney. 2016. "Intersectionality as Education Policy Reform: Creating Schools that Empower Telling. *Penn State Perspectives on Urban Education* 13, no. 2 (Winter 2016–2017). http://www.urbanedjournal.org/volume-13-issue-2-winter-2016-17/intersectionality-education-policy-reform-creating-schools-empower.

Bell, Monita K. 2016. "Teaching at the Intersections." *Teaching Tolerance* 53 (Summer 2016). https://www.tolerance.org/magazine/summer-2016/teaching-at-the-intersections.

Grant, C. A., and Elizabeth Zwier. 2012. "Intersectionality & Education." In *Encyclopedia of Diversity in Education*, edited by J. Banks, 1263–1271. Thousand Oaks: Sage.

Gray, Emma, and Jessica Samakow. 2015. "11 Things White People Need to Realize About Race." *Huffington Post: Black Voices*, July 23, 2017. https://www.huffingtonpost.com/entry/11-things-white-people-need-to-realize-about-race_us_55b0009be4b07af29d576702.

Krell, Elias Cosenza. 2017. "Is Transmisogyny Killing Trans Women of Color? Black Trans Feminisms and Exigencies of White Femininity." *Transgender Studies Quarterly* 4 (2): 226–242.

Martinez, D. J. 2016. "Systemic Racism and Misogyny Are Killing Queer and Trans People of Color Every Day." *The Seattle Globalist*, June 13, 2016. http://www.seattleglobalist.com/2016/06/13/racism-misogyny-killing-queer-and-trans-people-of-color-orlando/52499.

West, Cornell. 2000. *Race Matters*. Boston: Beacon.

PART IV

Vulnerability in the Academy: Women Explore Emotionality, Affect, and Self-Care

CHAPTER 14

You Can't Un-See Color: A Ph.D., a Divorce, and *The Wizard of Oz*

Meghan E. Barnes

I taught middle school for five years before deciding that I was ready to pursue my Ph.D. In the Skype calls and email exchanges with the man I hoped would be my major professor, we discussed my approaches to, beliefs about, and inquiries into teaching. Although I look back on my pedagogical choices now and find some of them to be a bit problematic, at the time I was a firm believer in service-learning. In one of our last email exchanges before I formally accepted the invitation to return to grad school, my major professor suggested that I write a book chapter about the service-learning work I had done with my middle school students. No one had ever suggested that I write something for publication. I was overwhelmed with excitement and nervousness at the thought of such an undertaking.

One Saturday morning a few weeks later, I pulled into the parking lot at Caribou Coffee, ready to spend the next few hours banging out a draft of the service-learning chapter. Before I jumped out of the car, my dad called. I proceeded to spend the next ten minutes telling him about the invitation to write a chapter and my ideas. At the end of my monologue, there was a prolonged (and unexpected) pause on the other end of the

M. E. Barnes (✉)
University of North Carolina, Charlotte, NC, USA

line. My dad, who had earned his Ph.D. in Civil Engineering decades earlier, didn't join in my excitement or ask for details about the chapter. Instead, he offered the following admonition:
"Don't let your ego get the best of you. A lot of people get into Ph.D. programs and end up getting divorced. I just want you to be careful and not forget your husband."

I was surprised by his warning and flippantly responded that of course I would never forget my husband, that I was just excited about the chapter, and that my relationship with my husband was on solid ground. I got off the phone, walked into Caribou, and began to take my first peek into the colorful Land of Oz.

The film adaptation of Frank Baum's (1900) novel *The Wonderful Wizard of Oz* first appeared in US movie theaters in 1939. As was the norm of that time period, the film began in black-and-white. Fearing that her loathsome neighbor would take her dog away, the story's main character, Dorothy, decided to run away from her home in Kansas. But after an encounter with a fortune-teller who suggested that her Auntie Em was ill, Dorothy returned home—just as a tornado struck. Unable to get into the storm cellar, Dorothy sought safety in her bedroom, where she ultimately hit her head and entered the dreamland of Oz. Dorothy's awakening in Oz was quite a dramatic one: Not only did the film transition from black-and-white to Technicolor, but also Dorothy contributed to the death of the Wicked Witch of the East. Upon her arrival in Oz, Dorothy learned that the only chance she had of returning to Kansas hinged on her ability to reach the Emerald City and meet with the Wizard of Oz. Along her journey to the Emerald City, Dorothy met a Tin Man, a Lion, and a Scarecrow. Though Dorothy didn't belong in the Land of Oz and was in fact eager to return home to Kansas, she had a positive influence on the characters there and she learned more about herself and her world as a consequence of her adventure. Although there were a number of influential women in the Land of Oz (namely Glinda, the Good Witch of the North, and the Wicked Witch of the West), Dorothy was ultimately dependent on a man (the Wizard of Oz) to get what she wanted most: to return home to Kansas. Dorothy's adventures in Oz bear a strong resemblance to the experience of getting a Ph.D.

The world of academia, like the world of work in general, wasn't built for women (Drame et al. 2012; Friedan 1936; Knights and Kerfoot 2008; Wolf 1991). The process of completing a dissertation, for instance, demands long stretches of time to write, without interruptions from for-profit work, children, chores, or other social responsibilities. Women who, for better or worse, have traditionally been expected to care for households and children often struggle to find the silence and isolation needed to complete the courses and/or dissertation required to earn a Ph.D. And, regardless of gender, those without funds for food, home, and general livelihood are inevitably barred from years of unpaid reading, writing, and research.

Of course, as gender roles shift in society (albeit slowly) and opportunities for scholarships and financial aid flourish (although these, too, are under fire), graduate programs are matriculating and graduating more diverse applicants (American Association of University Women 2004; Drame et al. 2012; Knights and Kerfoot 2008). However, even as students become more diverse (in terms of race, gender, socioeconomic class, language, able-bodiedness, sexual orientation, etc.), the processes and requirements for receiving a Ph.D. (or tenure for that matter) have remained largely unchanged (Drame et al. 2012; Mason et al. 2013). Thus, the academy is loath to accommodate the changing needs, interests, and lives of its students. Instead, students from traditionally marginalized groups are expected to change their lives to fit into the academy—a system that was initially built to keep them out (Drame et al. 2012; Wolf 1991). In this chapter, I focus on my experience as a woman entering the academy.

Similar to Dorothy walking into the Emerald City, when a woman enters academia, she is walking into a (wealthy, white) man's world. Even a woman's choice to enter academia is often met with derision from other academics and her peers. For when a woman enters the academy, she has inevitably left something behind: a husband, a child, and a home (see also Davila and Aviles, this volume). She is, in effect, making a selfish choice by conceivably choosing herself over her relationships.

The already fine line that exists between selfishness and self-care is almost imperceptible when it comes to women. Womanhood has been and in many cases still is, synonymous with selflessness. Society expects women, particularly white women, regardless of their own identities, to sacrifice their bodies to motherhood and their personal lives to the betterment of their children and family (Friedan 1936). I've been alarmed at the extent to which twenty-first-century women my own age sacrifice their own personhood to their children—adopting Instagram names like "AmandasMom" or "MrsRichard." So, when a woman chooses to enter the historically "man's world" of academia, it is inevitable that she will experience tension as she moves between her personal and professional lives, as she attempts to manage the relationship between selfishness and self-care, and as she struggles to determine what it means to be a woman.

In this chapter, I draw on my personal experiences while a doctoral student to consider the following questions: In what ways do women mold their personal lives to fit and/or push against the age-old structures of academia? Do women feel the need to camouflage their identities in the academy, so as to be perceived as belonging and knowledgeable? How do women traverse the space between their academic and personal lives? and How do women negotiate their gendered, sexual identities into the academic world?

My aim is not to tell anyone else's story or to generalize my own. I recognize that womanhood and gender, in particular, are powerful terms and identities that carry with them a host of meanings. I identify as a cisgender, heterosexual white woman, and it is those identities that shape the stories and perspectives that I discuss here. Like Dorothy's adventures through Oz, my progression through my Ph.D. program was wrought with tension as I struggled to maintain relationships outside of academia, to care for my physical and emotional well-being and to strike a balance between my work and personal lives. In particular, I draw on three salient aspects of *The Wizard of Oz* to organize the vignettes and thoughts that follow: (a) The Land of Oz was a land of color, unlike Dorothy's monochromatic home in Kansas, (b) Dorothy sought the help of the enigmatic Wizard of Oz to help her and her newfound friends get what they desired most, and (c) There was both a literal and figurative shroud of mystery surrounding the grand Wizard of Oz, who ultimately turned out to be a middle-aged human (i.e., not magical) man.

The Land of Color

It was a Saturday in October, and I was halfway through the first semester of my Ph.D. I had spent the previous week reading about different qualitative data analysis methodologies and considering the potential colonizing effects of ethnographic research. My brain felt hazy with all the new terms, theorists, and concepts that I was learning. But I was eager to keep learning and to deepen my level of understanding. On this particular Saturday, my husband and I were going to a friend's house to watch a football game with about eight of our closest friends since undergrad.

I've always been pretty disinterested in football, so (for me) these weekend gatherings were more about conversation and seeing friends than about enjoying the game. But this Saturday was different. Not only did I feel like I was having to pull myself begrudgingly away from school work and reading just to leave the house, but I struggled to stop thinking about school work once we got to our friend's house. I felt, perhaps for the first time, disconnected from their lives and topics of conversation. The jobs, social lives, and children my friends talked about seemed to exist in a world distant from my own.

When my friends first found out I was going back to school, many responded with envy—inevitably expecting that I was going to relive undergrad. I can't say that my expectations were significantly different from theirs. When I first started my Ph.D. program, I was shocked by the sheer number of hours I needed to work. Doctoral students are expected to teach undergraduate courses, to conduct research, to write for publication, to attend and present at conferences, and to serve the department, in addition to successfully completing their own coursework and dissertation. As the weeks and months progressed, I began to feel that the only people who understood the demands of a Ph.D. were fellow Ph.D. students.

The disconnect I perceived to exist between myself and many of my non-Ph.D. friends continued to grow until I felt completely isolated from my past relationships, pastimes, and interests.

When I started my Ph.D. program, it was as if I, like Dorothy in the Land of Oz, was seeing color for the first time. I grew up with two happily married parents and a younger sister. For as long as I can remember, I imagined having a life very similar to that of my parents—getting married, settling in one place, and having children. The first disruption to this imagined future happened when I chose to get my Ph.D. at a university that required my husband and me to move states (see also Tondreau, this volume). I didn't know at the time that this move would be the first domino to fall. The classes I took pushed me to look at my world through a more critical lens and to question the relationships, places, routines, texts, and words that had for so long defined me. It was during my Ph.D. that I finally started to consciously analyze my white privilege, to understand gender and sexuality as existing on a spectrum, and to develop the skills needed to be a critical consumer of life and society.

As my Ph.D. program progressed, my life became riddled with questions. Although I was already married, I began to question how that relationship would change as I continued to internalize what I was reading and learning about in school. How would my husband respond when I challenged some of our routines and goals as a couple? Would school drive a wedge between us, or merely leverage us to new planes in our relationship? I also started thinking more concretely about having children. I wondered what life with a baby would look like (see also Guyotte and Hick, this volume). How would I balance taking care of a child with the demands of a life in academia? *When* would I have a baby? Would it be smarter to have a baby during my Ph.D. program or to wait until after tenure?

As time went on, my interests in being married and one day having a baby faded. Although I have since met many women in academia who successfully balance marriage, motherhood, and their professional lives, early in my doctoral work I had met few. Further, there were very few women academics who talked openly about their personal lives. My interactions with women academics (even fellow students) were almost always relegated to discussions of writing, research, and teaching. I began to see academia as the (stereotypically) masculine and isolated place it was designed to be—a place free from children, romantic relationships, and personal problems and lives.

As a newcomer to this world, I (both consciously and unconsciously) tried to assimilate. I rarely talked about my husband, our past, our future plans, or our friends outside of academia—contributing to a very real sense that I was living two parallel lives. As time went on, I struggled more and more to reconcile those two lives or even to move back and forth between them. I was incredibly unfair to those around me and found that I was almost unable to have conversations with family or friends that didn't end with me criticizing them. My struggle to cross the chasm that was developing between my two worlds resulted in some very elitist behavior that, looking back, I'm not very proud of.

However, my relationship with my husband suffered the most. We struggled to talk about the divide that was consuming our marriage, and he refused to take an interest in my school work and resented school for changing the tenor of our relationship. He criticized me for being too challenging to talk to or spend time with, for questioning whether or not I wanted children, and for requiring him to put life on hold so that I could go to school. Ultimately, I found that I was unable to nurture my own personal learning and growth within the confines of my marriage.

Although plenty of my peers were critical and labeled me "selfish," I believe my decision to get divorced was a courageous act of self-care.

SEEKING HELP

It was pouring down rain the morning that I found out. It was four in the morning, lights were still on in the living room, and the TV screen glowed blue. I was alone in the bed my parents had given us as a wedding gift five years earlier, while my husband slept in the living room. Preferring the uncomfortable sofa to sleeping in the same room as me.

I woke up worried, a feeling in the pit of my stomach that things were off. I was supposed to run a half marathon in three hours, so I blamed my nerves on the race. But even after shaking off sleep and brushing my teeth, the nerves remained. I walked quietly into the living room and tentatively pick up my husband's cell phone from the coffee table. I pressed the circle at the bottom of the dark screen, and was met by lists of texts from one number. Over and over again, back and forth between my husband and his assistant, the words: I love you.

I quietly put a leash on my dog, slipped on shoes, texted my sister to come pick me up. And I left. Not to return until six months later when I would divide up the dishes and furniture, the meaningless artifacts of what would become a past life.

In the years following, there were feelings of guilt that I, as a woman, had failed at my marriage. That guilt was compounded with the fact that I had the luxury of being a full-time student: I didn't have a significant other or children to worry about and, although money was tight, an assistantship could be my primary source of income. And so, I often felt that I needed to make up for my desolate personal life by having a very robust and full professional one. I felt that I needed to be as busy as those around me and that somehow that busyness would give my life legitimacy. When I had been married and had taken a break from working, I had done it in the name of needing-to-spend-time-with-my-husband. But after the divorce, I had no excuse for taking breaks. So I just didn't.

I could feel myself morphing into the man that academia was built for: I used work to insulate myself from worries about children, a significant other, and money. As I rejected stereotypically "woman" responsibilities and interests (e.g., marriage and children), I turned to my work to give me an identity. But even by pouring myself into work, I reasserted my womanhood. Similar to the US housewives of the early to mid-1900s who busied themselves with chores around the home and volunteering at their children's schools (Friedan 1936), I was creating work for myself in order to both appear and be busy. However, also like the housewives, my busyness was neither wholly necessary nor fulfilling. So why did they do it? Why did *I* do it? In short: because I had imagined an audience to my life. I was making choices about how to spend my time based on what I believed others would find legitimate and worthwhile, rather than based on my own personal interests or goals. I was so concerned about rejecting the appearance of selfishness that I was unable to care for myself. The fine line between selfishness and self-care was, yet again, blurred.

During her time in Oz, Dorothy met a Scarecrow, a Lion, and a Tin Man. Each character had something they desired and believed that the Wizard of Oz would be able to grant them. Unlike Dorothy, the Scarecrow, Lion, and Tin Man were unaware of their deepest desires until the Wizard's gifts at the end of the story signified that they already had what they wanted all along: brains, courage, and heart, respectively. As much as I wish I had been more like Dorothy (who knew what she wanted and how to get it), I was, in actuality, more similar to the Scarecrow, Lion, and Tin Man. I thought that a life of reading, writing, teaching, and thinking could fulfill me. I poured myself into my degree. I made it my mission to be the most successful doctoral student I could be, and consequently, school became my entire life. I experienced some modicum of professional success, yes, but I also struggled to maintain out-of-school friendships and to take care of my physical and mental health. I gained weight, escaped my life to live abroad for a few months, lost too much weight, and had a couple panic attacks.

Finally, I began to recognize that not only was this life not sustainable, but it was unfulfilling. I had started my Ph.D. with intentions of being both professionally and personally successful. Somewhere along the way, however, academia became a zero-sum game: I could have either a full professional life or no life at all. My second panic attack was the Wizard's gift I needed because it forced me to pause and to realize that, like the Scarecrow, Lion, and Tin Man, I already had what I desired: family, friends, interests, and work. I just needed to care for myself in a way that allowed all of these parts of my life to intersect.

The Shroud of Mystery

I was hunkered down at my favorite coffee shop, having worn the same sweatshirt for two days, and doused my hair in dry-shampoo to try and mask the fact that I didn't shower that morning. It was early December and my dissertation was due to my committee in one week. As I stood up to get my third cup of coffee for the morning, I caught a glimpse of one of the women professors in our department. The antithesis to my disheveled and frazzled state, she was poised over her computer, no doubt writing what would turn out to be a brilliant journal article.

As I stood waiting for my coffee, I remember questioning how she managed to balance everything: she was a successful and well-respected Associate Professor, married, and mother to three young children. I, on the other hand, couldn't even manage to balance basic hygiene with writing a dissertation. So when she came up behind me in the coffee line I wanted to curl into my sweatshirt and disappear.

Instead, I turned to say good morning and glimpsed a stroke of distress cross her face. After saying hello, she asked:

"Can I get your opinion on something?"

I was at a loss as to what this professor could need my opinion on, but I nodded my consent.

"I have two twin girls; can I buy them one Barbie dream house? Or do I need to buy two? Can they share? Did you share with your sister?"

For the past three and a half years, I'd held professors on a pedestal. They were the elusive grand Wizard behind the curtain. But at this moment at the coffee shop, I felt that I had finally pulled away the curtain and seen the Wizard—and (s)he was human! At that moment, she wasn't concerned with the feminist critiques of gendered toys, she wasn't spending her Saturday morning writing an article, she was just trying to buy her kids Christmas gifts.

Academics often discuss the dark cloud of imposter syndrome: that feeling that at any moment someone will pull back the curtain and figure out that you, in fact, know nothing and have no business calling yourself an academic. For women in academia, the threat of the curtain being pulled back is perhaps even more pronounced than for men. For a woman to lay bare her humanity is also to reveal the fact that she isn't a man. By exposing her womanness (and all the historical, stereotypical, and socialized narratives associated with being a woman), the woman professor both confirms and challenges the fact that she's moving through a world that wasn't built for her. As a nascent academic, struggling to reconcile my personal and professional selves and to find a space for my womanness in academia, I needed this Barbie dream house moment. I needed a successful woman professor to peel back the curtain and to give me a glimpse into not only her personal life, but her gendered life, as well.

CONCLUSION

I still have moments where I wish I had never landed in Oz and seen the color there. In so many ways, life was incredibly simple and predictable before I decided to pursue my Ph.D. I had no idea that my choice to enter academia would mean that I would lose friends, get divorced, reconsider having children, struggle to balance my personal and professional lives, or question what it means to be a woman. But, like Dorothy, the fact that I've seen color only adds a new layer of complexity to my life, rather than one life replacing another. The people who care most for me will remain in my life (hopefully having forgiven my moments of elitism); experiences from my marriage will shape and help me to navigate my current romantic relationship; and memories from my early Ph.D. years will help me as I continue to balance my personal and professional lives.

I've learned that the line between selfishness and self-care is a fine and gendered one. I have no doubt that men and women receive different levels of criticism when it comes to distinguishing between selfishness and self-care. Although I saw my decision to go back to school as a form of self-care, my husband saw it as selfishness, in part because he thought it would take away from my ability to give birth to or care for future children. To my knowledge, he never faced criticism for being selfish when he chose to take on a job that demanded he work during the evenings and weekends (times that would typically interfere with time spent with children). I've given up, however, on the quest to identify universal definitions of self-care and selfishness, or to defend my choices to others. Acts and understandings of self-care are deeply personal. Like the Scarecrow, Lion, and Tin Man, I've found that I don't need to look outside myself to get what I desire most. Sometimes I just need to take the time to realize and nurture those desires.

Throughout my Ph.D., I expected there to be moments when I would pull back the Wizard's curtain to find the answer to how to balance my personal and professional lives or how to navigate being a woman in academia. Although I feel I've gotten better at managing the workload and not letting it seep (too much) into my personal life, I still find myself periodically glued to my laptop at one in the morning, writing, having forgotten to eat anything beyond a series of snacks all day. For me, the self-care needed to balance my personal and professional lives will be an ongoing quest. It's not something that I'm going to find and nail down, but instead something that I will constantly have to negotiate into my life. Similarly, I expect that I will continue to struggle with what it means to be a woman in academia. I will simultaneously question how vulnerable I can afford to be in the academy and will push against the very fact that I'm in a vulnerable position as a woman. I will both reinforce and chip away at the masculine structures and traditions that define my profession. Hopefully, though, the chipping away will slowly start to overtake the acts of reinforcement.

The Wizard of Oz ended as Dorothy closed her eyes, clicked her ruby slippers three times, and woke up back in her bedroom in Kansas. Although she returned to a world dominated by shades of black, white, and gray, she didn't leave the color of Oz completely behind her. Instead, she recounted her adventures to her family and friends—in effect, keeping the color alive. For Dorothy, there was "no place like home." Although I loved *The Wizard of Oz* growing up and have no personal vendetta against Dorothy, I think she got it a bit wrong in the end. Instead, I think Dorothy could've taken some notes from Thomas Wolfe's (1940) titular admonition: "You can't go home again," for once you see color, the whole world—even home—is altered.

> It was lunchtime and I was sitting on the patio of a Mexican restaurant with my husband. I remember feeling relieved that we were sitting outside because there was no way I could take my sunglasses off to reveal my eyes—red, puffy, heavy with tears cried and still to come. My husband offered an ultimatum: either I give up the Ph.D., find a job teaching middle school again, and have a baby, or our marriage was over. And there was a moment that I wished it all away: I wished I'd never thought about going back to school, that I'd never met my major professor, that I'd never been asked to write that chapter on service-learning.
>
> And then I breathed out. And in that breath, realized that I could never unsee what I had seen. I'd arrived in the Land of Oz, I'd traveled to the Emerald City, and I'd seen the man behind the curtain. The world had become a more complex, exciting, mysterious, and colorful place—and there was no way I could fully return to my sepia-toned former life. And

even though I wouldn't admit it for many months, it was in that moment, sitting in that Mexican restaurant, faced with the possibility of never seeing color again, that I decided not to turn back.

References

American Association of University Women. 2004. *Tenure Denied: Cases of Sex Discrimination in Academia*. Washington, DC: AAUW Educational Foundation and AAUW Legal Advocacy Fund.

Baum, Frank. 1900. *The Wonderful Wizard of Oz*. Chicago: George M. Hill Company.

Drame, Elizabeth, Jennifer Mueller, Raquel Oxford, Sandra Toro, Debora Wisneski, and Yaoying Xu. 2012. "'We Make the Road by Walking': A Collaborative Inquiry Into the Experiences of Women in Academia." *Reflective Practice* 13, no. 6 (October): 829–841.

Friedan, Betty. 1936. *The Feminine Mystique*. New York: W. W. Norton & Company.

Knights, David, and Deborah Kerfoot. 2008. "Editorial: Breaking Boundaries: Women in Academia." *Gender, Work & Organization* 15, no. 3 (April): 231–234.

Mason, Mary Ann, Nicholas H. Wolfinger, and Marc Goulden. 2013. *Do Babies Matter?: Gender and Family in the Ivory Tower*. New Brunswick: Rutgers University Press.

Wolf, Naomi. 1991. *The Beauty Myth: How Images of Beauty Are Used Against Women*. New York: Harper Collins.

Wolfe, Thomas. 1940. *You Can't Go Home Again*. New York: Harper & Row.

CHAPTER 15

Doctor of Vulnerability and Resilience

Janine de Novais

RECKONING

In August 2017, a tweet from one of my most beloved academic heroes, Tressie McMillan Cottom, stopped me dead in my digital tracks. Cottom ranks high among academics who inspire me because of the ways she puts original and impactful ideas to work in the world. Within her wide-ranging expertise, Cottom (2017) is a proponent of and brilliant practitioner of digital sociology, which may have something to do with her Twitter acumen. On that platform, Cottom weaves 140-character slices of personal narrative with critical insights into the intersections of race, culture, democracy, and education. Her tweet came at the end of the summer after my graduation and maybe that is why it rang like a bell inside of a set of thoughts that I had been keeping quiet. It reverberated, through a series of tweets:

> After a successful thesis defense today, I did what is becoming my ritual: I talked with the new graduate about the trauma of finishing.
> Starting my third year as a tenure track faculty, I am only halfway through recovery.

J. de Novais (✉)
University of Delaware, Newark, DE, USA

© The Author(s) 2018
S. A. Shelton et al. (eds.), *Feminism and Intersectionality in Academia*,
https://doi.org/10.1007/978-3-319-90590-7_15

All of this is especially true for black and brown folks going through grad school, with, I suspect, special trauma if you're also a woman.

Plenty of ink has been spilled about the trials of graduate school, so the sentiment itself was not surprising. What caught my attention was Cottom's blunt diagnosis: "trauma." I took that word in, anxious about its heavy resonance. Was that why, in the week following my dissertation defense, I had incredibly vivid flashbacks of it? Was that why, even though graduation had been one of my best days in recent memory, some part of me couldn't quite connect with the joyful celebration on that day? Was that why, as a new year and ostensibly an exciting new professional life drew near, I fantasized about running away to a remote beach and just sitting there in absolute silence? Was Cottom right?

The overwhelming recognition of others on Twitter seemed to suggest that she was. In their replies to her tweets, they parsed their nuanced experiences, their particular version of the trauma of graduate school. I sat with the idea for some time. I dug up memories and feelings, and I retraced my steps, some recent, some more remote, and all difficult. I concluded that for me graduate school was not so much a trauma as it was a reckoning. A reckoning with myself.

Mindelo, Cabo Verde, Circa 1990

I am thirteen years old, maybe close to fourteen. Lately, I have been feeling a new kind of ease, an unprecedented comfort in my own skin. The years of excelling in school have added up to a sense of my own capacity to control at least that aspect of my life. In school, I feel like my mind is perfectly suited to the challenges presented to it. It is a perfect symmetry that is absent in the rest of my life. How I will be valued by the adults around me is usually unclear and unreliable. Except when I achieve in school. Then, it is clear that they are proud of me. Ever so slightly, there is now more joy than labor in school work; there is pleasure. Not everyone notices, but some people do. I don't mind how subtle the change is because it makes moments of feeling comfortable in myself ever-surprising. This feeling of confidence is new, and I cherish it appropriately, like a revelation.

I am sitting at the beach, at dusk, my favorite time of day. I am flanked by my two best friends, Suzanna Helena and Alexandra Sofia: Su and Xa, for short. I have been best friends with Xa since the 4th grade.

We bonded as the two kids at school who never got attention from popular girls or boys but who always were the teacher's favorites. Su broke rank with the cool girls toward the end of 7th grade to become one of us. We never understood why she squandered precious social standing to join our nerdy pursuits: math games, friendly competitions during examination periods, memorizing Madonna lyrics, customizing our Keds sneakers, and watching "Dirty Dancing" until the VCR was burning hot.

We are lost in conversation as we often are, forgetting homework and dinner time. We are talking about the future. Xa will go to Portugal and study law. Su will study economics and manage her family's multiple businesses. I will move to New York. Will I still be a novelist, or a poet, they ask? I say I will maybe be a sociologist. "So, a professor?" Xa asks. I shrug and say "Yes, or some kind of intellectual person." The word, "intellectual," is not a precious word for us. It is a familiar word that goes with me, like "lawyer" goes with Xa and "entrepreneur" goes with Su. The future looks bright and concrete for all of us. Fully realizable.

This dusk-lit memory comes to me easily and always has. It is flooded with details that my memories usually lack: the smell of the ocean and how sand covered some parts of our bodies—elbow here, shin there, arm here, and toes there. The frizz making our hair look wild, the dance of our eyes above our cheekbones, the joy we felt at the plans we made, and how we reveled in who we were. We felt so absolutely sure of our abilities to move through the world and to bend it to the arcs of our dreams.

Over a lifetime, we know that it is common for women to lose that feeling. Our patriarchal world is engineered to create womanhood through a subtractive process, an exercise in caging what begins as a wild and free humanity (see also Matias and Jones, this volume). I was not an exception to those rules. My coming into adulthood, like that of so many women, was characterized by struggles of worth. In all this struggle, my intellectual identity was a singular comfort; from high school through college, I soared. I felt a sense of coherence, a sense of purpose, and sometimes, I even felt my self-consciousness disappear. Through my twenties and into my thirties, I joked that my intellectual identity was "the one part" of me that was immune to the dramas of worthiness that plagued "the other parts." That is the person I was when I leapt forward into the long-deferred dream of graduate school.

It might be more accurate to say I ran, rather than applied, to graduate school. I was a single mother of a 4th grader, having spent my twenties breaking my heart in vain, trying to keep my family together.

Having mended that broken heart, I came to graduate school at thirty-four years of age, single, and with a kid. I felt immediately out of place. My peers were younger, or if they were old enough to have families, they had nuclear ones and lived in spacious homes. My son and I cozied up in a one bedroom—the only kind of rent that we could afford. As a mild panic took over early on, I told myself that this was probably because my life circumstances were so atypical. What else could be making me anxious? After all, I had been, in some ways, making my way to graduate school my whole life. Not only was I fulfilling a lifelong dream, but I was also in a space—the university—in which I was accustomed to thriving. Everything, as they say, was finally coming up roses.

CAMBRIDGE, MASSACHUSETTS, CIRCA ANY TIME BEFORE GRADUATION

I am in graduate school at Harvard. It doesn't matter which year it is specifically, as every year looks the same. In the pages of my journals, there is a never-ending cycle of elusive and sparse good moments, interspersed with increasingly low and dark ones. It seems that coming here, to graduate school, was a mistake. It was only a way to guarantee that the lifelong expectations that I set for myself will not be met; I have set myself up for failure. The worse feelings come and go, and there are bright spots: a milestone completed here, a positive comment from the adviser there, and the supportive compliments from colleagues somewhere. But when the good feeling dissipates, I cannot remember it long enough to believe it ever happened. I gain no traction on this loop. The depressive bouts feel like a brand-new nightmare each time. The repetitive ebb and flow of moods do not reduce their impact. The self-doubt encroaches on productivity, and I distance myself from the work. Eventually, a kind of paralysis sets in. Each day kept away from work is a day closer to a kind of despairing fear that I do not, in the end, have what it takes to pull this off.

As soon as I can, after one of these bouts, I pick the work back up. I am battle worn and bruised but relieved to fight another day. On and on, this is the cycle, and I do not understand it. How is it that my intellect has also fallen prey to self-doubt and insecurity? The only thing that exceeds my utter confusion is my sadness. I am so sad that I do not seek help, even though I need it. I stubbornly cannot accept that—as with other aspects of my life—my intellectual life is tarnished by this feeling that I am not good enough. It feels unfair to lose my only respite, and I feel untethered.

In the summer before my purported last year, I witness, in quiet, internal horror, myself shut down. I run home to my native Cabo Verde for the summer, knowing that I will not get any work done there. In my hometown, I try to accept that I am quitting graduate school, that I am that cliché. I try to make peace with failing so publicly and loudly—failing at Harvard. Which is to say, failing to be who I thought my whole life, that I was. I try the taste of that story of my life and spit it back out. When I get back on the plane to return to the USA, I know two things. I know that I have added another year to my doctoral career because I am not ready for the challenge it poses me. And I know that if I am going to meet that challenge and graduate, I am going to have to change.

Role Model Interlude

There was a discourse of Graduate School Is Awful all around me. The consensus was that what I was going through was normal and no impediment to the so-called progress to a degree. This attitude was well-documented by people's eye rolls, sighs, and dismissive nods of recognition whenever I tried to say that I was having a hard time. Weren't we all? In fact, we might whisper or, if we are feeling particularly petty, even chuckle at someone who had really fallen off the grind. Didn't they know the pain was part and parcel of the experience? There were oblique references to The Bureau of Study Counsel, which as the name suggests was an academic counseling service that everyone had frequented at some point. But no mentions as to what specifically made everyone go. When I attended one of its programs, for folks experiencing writer's block, we all voraciously engaged the free-writing exercises. The tension generated by a room full of adults who were confounded and terrified by their own failure could have been cut with a knife, but nobody dared do it.

My emotional rollercoaster was thus implicitly dismissed as grown-up growing pains, the price of the ticket. Serious mentions of mental health happened, but only if someone hurt themselves. Most talks of what ailed us preferred the well-worn tropes: dysfunctional advisers, the pitfalls of data sets, or the dramas of fieldwork. Much was said, but never too seriously, about the so-called Impostor Syndrome (see also Barnes, Flint, and Tondreau, this volume). One day a colleague laughed and told me:

"I heard on a podcast that it's not called a syndrome anymore because that was too pathologizing, you know? It's so common, like, everyone has it, so it's just called impostor experience now." There: so many graduate students have it, it's like you don't even have it.

Amidst all this hypocrisy and evasion and posturing, my friend Dana stood out. A few years ahead of me in the doctoral journey, Dana was everything an advanced doctoral student should be. She was well-read, effortlessly brilliant, and often outshined our faculty during seminars. She was generous with peers like me, sharing everything she knew, pointing me in the right directions. A better pedagogue and researcher than most, she was deep into her dissertation work. The project entailed not only innovative, socially impactful research but also creative and field-shaking methodological innovations. But she was struggling. One moment Dana was on top of the world, excited to share her latest insights. The next, she was drowning in a disbelief that she could move forward. I remember the day when Dana's unabashed expression of exhaustion and despair—bursting into tears—reduced our small writing group to a startled, cruel silence. To empathize with her sitting there and crying was too risky because it meant admitting we knew what she was feeling. I remember that for her own sake, and ours, Dana bravely convened a small book club for interested graduate students. The book we read was Brené Brown's *Daring Greatly* (2012). Dana was a harbinger of the challenges that were to come. She modeled the kind of emotional honesty and courage that those challenges would demand of me.

Constructing an Emotional Architecture

I remember picking up *Daring Greatly* once more at the start of my last year in graduate school, with the bulk of my dissertation writing ahead of me. This was in the wake of almost walking away. Since first discovering her in 2010, I had more than once come to Brown's work in a state of complete confusion. Her work on shame and vulnerability had, among other things, an incredibly prescient set of insights about the ways in which both our upbringing and our culture conspire to exacerbate our struggles around worth (Brown 2010, 2012). Her central thesis, because it tracked on such foundational phenomena in human development and interaction, illuminated different aspects of my life, depending on what questions troubled me. Once, it helped me make sense of aspects of my childhood. Another time, it helped me understand my mother's childhood—and by extension, our relationship as adult women. It also afforded me important insights into my failed relationship with my son's father. I was not surprised therefore, when inspired by Dana's example years earlier, I picked up the book and it cast much-needed light on my graduate school struggles. The question I brought to Brown this time was simply this: How could I build the kind of emotional architecture that I needed in order to achieve my most desired accomplishment—writing a dissertation and graduating? Unsurprisingly, Brown "answered" me in the usual, resounding way.

Self-compassion and Understanding

Brown stresses that shame afflicts many domains of our lives, including the spheres of work and productivity. Rather than relegate shame to more private or personal domains, she reminds us that any creative work, any sharing of one's own ideas, entails risk and vulnerability—and shame. She defines shame as simply: "the intensely painful feeling or experience of believing that we are flawed and therefore unworthy of love and belonging" (Brown 2012, 69). In that definition, I saw the experience of graduate school as one where I was often in close contact with the threat that I was flawed, unsuited for the task before me and unworthy of being there. Shame and self-loathing were exacerbated in graduate school because, as a processual matter, graduate school connected my self-worth to my work. And then it proceeded to evaluate that work—and therefore evaluate me—relentlessly. Academia did not have to work very hard for the connection between my precarious self-worth and my work to thicken to the point of toxicity. Here is how Brown helped me finally understand the stormy weather I had found myself in, year in and year out:

> Because of how you were raised or how you approach the world, you've knowingly or unknowingly attached your self-worth to how your product or art is received. In simple terms, if they love it, you're worthy; if they don't, you're worthless. (Brown 2012, 128)

My inner voice was even more unforgiving: "If my work is not perfect, I'm worthless and my whole identity as someone who has a calling for the intellectual life—or someone who has a calling at all, is a sham." Once I started to explore my experience from this vantage point, as painful and scary as it was, I started to see myself with more clarity and compassion. Suddenly, the struggles I had were legitimate. In programs that train artists, there is often ample attention paid to issues of identity, vulnerability, and worthiness. It is understood that to produce work creatively, that is connected to oneself, puts one in the state Brown aptly calls "excruciating vulnerability." It seemed that I should have been given, if not more support around this predictable socioemotional challenge, then at least a heads up. It seemed to me that graduate school admitted only to be training researchers, when really it was cultivating intellectuals—something akin to training artists.

Abandoning Perfectionism

I struggled mightily with perfectionism, and while it cost me greatly and delayed every aspect of my work, I embraced it at first (see also Hick, this volume). For the bulk of my doctoral studies, I misperceived my perfectionism erroneously as some great quality of my character. This is what perfectionists do, I learned from Brown (2012, 128). We flatter ourselves into thinking that we are the way we are because we are striving for excellence. Not so. In sharp contrast to people with a strong sense of their own worth who do strive for excellence in a healthy way, Brown argues that perfectionists strive for impossible standards precisely because they have an almost existential fear of being unworthy. Perfectionists are always "hustling" to prove their worth. One becomes, as Brown puts it, and as I certainly was, a prisoner of a cycle of "Please, Perform and Perfect" (Brown 2012, 128–130). In my case, whenever I became painfully aware of my own inability to "perfect," I froze. Hours of being unable to touch my work, to write one word, to analyze one piece of data, became days. A sequence of three or so terrible days led to weeks-long bouts of work avoidance. Once re-reading Brown's book gave me these insights about perfectionism, I was able to see and then disrupt those patterns.

Practices of Awakening, Observing, then Loving My Mind

It is this process of recognizing and understanding my struggles that I describe as creating an emotional architecture. I recognized that there were existential stakes for me embedded in graduate school that could not be higher. This is why it was so hard. I then understood that I had to conceive and then construct, through everyday practices, the structure that I needed for sustenance. For a healthy and productive life of the mind. For not only getting through a dissertation but also making a considerable developmental leap in middle age.

Beyond Brown, I dove into work about cognition and socioemotional well-being. From hacks to laboratory experiments, from classics to the week's latest podcasts. Overwhelmingly, the key, resonant ideas were all the same. That neurological and biological productive states can be primed, that therapy is as essential a kind of hygiene as brushing one's teeth, that it takes repetition to instill a new habit, and that the mind can be trained to veer toward different attitudes and defaults. All in all, this was distilled into beginning my days with exercise, ending them with journaling, and going to therapy once a week. Taken together, these were practices of awakening my mind.

Still, all of this important socioemotional labor through both integrating Brown's ideas and teachings and working with my own therapist took a toll. My mind began to feel perhaps too awake, and slowly but surely I started to feel a distinct need to reduce all this processing of experiences, and x-raying of complicated emotions. After all, the primary task at hand was still to write a dissertation. I couldn't wear my mind out from bringing up too much stuff, especially when my mind was precisely the instrument I was betting my future on. It was out of the realization that sometimes the reflections about my state of mind could overwhelm me that I made my way to meditation.

If therapy and Brown's teachings allowed me to take my feelings seriously, meditation reminded me that they were not that serious. If all the work on self-worth was waking my mind, then meditation allowed me to observe my mind. The central tenets of meditation practice, including practicing detachment from thoughts and experiencing the very human scale of my own life, produced a perfect balance to the deep, often encroaching work in therapy. Meditation allowed me to watch my mind perform a kind of relentless number on me: my comparing mind insisting that everyone was better, faster, and stronger than me, and my ego raging with insecurity and repetitive regret for all my mistakes. Observing the harshness of my inner critic deepened my self-compassion. On the cushion every morning, I came to my own rescue and made myself okay.

The greatest gift followed from this juxtaposition of an awakened mind with an examined one. Over time, these practices made me feel more kind to myself than I had ever been. I felt full of care for myself.

Careful. And slowly but surely, I started to feel a deep connection to and pleasure in my own intellect—something that felt long lost. My mind returned to me as not merely as a tool for plowing through graduate school, not just a means to an end, but as a wonderful, foundational part of myself. My mind reappeared as one of the places where I experience the most joy. Reading for pleasure, listening to podcasts, dancing in my kitchen, having hour-long phone calls with my friends, and returning to my creative writing, all this came back with great force. I grew to love these times spent inside my own head, not working but playing. I found the rhythm of my intellectual life again—the operative word being *life*.

Vulnerability and Resilience

If it were that simple, it would not be real life. One last hard lesson had to be learned. Despite my hard-fought new insights and my great new practices of self-care, I still struggled with my demons, and perfectionism still tripped me up. I still screwed up. And so it was, that on a given morning, having not slept the previous three days, I submitted a draft of my dissertation to my committee at the very last minute of the deadline. Reverting to old habits, I found the shame of missing the deadline too much to stomach, and it blinded me to the fact that a late draft is better than an inadequate one. No sooner had I sent the draft than I received word from my adviser, on behalf of my committee, that this was an unacceptable performance. The worst nightmare made real: actual failure. Yet, as I read her recriminating words in an email, I also realized that I was standing at this particular place for the last time. Surprisingly, I did not feel the deep shame I feared I might feel in such a moment. I felt just guilt. Here is Brown (2012) on the crucial difference:

> When we apologize for something we've done, make amends or change a behavior that doesn't align with our values, guilt—not shame—is most often the driving force... It's an uncomfortable feeling but one that is helpful. The psychological discomfort, something similar to cognitive dissonance, is what motivates meaningful change. (72)

Unlike shame that strikes at the very core of one's self-worth, guilt triggers one's capacity to do better. I could not wait to get to work and make amends. I understood exactly what had gone wrong, and why, and I had absolute confidence that it would not happen again. I felt, at that moment, liberated. To this day, I have a visceral memory of that morning. I wrote an email to my closest friends, processing in real time. I told them that in order to get through the morning I was having, "I needed to be honest." It was the kind of email, perhaps not unlike this chapter, where you know you said too much, exposed too much, but did it anyway.

With a new dissertation deadline, I got to work on my final draft and for the first time, I couldn't wait to get to it. The weeks that followed had a powerful quality to them; they felt dense with a challenge that I felt finally suited for. I didn't sleep much, but I didn't care much for sleep either. I sometimes wondered if I was in what Csikszentmihalyi (1990) calls flow. During the few breaks I took, I made sure to journal and to commit these crucial lessons to memory. Four weeks later, I submitted a revised draft of my dissertation that felt final, felt strong, and felt like the best possible representation of my study, the clearest and most compelling rendering of my thinking. It felt like a good piece of work that nonetheless felt completely separate from me, as a person. When I finally defended my dissertation, the most distinct feeling I had was wholly unprecedented in my life: I felt a steadiness within myself.

In her research, Brown (2012) finds that when people are trained to connect their worth with their work, as we are trained to do in graduate school, both explicitly and implicitly, there is a high incidence of "disengagement, blame, gossip, stagnation and a total dearth of creativity and innovation" (65). That is a pretty apt description of graduate school at its most dysfunctional but alas, its most common. Brown argues that cultures that cultivate vulnerability and resilience empower people to produce creatively, to take risks in that productivity, and to eschew perfectionism in favor of soliciting input, collaboration, and constructive criticism. My experience has taught me that a great deal of that signature pain of graduate school would be averted and a great deal of productivity would be achieved if doctoral programs engaged students proactively with a simple idea: Graduate school is as much an intellectual challenge as it is a challenge of adult development. I believe much trauma would dissipate if programs instructed students, with the clarity of purpose with which they teach them the methodologies and mores of academia, about practices of socioemotional health. If advisers and mentors, instead of guarding the worst kept secret—that graduate school holds up a mirror to all that you are—honestly prepared students for that reckoning. If supports were put in place to help students build the necessary emotional architecture to sustain themselves, just as they build their dazzlingly competitive CVs (curriculum vitae).

Instead, we encourage students to hide when they fail or fear failure. It is ironic to me that scholarly communities can show such lack of curiosity about what is a deeply rich terrain of cognitive and affective entanglement. We spend most of doctoral study avoiding the most complex problem to solve: ourselves. It is always surprising to me how uncomfortably people react to me when I suggest any of this. Interestingly, these public moments when people avert their eyes or quickly change the subject are often followed by private moments where individuals thank me for "keeping it real" and "sharing." Academia lacks an honesty that, Brown suggests, every segment of our society lacks: honesty about the shame that attends to failure, real or feared, whenever we attempt something new, something hard, and something that comes straight from inside. But while I know it to be rampant in society, this kind of intellectual incoherence and emotional immaturity seems a particular tragic failure in the academy. After all, are we not supposed to be the enlightened ones?

I like to joke that I graduated with a second degree, a doctorate in Janine. But I am not kidding when I say that the opportunity to begin to understand my way out of my entanglements with self-loathing and perfectionism, such that I could regain a sense of joy in my work, is by every measure the greater achievement of my doctoral career. I do not expect to ever again feel that unflinching, untarnished power I felt as a young girl, when I plotted my future with my best friends back in Mindelo. But fighting my way through graduate school reconnected me with an even mightier power: one that cracks, that shudders, and that bends but does not break, because it is made from that threaded web of vulnerability and resilience. It is a soul, that mysterious thing which every good education cultivates.

References

Brown, Brené. 2010. *The Gifts of Imperfection: Let Go of Who You Think You're Supposed to Be and Embrace Who You Are*. Center City: Hazelden.
———. 2012. *Daring Greatly: How the Courage to Be Vulnerable Transforms the Way We Live, Love, Parent, and Lead*. New York: Gotham Books.
Cottom, Tressie McMillan (@tressiemcphd). 2017. "After a Successful Thesis Defense Today I Did What Is Becoming My Ritual: I Talked with the New Graduate About the Trauma of Finishing." *Twitter Post*, August 4. https://twitter.com/tressiemcphd/status/893628620425613313.
Csikszentmihalyi, Mihaly. 1990. *Flow: The Psychology of Optimal Experience*. New York: Harper & Row.

CHAPTER 16

Teaching and Learning Within Feminist Dystopias

Alyssa D. Niccolini

THE RED BAG

The Teacher lays on the Examination Table and the Director runs the scanner along the length of her body. It hovers curiously like an animal or insect above the clavicle. The Assistant Director moves closer, tipping over the Teacher's red bag propped against the table leg.
"What is it?"
"An incipience of some sort," answers the Director.
The Assistant Director nods solemnly. "The Reviewer will watch it."
The Director turns to the still body, "You may go to class."

Inheritances are tricky things. They are things we are given to carry on, at times with and at times without consent. Wealth, names, traumas, estates, systems, skins. We inherit cells with coded stories from the past. What are tortured mother rats revealing to scientists in their disturbed pink litters? Is it twelve generations of trauma we now carry? *Your great-great-great grandmother's experiences live on in your genes* the headlines promise. As if feminist writers haven't been saying the same thing for years (see also Jones, this volume).

A. D. Niccolini (✉)
Teachers College, Columbia University, New York City, NY, USA

© The Author(s) 2018
S. A. Shelton et al. (eds.), *Feminism and Intersectionality in Academia*,
https://doi.org/10.1007/978-3-319-90590-7_16

I inherited a course on feminist dystopias. The course offered an introduction to feminist dystopian literature. Throughout the semester, we explored the dark imaginaries of women writers: Margaret Atwood, Joanna Russ, Octavia Butler, Charlotte Perkins Gilman. I was elated when I was given the course. I was excited to teach the books, humbled that I'd been entrusted to pass on these women's stories, and as an adjunct, I was thrilled that it wasn't the dreaded freshman composition class.

One of the feminist dystopian novels we read was Octavia Butler's (1979) *Kindred*. Butler has been celebrated as the first woman of color to find success in the male- and white-dominated science fiction genre. *Kindred* asks readers to imagine what it would be like for a black woman in 1976 to be transplanted to the days of slavery. Dana is a writer, but works for a temp office she argues operates like a "slave market." After a recent move with her white husband Kevin, she is overcome by bodily seizures wherein she gains a capacity to time travel. She is only able to return to the present when she feels her life is in danger. The time-traveling episodes wreak havoc on her body—making her dizzy, weak, and disoriented for increasingly longer periods of time. In her trips to the early 1800s, she is repeatedly faced with the task of saving Rufus, the white son of a slave-owning family in Maryland. She develops a complex relationship with Rufus and eventually learns he is a distant relative through the rape of one of his slaves, Alice. At some points, Kevin is also pulled into the past, raising uncomfortable questions about his complicity in past and present systems of oppression.

Past and present, here and there, blur as Dana toggles between the 1800s and 1976. In a final grueling trip, Rufus attacks Dana, saying she bears an uncanny resemblance to Alice, who has died by suicide. The viciousness of the attack hurls her back into the present, but she finds she has lost the arm Rufus had been violently holding onto. The grip of the past persists through time and space.

Dana's body, to the very possibility of her existence, is entangled in violent inheritances. These inheritances are part of her body down to the twisted ropes of her very DNA. These inheritances also live in our cultural DNA. Like Rufus' grip on Dana's arm, *Kindred*, Alys Eve Weinbaum (2013) argues and captures "the afterlife of slavery":

> Butler's representation of historical continuity, overlap, and transformation [...] not only allows for apprehension of the ideology of dominant economic systems and cultural processes, but it also gives us access to *residual*

16 TEACHING AND LEARNING WITHIN FEMINIST DYSTOPIAS 181

(formed in the past but still "active" in the present) and *emergent* ("alternative" and yet often inchoate) ideological and cultural processes that continuously exert pressure on, compete with, and in the process reshape dominant ones. (51)

Inheritances have afterlives. They are residues that are "active" on cultural processes. They live in our bodies and act on, exert pressure on, and reshape the present. This chapter labors to think through the inheritances I brought to the feminist dystopian classroom that I inherited. While many of these inheritances have created spaces beneficial to me, and perhaps even some of the students I taught, they have also carried with them skins, systems, and traumas.

Let me begin with an incomplete accounting of my inheritances:

I inherited a space to teach in the academy fought for by others before me. In particular, without the intense work undertaken in the 1970s, '80s, and '90s to create Women's Studies and Gender Studies programs, an accredited course like "feminist dystopias" fulfilling major degree requirements likely wouldn't have been imaginable.

Certainly, inheritances of white privilege put me in front of the degrees, the social and economic capital, histories, and experiences that put me in front of that class. What other bodies might I have been standing in front of (*before—over—on*)?

But we all know adjuncting is not the inheritance we want. As an adjunct (and someone on the market for a tenure-track job today), I am among the legions hoping to one day inherit an office with a door, a contractual promise, a declaration that I am worthy. We're easy to find (and replace).

And so, while I was blessed to inherit a space and department to teach in, I also inherited a space of contingency, a home among the precariat. We come and go, gaining temporary access to institutions, being entrusted with semester-stickered cards that slide us past security for a few months at a time. We move through institutional spaces like ghosts, unseen to each other, a zombie of conjoined bodies stitched together with the threads of insecure contracts.

It is only now that I look up adjunct:

> a thing added to something else as a supplementary rather than an essential part.
> Synonyms: supplement, addition, accompaniment, complement, companion, extra, add-on, additive, accessory, appurtenance; attachment, appendage, addendum, affix, auxiliary. (Google Dictionary n.d.)

Women, and particularly women with children, make up the largest portions of contingent university faculty (Curtis 2014; Mason 2011). Women make up only 38% of university faculty overall with their highest representation at community colleges and their lowest representation at doctorate-granting universities (Mason 2011).

As adjuncts, we learn to love our contingency. *I'm getting paid to do what I love*, we tell ourselves. *What other job would/could fit so nimbly between childrearing and dissertating?*, we coo. *This will help prepare me for a tenure-track job*, we promise (*I'd be an imposter anyways*, we fear). *This is just temporary*, we repeat to ourselves delirious from exhaustion in an empty classroom on a Tuesday night at ten o'clock with a block of Staples poster paper held like a shield between our body and the inherited anger of a white male student discussing his grade.

So, I inherited a space of contingency, of impermanence. This does not feel all that unique in a neoliberal present and certainly is nothing new for those who live in this country without a cloak of white privilege.

And I inherited a body of feminist dystopias I was entrusted to teach: a canon of women's literature whispering warnings to other women. *Pay attention. Look around. Don't be fooled. Imagine this.*

How should I have prepared for this honor, this challenge, and this burden? How should I have passed on the complicated inheritances of feminism?

Questions I am still unsure about: What is a feminist dystopia? Is being a feminist dystopian? Are feminist dystopias places feminists resist living "dehumanized and fearful lives"? (Merriam Webster Dictionary n.d.) Do we need a genre of literature to stake out territories safely immured in fiction to house, like concrete around nuclear waste, our feminist anger, shock, fear, and despair?

So why does a genre termed "feminist dystopian literature" exist? A journalist interviewing Margaret Atwood muses, "Do dystopian novels, I wonder, actually do anything? Can they change behaviour? They are, [Atwood] says, more like weathervanes than guides on averting disaster" (Higgins 2016, para. 15).

If feminist dystopias aren't imaginary, are they descriptive of the horrors of being feminists and women in the face of the present? While some might argue it's unethical to escort students into such unhappy spaces, I wonder if it is my white feminist naiveté or hubris that actually believes that my privileged white body has anything to teach this assemblage of different bodies—black bodies, brown bodies, queer bodies, bodies that may have been raped, bodies that may have been abused or assaulted, bodies that may be chronically ill or disabled, bodies that may be living with eating disorders, bodies that may have endured or are enduring the ravages of poverty, bodies that may have crossed deadly borders and been tangled in snares of (un)documentation, bodies that may bend and pray to something other than a Christian god, and bodies that may stray, however boldly or miniscully, from an imaginary norm—does my white privileged body have anything to teach these bodies about people leading dehumanized and often fearful lives?

I was surprised when I enter the room and it was full.

Empty Spaces

The Teacher places her red bag on the desk in the empty classroom. Empty classrooms unnerve her. Someone made up a word for the strange feeling spaces intended for groups of people have when they are empty: kenopsia (Hunter 2010). The room is charged as if it both misses and anticipates the intensities it was intended to contain—a strange pulsing of both past and present, bodies that were and bodies that are to come. She feels a panicky rush as she empties her red teaching bag.

Mixed Legacies

In class, we began with a staple of feminist literature, Charlotte Perkins Gilman's short story "The Yellow Wallpaper." Originally published in 1892, Gilman's text was long out of print and was eventually recuperated by the Feminist Press in 1973. Gilman's story went onto be named one of the top ten best-selling works of fiction by a university press (Lanser 1989).

The setting of the story is simple, a single attic room with barred windows (perhaps because it was formerly a nursery) in a "colonial" manse. An unnamed white middle-class female protagonist has been sent to this room to rest her nerves after childbirth by her well-intending doctor husband, John. She has been forbidden from writing and barred from social contact, save visits from John and his housekeeping sister Jane. Alone in the attic room, she unsurprisingly "goes mad," becoming consumed with the elaborate yellow wallpaper adorning the walls. Increasingly convinced a woman is trapped in the paper's patterns, she rips and shreds the walls to free their captive. The story ends with her husband fainting on finding her crawling around the room shouting, "I've got out at last."

The story unsettled readers. A male editor of the *Atlantic Monthly* justified not printing the story because "he could not forgive myself for making others as miserable as I have made myself" (Lanser 1989, 417), though Susan Lanser then questions why Edgar Allen Poe's works were then so celebrated at the time. Sara Ahmed (2010) has acknowledged, and urged us to celebrate, this feminist capacity "for making others miserable" by pointing out inequities. Gilman is then part of a longline of what Ahmed calls *feminist killjoys*.

In "Why I Wrote the Yellow Wallpaper," however, Gilman (1913) argues she penned the story to save other women from the "rest cure":

> [A doctor] put me to bed and applied the rest cure, to which a still-good physique responded so promptly that he concluded there was nothing much the matter with me, and sent me home with solemn advice to "live as domestic a life as far as possible," to "have but two hours' intellectual life a day," and "never to touch pen, brush, or pencil again" as long as I lived. This was in 1887. (271)

Gilman shares in the letter how the treatment brought her to the "borderline of utter mental ruin" (271). Admonished that her story might drive other readers themselves mad, Gilman argued that the story "was not intended to drive people crazy, but to save people from being driven crazy, and it worked" (271) since the rest cure was soon abandoned by the medical community.

Barred from an "intellectual life" and "infantalized, immobilized, and bored literally out of her mind," Gilman's narrator and story became ready feminist touchstones (Lanser 1989, 418). When I taught "The Yellow Wallpaper," I shared in a history of feminist enthusiasm for the text. While perhaps not "feminist dystopian" in the strictest sense, it could be well argued that an attic prison bedecked in garish yellow (or America at the turn of the century, for that matter) is just as dystopian a territory for women as Atwood's (2006) Gilead in *A Handmaid's Tale*. (It could be well argued that America in 2018 is also just as dystopian.)

I had taught "The Yellow Wallpaper" before, and students generally read it, liked it, and "got it." I thought it did nice work in illustrating first-wave feminist sentiments and women's oppression at the turn of the century. But what exactly did they "get"? Gilman's celebration as a white feminist is fraught with the politics of White Feminism. I capitalize White Feminism to signal a strand of feminism that wittingly or unwittingly elides, buries, or speaks over the knowledges, histories, and experiences of women of color. As I write this chapter, I am learning about my own inheritances of, and complicities in, White Feminism. For example, aside from Gilman's explanation letter, we read no criticism of the short text in class and quickly moved onto the meat of the course—three feminist dystopian novels. I see now, however, how this course selection carries with(in) it uncomfortable inheritances that I neglected to teach. As Denise Knight (2000) points out in her article, "Charlotte Perkins Gilman and the Shadow of Racism," "Gilman left a mixed legacy" (168).

We might have read, for example, Susan Lanser's (1989) well-known essay "Feminist Criticism, 'The Yellow Wallpaper' and the Politics of Color in America." Lanser argues that second-wave feminism's rediscovery and recuperation of forgotten, hidden, or maligned feminist texts were often problematic since some feminist readers were quick to see "men's writings as ideological sign systems and women's writing were representations of truth" (422). She points out that "virtually all feminist discourse on 'The Yellow Wallpaper' has come from white academics and that it has failed to question the story's status as a universal woman's text" (423). To combat this triumphalist essentialism of "women's writing" and experiences, she submits:

> I believe we have also entered a moment not only of historical possibility but also of historical urgency to stop reading a privileged, white, New England woman's text as simply—a woman's text. (Lanser 1989, 424)

I was a "privileged, white, New England woman" teaching "a privileged, white, New England woman's" story as a foundational feminist text.

Lanser points at that Gilman wrote the story while in California at the height of the so-called Yellow Peril, a time pitched in national anxieties around race. This, of courses, tinges new readings of the threat to white womanhood lurking within ornate, orientalized yellow wallpaper in a "colonial" estate. In class, we also read more than Gilman's famous short story. We ended the semester with her full-length novel *Herland*, which imagines a remote area cut off from the rest of the world after a volcano eruption and inhabited solely by women (Gilman [1915] 1979). Completely self-sufficient, the women reproduce through a process of parthenogenesis, a form of reproduction that doesn't involve a partner.

Gilman's aunt was Harriet Beecher Stowe, author of *Uncle Tom's Cabin*, and she often boasted of her "Beecher blood." Though Gilman celebrated her family's "progressive" legacy, Denise Knight (2000) reveals how Gilman equally celebrated her family's inherited intelligence and oratory skills. Knight argues that while Lanser excavates "subliminal" signs of racism in Gilman's work, more "overt and unapologetic" (162) examples stand in plain sight such as her novels, short stories, and personal letters. John Mertstock (2001) links up Gilman's descriptions of *Herland's* women as of a "'pure stock' of two thousand uninterrupted years" (122) aligned with eugenicist dreams of a master race:

> Scientific jargon like "pure stock" exists throughout the novel, aligning human reproduction with genetic engineering in animals and giving the whole process a dystopic rather than utopic tone. In Herland, the cultivation of their race into "perfect" Aryan, community-driven breeding machines projects *Herland* as an allegory for what she thought could be achieved using social Darwinism and eugenics. (Mertsock 2001, 36)

Though we used an intersectional feminist framework to think through the course, I was so entangled within legacies of White Feminism that I was immune to the possibility her work might smuggle legacies of white supremacy.

Line Up

The Teacher makes it through the final minutes of class without incident. She announces the next reading and the students line up neatly at the closed door. The Reviewer moves down the line and scans each body carefully. Her cheeks burn with hope and terror as the Reviewer proceeds further and further down the line of students without alert. The final student's body is soundlessly scanned. She may see them again.

Not a Policy Guide

Feminist dystopian literature is perhaps most readily associated with our second course text, Margaret Atwood's (2006) *The Handmaid's Tale*. This was years before Atwood became hot, before the Hulu show, before pussyhats, before 2016 and collective wokeness on Facebook, and before such dystopian futures seemed possible for many.

Atwood's novel features a dystopian not-too-distant future where war and environmental devastation have wrought widespread infertility. In the Republic of Gilead, a militarized authoritarian regime fueled by Christian fundamentalism, women have been stripped of their civil and property rights. Reading has been outlawed, and women require passes to go outside. Organized into castes, women's lives are intensely regulated and surveilled. Offenders to the Republic's strict rules are publicly hanged on The Wall. A minority of fertile women, deemed handmaids, have been forced into slavery to be reproductive surrogates for the ruling class. In ceremonial rape, ruling-class wives clutch handmaid's wrists while their husband thrust toward futurity. Meanwhile, a rebellion is stirring.

The Handmaid's Tale is in some ways an inheritance I refused. It was in my mother's stash of books in the basement. I often went into the cellar and ran my hands along her paperback books: *Beloved, Dead Souls, A Raisin in the Sun, The Feminine Mystique, Manchild in the Promised Land, The Women's Room*. My mother had often urged me to read *The Handmaid's Tale*, but the cover looked boring.

"It's really good," she said again and again. Like a good undutiful daughter, I didn't listen.

The 2016 election spurred renewed interest in both Atwood's works and dystopian literature writ large. *Animal Farm* and *1984* became sudden bestsellers on Amazon.com, and sales of *The Handmaid's Tale* soared (Alter 2017). Readers worldwide felt dystopian literature might offer pedagogies on how to navigate a tense geopolitical climate.

Direct allusions to *The Handmaid's Tale* were widespread at pre- and post-election protests. A *Bustle.com* piece by Sara Levine (2017) showcases images of Atwood-inspired protest placards:

"The Handmaid's Tale is not an instructional manual"
"Make Margaret Atwood fiction again!"
"*Nolite Te Bastardes Carborundorum*"
"Not a policy guide book" (accompanied by a cover of *The Handmaid's Tale*)
"No! To the Republic of Gilead"

Beyond placards, *The Handmaid's Tale* has inspired politicized feminist cosplay. Women dressed in the handmaid's red cloaks and bonnets have shown up in courtrooms, in Washington, at protests, and at other spaces where women's rights are under threat. A reporter asks, "Is this bonnet the new pussy hat?" (Bobb 2017).

Many have felt the 2016 election has thrown us, perhaps akin to Dana, into a regressive past. Celebrity statistician Nate Silver, hurled to infamy after predicting Hillary Clinton would win, showed a map of America is only men voted and another if only women voted—almost entirely republican-red if only men and entirely democrat-blue if only women. The report sparked the hashtag #repealthe19th, referring to the 19th Amendment of the US Constitution, which granted women the right to vote. But Silver was infamously wrong about the election outcome, beguiled most strikingly by college-educated white women. (The majority of the students I teach are white women being college-educated by a white college-educated woman.)

The hashtag #repealthe19th stings my body, but my feminist inheritances are heavy, weighty, ungainly things I was and am unsure how to pass on. I am indebted to first-wave feminists for my inherited rights. In October 2016, I felt an intense surge of emotion seeing images of Susan B. Anthony's gravestone dotted with "I Voted" stickers circulating on my Facebook feed. It was the online content of women of color who pointed out to me white women suffragists' complicity in white supremacy and the complexity of my inheritance of enfranchisement. I read for the first time: "It is not fair that a plantation Negro who can neither read or write should be entrusted with the ballot" (Fields-White 2011, para. 23) or Founder of the League of Women Voters, Carrie Chapman Catt's promise, "White supremacy will be strengthened, not weakened, by women's suffrage" (Sanghani 2015, para. 27).

If the election made plain the tenuous gains of first-wave feminists, Atwood feels contemporary feminism is grappling with the elemental: "First wave, the vote. Second wave, the image. Now it's about violence and rape and death: we've got down to the nitty-gritty." US readers, in particular, felt the handmaid's loss of bodily and reproductive autonomy was uneasily familiar (Higgins 2016, para. 8). As Atwood related in a recent interview, "When *The Handmaid's Tale* was published [...] the novel was reviewed by British critics as an enjoyable fantasy, and by the Canadians with a certain anxiety ('Could it happen here?')". In America, though, there was a sense of: "How long have we got?" (Higgins 2016, para. 9).

Angelica Jade Bastién (2017) points out that we don't even need to go back as far as slavery to see the bodies and reproductive rights of black women being exploited and controlled. She reminds us that women of color as young as nine years old have been forcibly sterilized in the USA as recently as 1974 (Bastién 2017).

Noah Berlatsky (2017) criticizes both Atwood's novel and its popular Hulu adaptation for erasing black people from Gilead. In a brief line in the novel, it is revealed that the "Sons of Ham," assumedly people of color, were "relocated" to bolster the regime's eugenicist dreams. In addition to flippantly erasing people of color in this line, Berlatsky argues the book and show exploit the very real pain and suffering endured by black women during slavery and use it to imagine a dystopia for white women. Berlansky explains:

> In Western fiction, dystopic stories often ask, "What if this atrocity had happened to white people instead?" That was the formula more than 100 years ago, when H.G. Wells wrote *The War of the Worlds*, its narrator comparing the Martian invasion of Britain to Britain's ruthless invasion of Tasmania. It's the formula in Universal Pictures' new franchise-starter *The Mummy*, which envisions a Middle Eastern woman bringing war to London, as Brits and Americans brought war to Iraq. And it's the basis for Margaret Atwood's 1985 novel *The Handmaid's Tale*, which imagines a world in which white women are enslaved and sexually coerced as black women were under American slavery. (para. 2)

We see echoes of this in how the white handmaids are barred from reading, a common practice during slavery. Butler cites this practice in *Kindred*. Dana is simultaneously mistrusted, envied, and exploited for her literacy skills, highly uncommon for both white men and women in nineteenth-century America. In a cruel irony, Rufus' father bars her from the books in his library, but then asks her to teach Rufus to read. He later whips her senseless when he suspects her of teaching other slaves to read. As Butler (1979) writes, "Repressive societies always seemed to understand the danger of 'wrong' ideas" (141).

Navigating the Gaps

When Dana in *Kindred* travels to the past, she must reconcile the painful knowledge that she is genetically tied to a slave-owning family through unspeakable violence. Inheritances are tricky things. They may hurt us, help us, hurt others, hide in plain sight, be painfully obvious, surprise, and dumbfound us at once. They're ungainly things we have to reckon with, benefits and burdens that live in our bodies and grip us violently in the present.

Feminists, particularly those who are white, carry simultaneously the burdens and benefits of White Feminist histories. What responsibility do those of us teaching future college-educated women have? What inheritances do we want—do we need—to pass on? What things do we carry unaware in our red teaching bags? As a feminist teacher, I need to vigilantly sit with, reflect on, return to, learn and relearn, teach and reteach—like a dizzy time-traveler—these inheritances.

I can't help but think how a neoliberal-driven, contingent-teaching-reliant university makes writing, research, and an "intellectual life" whereby such can work happen nearly impossible. Are we being administered whatever the opposite of the rest cure might be? Are we the women in the university attic?

Inheritances have afterlives. They are residues that are "active" on cultural processes. They live in our bodies and act on, exert pressure on, and reshape the present.

I am not suggesting there can ever a complete and final reckoning for all that's smuggled within the gaps of the stories we teach. Neither am I foolish enough to think that with enough training, mentorship, institutional support, funding and research time, an office, a golden nameplate, and possibility of tenure, I could ever provide a complete accounting of, or redeem my complicities within, White Feminism's "mixed legacies." Yet, the writing of this chapter has given me a small space to read and reflect, work that is vital to teaching and learning. As feminist educators, we need collective spaces to share such stories and knowledge—spaces like this very book. We must find, nurture, and multiply these small spaces among ourselves, our students, each other, while acknowledging they demand time, energy, and resources we don't always have. They may leave us dizzy, disoriented, drained, caught between past and present, here and there, tied to violent legacies we may not want.

And each time we do the work, we must be ready to lose a limb.

> It is the Teacher's turn to be scanned. The Reviewer moves the scanner slowly along the lengths of her body, the wand an unruly insect or animal.

When she reaches the clavicle, a beep, sudden, but somehow calm and perhaps even expected, echoes in the room. The Reviewer places the scanner in her red teaching bag and faces the line of waiting students. "Your new instructor will be announced before midnight." The students file out. She flicks off the classroom lights leaving it to buzz in the darkness.

REFERENCES

Ahmed, Sara. 2010. *The Promise of Happiness*. Durham: Duke University Press.
Alter, Alexandra. 2017. "Uneasy about the Future, Readers Turn to Dystopian Classics." *The New York Times*, January 27, 2017. https://www.nytimes.com/2017/01/27/business/media/dystopian-classics-1984-animal-farm-the-handmaids-tale.html?_r=0.
Atwood, Margaret. 2006. *The Handmaid's Tale*. New York: Everyman's Library.
Bastién, Angelica Jade. 2017. "In Its First Season, The Handmaid's Tale Greatest Failing Is How It Handles Race." *Vulture*, June 14, 2017. http://www.vulture.com/2017/06/the-handmaids-tale-greatest-failing-is-how-it-handles-race.html.
Berlatsky, Noah. 2017. "Both Versions of The Handmaid's Tale Have a Problem with Racial Erasure." *The Verge*, June 15, 2017. https://www.theverge.com/2017/6/15/15808530/handmaids-tale-hulu-margaret-atwood-black-history-racial-erasure.
Bobb, Brooke. 2017. "The Handmaids Take Washington: Is This Bonnet the New Pussy Hat?" *Vogue.Com*, June 28, 2017. https://www.vogue.com/article/fashion-runway-the-handmaids-tale-protest.
Butler, Octavia E. 1979. *Kindred*. Boston: Beacon Press.
Curtis, John W. 2014. "*The Employment Status of Instructional Staff Members in Higher Education, Fall 2011.*" Washington, DC: American Association of University Professors. https://www.aaup.org/sites/default/files/files/AAUP-InstrStaff2011-April2014.pdf.
Fields-White, Monee. 2011. "The Root: How Racism Tainted Women's Suffrage." *NPR.Org*. March 25, 2011. https://www.npr.org/2011/03/25/134849480/the-root-how-racism-tainted-womens-suffrage.
Gilman, Charlotte Perkins. (1892) 1973. *The Yellow Wallpaper*. New York: Feminist Press (Reprint).
Gilman, Charlotte Perkins. 1913. "Why I Wrote the Yellow Wallpaper." *The Forerunner* 4: 271.
Gilman, Charlotte Perkins. (1915) 1979. *Herland*. New York: Pantheon Books (Reprint).

Google Dictionary. n.d. "*Adjunct Definition—Google Search.*" Accessed December 8, 2017. https://www.google.de/search?q=adjunct+definition&oq=adjunct+-defini&aqs=chrome.0.0j69i57j0l4.5262j0j4&sourceid=chrome&ie=UTF-8.

Higgins, Charlotte. 2016. "Margaret Atwood: 'All Dystopias Are Telling You Is to Make Sure You've Got a Lot of Canned Goods and a Gun'." *The Guardian*, October 15, 2016. http://www.theguardian.com/books/2016/oct/15/margaret-atwood-interview-english-pen-pinter-prize.

Hunter, Hayden. 2010. "Kenopsia." *Tumblr*. http://www.dictionaryofobscuresorrows.com/post/27720773573/kenopsia.

Knight, Denise D. Knight. 2000. "Charlotte Perkins Gilman and the Shadow of Racism." *American Literary Realism* 32, no. 2 (Winter): 159–169.

Lanser, Susan S. 1989. "Feminist Criticism, 'The Yellow Wallpaper,' and the Politics of Color in America." *Feminist Studies* 15, no. 3 (Autumn): 415–441.

Levine, Sara. 2017. "These Margaret Atwood Signs Are Chilling." *Bustle*, January 21, 2017. https://www.bustle.com/p/these-margaret-atwood-signs-at-the-womens-march-will-give-you-the-chills-32074.

Mason, Mary Ann. 2011. "The Pyramid Problem." *The Chronicle of Higher Education*, March 9, 2011. https://www.chronicle.com/article/The-Pyramid-Problem/126614.

Merriam Webster Dictionary. n.d. "Definition of Dystopia." Accessed December 8, 2017. https://www.merriam-webster.com/dictionary/dystopia.

Mertsock, John S. 2001. "Racism and Xenophobia in Charlotte Perkins Gilman's 'The Yellow Wallpaper,' Herland and With Her in Ourland." English Master's Thesis, Brockport, NY: The College at Brockport: State University of New York. https://digitalcommons.brockport.edu/eng_theses/76.

Sanghani, Radhika. 2015. "The Uncomfortable Truth about Racism and the Suffragettes." *The Telegraph*, October 6, 2015. http://www.telegraph.co.uk/women/womens-life/11914757/Racism-and-the-suffragettes-the-uncomfortable-truth.html.

Weinbaum, Alys E. 2013. "The Afterlife of Slavery and the Problem of Reproductive Freedom." *Social Text* 31, no. 2 (June): 49–68.

CHAPTER 17

Re-introducing the Phoenix Within

Cheryl E. Matias

Recently, one of my doctoral students, Danielle, asked me, "What do you need to stay in academia?" She asked me this after riding along with me on my bumpy road toward tenure—an emotional bumpiness due to institutional resistance to my research and to my racial identity as a Brown-skinned Pinay motherscholar teaching white teachers about their whiteness. The question was so poignantly direct that it made me physically grimace. I froze, heart pounding ferociously in my chest. I found myself so communicatively immobilized that I simply drew in a breath and stared. I had no answer then. I'm not sure that I have a solid answer now. But as time passes, I am still haunted by that question. Because its seemingly simple quandary forces me to find an answer, and by attempting to answer it, it plunges me into a deeply complex identity crisis. Embedded in this answer, I am forced to identify myself as something I never thought I was, while simultaneously conjuring up fear of not being identified as it, or even losing it. Suffice it to say, as a once emboldened, young, radical activist and educator, I have always detested the discriminatory and elitist practices of the ivory towers, but now, as an associate professor, I am perched upon its balcony afraid to or, dare I admit, refusing to leave. As post-colonial, indigenous scholar Dr. Eve Tuck reminds

C. E. Matias (✉)
University of Colorado Denver, Denver, CO, USA

me in her mentoring dialogues at the annual American Educational Research Association Conference (AERA), "Does tenure mean forever or does it mean for just ten years?" Or, as Dr. Maria Salazar, another motherscholar of Color, has reflected in our ongoing dialogue, academy life gets "easier" as a tenured academic. However, upon this discovery, she immediately questioned herself as to why. Was it because she is conforming to the academy, losing who she was, or molding into anew? As critical scholars, we are familiar in deconstructing what is lacking but being asked forthrightly "What exactly do I need in order to stay put?" put me in an existential crisis. *Hold up, am I an academic now?*

There are many reasons why that question still resonates with me. However, this chapter will focus on the vulnerabilities such a question surfaces, precisely because the ivory towers are imbued with so much hegemonic whiteness and cis-gender patriarchy that being an "unapologetic" woman of Color, let alone a motherscholar of Color in the academy, freaks them the f out. The dynamics are eerily similar to President Obama's presidency. Meaning, upon his advancement as the first Black president—let alone any person of Color—into the Oval Office, white racists could not handle themselves. This became a predicament that has now led us to the current racial climate, whereby white nationalists (otherwise racists) feel entitled to take to the Charlottesville streets (Yan et al. 2017). In the streets, they are rallying their racist ideals in public—yet, ironically, behind masks. Clearly, racists cannot stand it when people of Color advance, mobilize, and are educated—just as sexists cannot stand it when women advance, mobilize, and are unapologetic of their achievements. The question that needs to be answered is why must I, as a woman of Color, be apologetic to these oppressive institutions, when whiteness and patriarchy were what held me back in the first place? Instead of being unapologetic, I feel like I deserve an apology from people who employ this emotionally deflective way of dealing with one's own racist and sexist inclinations toward my success. Yet, quandaries of "Shouldn't I just be grateful to be an academic in the first place?" made me feel foolish for asking. Ringing in my ears is the endless barrage of microaggressive inquiries such as "You're a professor?! Do you really have a Ph.D.?"

This chapter draws from my own experiences, stories, and personal narratives to illustrate just how tortuous life is within the academy. Though such stories may initially seem commonplace, blatantly disrespectful, or seemingly ungrateful, speaking *our* (as in people of Color, more precisely, women of Color) Truths is a bold move in the academy that needs to be continuously heard and respected. In fact, even in my own tenure case, one of my administrative letters tried to condemn this approach, claiming that my story is dangerous because it is "a single story" (Adichie 2009). And, embarrassingly, she cited and re-appropriated Chimamanda Ngozi Adichie's (2009) TED talk's main argument. According to Adichie, the single story that is dangerous is the white western narrative that dominates the schematic canon, not the marginalized stories of women of Color. Yet, this line of reasoning from such an administrator (much like the Kentucky clerk, Kim Davis, who refused to give a marriage license to a couple for being gay, claiming it was against her religious rights, was likened by her lawyers to Martin Luther King, Jr.) is grossly employed (Tashman 2016). In fact, it is a manipulative mechanism of whiteness because it is an ahistorical excuse to re-appropriate civil rights or marginality in favor of folks in power at the expense of those who are already oppressed. It is tantamount to a man saying women's rights or accusations of rape are an infringement of his civil liberties and privacy. Therefore, I do not share these stories without reservations. Indeed, there is an element of fear of those in power, precisely because those folks are most fearful of being exposed for their bias, bigotry, and thirst for power, rather than to learn from them. And in their fear and abuse of power, they will do anything to silence our stories. So I conclude that these stories, then, are powerful and must be heard.

Employing Duncan-Andrade's (2009) typologies of hope, these stories better explicate how hope moved, distorted, and evolved throughout my stay in the academy thus far. Although this personal revealing is quite embarrassing for me, I provide them to other women of Color who are considering entering or are currently on the same road to tenure in the academy as a way to understand how hope matures. Each typology of hope will be illustrated in a narrative of my experiences below.

Hokey Hope

During my doctoral classes, we freely deconstructed the depths of white supremacy, patriarchy, and capitalism in current society and how education is both implicated in replicating such power structures as social reproducers and transformative in changing the existing social structures. Therefore, one can understand how coming out of my doctoral program armed with knowledge of social justice education, critical race theory, and culturally responsive teaching, I had a vision of hope that encompassed taking on the world's injustices. Yet, in my twelve years of access to higher education, surpassing the educational journey of my immigrant parents, I overlooked how far away I have drifted from the struggles of my parents and who I was before all the fancy degrees. Sadly, as Duncan (2009) states, hokey hope "is a false hope informed by privilege and rooted in the optimism of the spectator who needs not suffer" (183). Despite growing up with constant racial, gender, and sexual microaggressions, I question whether I have been so seduced by the rhetoric of social justice that I had forgotten what it feels to be on the other end? Because of this hokey hopeful thinking, I did not fully understand the degree to which such a mission will exact an emotional, physical, and psychological cost. In my mind, any good deed, such as ridding the world of white supremacist ideology, would be benevolently recognized. I mean, is it not commonplace parlance that no good deed goes unnoticed?

In my blissful mission to reeducate folks on issues of race, there are two things that I grossly overlooked. One: should a good deed need to be noticed? If so, what does such a recognition look like? And two: What type of noticing is being done and how would that visibility impact me? This naïve ignorance, largely based off my blinded hokey hope to dismantle white supremacy, would later bite me in the ass.

CRITICAL HOPE

Duncan (2009) then describes the antithesis of false hopes such as hokey and mythical hope by articulating critical hopes that encompass the reality of human suffering. He writes, "Any growth in such an environment is painful because all of the basic requirements for healthy development (sun, water, and nutrient-rich soil) must be hard-won" (186). Understanding this new concept of hope helps me better understand my first seven years in the professoriate. Essentially, I realized with all that I went through, I was merely tearing down my once hokey hopeful wishes of dismantling whiteness and developing the fortitude of critical hope. Such a tearing down was arduous because I was confronted with ceaseless resistance, hysteria, and passive aggressive responses. Specifically, the resistance to my identity as a Brown-skinned "unapologetic" Filipina who refused to *nurse* (in reference to the historical immigration of Filipina nurses) the white fragilities of my colleagues and students entrenched in whiteness was overwhelming. Though I was hired to do a job and teach race and whiteness, there were too many white emotionalities that attempted to thwart my career path. In fact, by year two, there was much discomfort in listening to another colleague's presentation on race and racism inside the teacher education program (and knowing I was a scholar of whiteness) that the majority of white faculty projected their emotional angst onto me in a closed meeting held by the dean—a meeting where I (an untenured faculty member at the time) was denied my right to have a mentor present, and where no other members of faculty were allowed to attend (including the faculty diversity committee). I wrote about this experience in some of my later publications.

By year five, an "anonymous" caller attacked my scholarship, forcing the institutional review board (IRB) of my university to scrutinize all of my IRB statuses (which proved to be sound). Then in year six, I was attacked by ultra-conservative media that misquoted one of my articles. From this media frenzy, my family and I suffered harassing and borderline threatening emails, voicemails, packages sent to my office, and countless social media stalking. My family and I were not given any protection by my administration (no counseling, no public statement decrying the harassment or even supporting academic freedom, no extra security, not even offering to pay for my parking so that I could park closer to my building for my night classes, especially since I was pregnant at the time). Ultimately, the administration's lack of response clearly showed their level of investment to my scholarship and safety. By year seven, I had earned several local and national awards for my work on diversity, yet with each publication, award, or grants earned for creating a national conference on race in my local community, I was given less and less support. It came to a point where it became excessively difficult to even teach courses on race or even to teach any courses within the program. According to administration, there were always new, unwritten procedures of who gets "dibs" on courses, even if the course was housed in my own program where there were only three identified tenured faculty members. These institutional passive aggressive tactics were indicative of the resistances many will experience in academia, especially when their scholarship directly attempts to dismantle white supremacy in education, including academia. And, yet, despite the hope of producing a more racially just P-20 educational system, all of these resistance and passive aggressive tactics were (are) painfully traumatic to me, as a researcher and human being. In a sense, it reminds me of the critical hope Duncan (2009) points out: that the work is only relevant when resistance is constantly trying to suppress it is a sad reality. Yet, it is a reality that I am willing to engage in for the hope of a better tomorrow.

From the Ashes I Am Anew

Duncan's (2009) typologies of hope provide a formidable framing for my experiences as a Brown-skinned Pinay working toward tenure in the ivory tower. Sadly, I acknowledge that my experiences are not so different from the many other women of Color faculty and/or motherscholars in the academy. However, now as a tenured faculty member, it does not touch upon the inner peace I find now in the work I do and the hope I will forever hold despite it all. It is as if I am reborn, despite the fires of yesteryear. Suffice it to say that I have burned in the flames in the hellishness of the academy but instead of withering into ashes, I grew anew. Or metaphorically, I was reborn a phoenix of hope. In fact, my eyes are now wide open (unlike how they were bright eyed in the early days), and I still plunge forthright into the fire, hoping that with each plunge a person, a group, or an institution might open their hearts to a more racially humane coexistence, even if it means forcing them to feel the loss, discomfort, and humility of divorcing themselves from a familiar world, one which we all know is too embedded in whiteness. I am not saying that there is some ultimate moral to my story or that I am now supremely confident in my path. However, echoing in my heart is "What do I need now in the academy to stay?" I can say here are some things I would want: My own classes on race, respect from colleagues, grants or research assistants to support my scholarship, or simply the benefit of the doubt, yet all those will never come nor should I place my sense of worth on whether they ever do come. In the end, or perhaps it is my new beginning, I have my mind, heart, and soul, just as I did over eight years ago when I entered the academy. And that is far more priceless, fearless, and sexy than anything they could ever provide. And with these words I pass onto other women of Color and motherscholars in the academy a renewed sense of hope that, although tarnished by the many microaggressions one experiences in the cis-gender heteropatriarchal white supremacist academy, will never be burnt out... precisely because you are not alone. You never were. The ivory tower can do all that it wants to isolate your experiences, deny your humanity, or overlook your accomplishments, but all that BS is irrelevant. At the end of the day (and the beginning of your inner phoenix) realize there is a network of phoenixes already beckoning you to fly. And, this time we soar together. Salamat po.

Special Note

To my doctoral students who push me to rethink who I thought I was or think I am every day.

References

Adichie, Chimamanda Ngozi. 2009. *The Danger of a Single Story*. TED Global 2009. Oxford. https://www.ted.com/talks/chimamanda_adichie_the_danger_of_a_single_story.

Duncan-Andrade, Jeffery M. R. 2009. Note to Educators: Hope Required When Growing Roses in Concrete. *Harvard Educational Review* 79, no. 2 (Summer): 181–194.

Tashman, Brian. 2016. "Kim Davis' Lawyer Compares Her To Martin Luther King Jr." *Right Wing Watch*, January 19, 2016. http://www.rightwingwatch.org/post/kim-davis-lawyer-compares-her-to-martin-luther-king-jr/.

Yan, Holly, Devon M. Sayers, and Steve Almasay. 2017. "Virginia Governor on White Nationalists: They Should Leave America." *CNN.Com*, August 14, 2017. http://www.cnn.com/2017/08/13/us/charlottesville-white-nationalist-rally-car-crash/index.html.

Afterword

While this book originated in ruminations on different pathways for women in academia, the authors in this volume represent an even greater diversity of experiences than what we envisioned during our first NCTE session. As we editors solicited authors for each of the sections and started to read the chapter drafts, we said repeatedly to one another how excited we were about this work, how honored we were to be able to share the chapters crafted by these smart women. We acknowledge and honor the risks that they had to take in writing and publishing their narratives. This book's authors have shared their struggles with managing their work and their commitments to self, family, and cultures. They have discussed the ways that they have found fulfillment in different types of career paths. They have explored the ways that other aspects of their identities, along with their gender, have impacted them. It is appropriate that the book ends with the section on vulnerability and self-care; emotions and our responses to them are vital for us to negotiate and center as we move through our lives as women in higher education.

We write this conclusion at a time when the U.S. President and multiple members of Congress have been accused by women of harassment and assault; a time when, in the State of Alabama, where Stephanie works and resides, a Senate candidate who faced a plethora of accusations concerning his previous pursuits of underage girls won his party's nomination and lost the main electionrace by less than two percentage points.

Yet this was an election in which women were a major electoral factor, and in particular it was Black women who voted in droves against this candidate. It is also a time when the #MeToo Campaign, which brings visibility to the pervasiveness of sexual harassment and assault, can be found everywhere on social media. It is a time when prominent, powerful men—at least some of them—have been held accountable for their predatory and inappropriate behavior. We wonder if history will look back on this time—following, as it does, the Women's March on Washington and all of the sister marches in the U.S. and other nations—as a crucible for women's rights and power.

While the experiences shared in this volume are diverse and come from many perspectives, they are not exhaustive. As women in academia, we should continue to share our stories even as they grow and evolve. We hope you have been troubled, inspired, moved, and touched by these narratives of women in higher education, stories of feminism and intersectionality, stories that are too often hidden and suppressed. We echo Lester's call to center intersectional understandings as a way to make change, and we recall Matias' exhortation to birth our inner phoenix and find the flock of fellow travelers to soar along with. We hope to start to make a space where more of us can share our voices, coming together in sisterhood and support as we did on that November night when this book first began.

Index

A
A.B.D., 22
able-bodied, 109, 112, 114
ableism, 105, 106, 109, 115
academia, 2–10, 16, 22, 26–28, 33–35, 46, 47, 69, 75, 85, 86, 92, 94, 97–99, 108, 118, 124, 133, 134, 136, 151, 156–158, 160–165, 173, 177, 178, 193, 197, 201, 202
academic, 2, 6, 7, 22, 33, 35, 37, 40, 42, 43, 45–47, 64, 69, 75, 76, 78, 84, 86, 87, 90, 91, 93–95, 99, 104, 106–108, 123, 131, 132, 134, 136, 137, 140, 158, 163, 167, 171, 194, 197
accessibility, 109–112
accommodation, 65, 105, 110–112
action research, 90, 91
activist, 149, 193
adjunct, 6, 9, 42, 64–66, 99, 105, 180, 181
administration, 16, 66, 88, 197
adulthood, 71, 169
advisor, 16, 18, 22, 30, 31, 40, 41, 43, 77, 82
African American, 76, 77, 79–81, 84, 120
Afro-Puerto Rican, 9, 118, 121, 123, 128
allyship, 123, 131, 135–138, 140, 141
ancestry, 8, 125
anti-feminist, 4
anxiety, 17, 18, 20, 21, 38, 63, 91, 127, 146, 149, 188
art, 29, 30, 33, 46, 173
assault, 53, 127, 202
assistive technologies, 103
Atwood, Margaret, 180, 182, 184, 186–189
audience, 2, 112, 132, 162
autoethnography, 123, 129
automatic door, 109, 115

B
baby, 16, 40, 41, 46, 50, 72, 127, 160, 165
becoming, 7, 22, 25–29, 31–35, 38, 42, 44, 45, 69, 86, 97, 119, 134, 141, 167, 183
bilingual, 120

binary, 45, 120, 121
Black Student Union, 77
Black women, 95–97, 189, 202
blood, 95, 186
book, 1, 3, 5–10, 46, 51, 63, 80, 147, 151, 155, 172–174, 187, 189, 190, 201, 202
Botswana, 78, 132
Brand, Dionne, 97, 98
breastfeeding, 42
Brown, Brené, 21, 172
Butler, Octavia, 180, 189

C
camping, 7, 61, 62, 64, 70
candidate, 4, 202
canon, 182, 195
care, 19, 29, 35, 50, 59, 83, 109, 113, 117–119, 123, 157, 158, 160, 162, 164, 175, 177
career, 2, 7, 8, 16, 19, 23, 27, 28, 31, 32, 39, 45, 64, 65, 68–70, 75, 77–79, 81, 83, 85, 87–90, 92, 93, 139, 171, 178, 196, 201
change, 21, 22, 32, 46, 51, 55, 79, 80, 83, 89, 91–94, 105–108, 112, 114, 115, 125, 127, 135, 140, 145, 157, 160, 168, 171, 176, 178, 182, 202
Charlottesville (Virginia), 121, 129, 146, 194
choice, 17, 22, 28, 157, 164
cisgender, 3, 47, 107, 148, 158
civil rights, 125, 195
classism, 124
clinical faculty, 6
Clinton, Hillary, 3, 4, 188
colleague, 17, 49, 51, 55, 56, 93, 111–114, 136, 137, 171, 197
college, 2, 15, 29, 33, 43, 66, 76, 78, 80, 87, 90, 107, 109, 113, 118, 128, 150, 169

college-educated, 4, 188, 190
college graduate, 108
colonialism, 122
color blindness, 133
Colorism, 122
communicate, 54, 140
community, 29, 60, 65, 76, 77, 82, 86, 87, 107, 109, 112, 114, 121–124, 128, 129, 150, 182, 184, 186, 197
compass, 26, 28, 30–35, 77, 84
compassion, 50, 141, 174, 175
compliance, 104, 105, 109
conference, 1, 2, 4, 7, 40, 93, 122, 194, 197
Congress, 86, 202
connection, 28, 76, 79, 122, 173, 176
consultant, 64, 65, 83
context, 4, 5, 68, 72, 79, 82, 86, 87, 93, 106, 109, 118, 122, 131, 132, 135, 137, 140, 145
contingent, 182, 190
cosplay, 188
Cottom, Tressie McMillan, 167, 168
cotton, 95, 96
counseling, 171, 197
countermemory, 38
counternarrative, 123
course evaluation, 49, 53, 59
cousin, 87
coworker, 114
Crenshaw, Kimberlé, 5, 6
Critical Race Theory, 123, 195
cry, 22, 52, 127
culturally responsive teaching, 195
curriculum, 78, 89, 128, 135–137, 139, 177

D
data, 4, 37, 40, 43, 80, 158, 171, 174
daughter, 7, 26–30, 32–35, 40, 43–47, 50, 56, 82, 187

deaf, 106, 107, 110
death, 7, 32, 33, 156, 188
decolonial, 131, 136, 138, 141
devalue, 8, 10
diaspora, 76, 81, 95, 121
dis/ability, 103, 106–110, 112, 113, 115, 135
discussion, 2, 3, 7, 9, 131, 136, 148, 149
dissertation, 22, 40, 41, 43, 55, 64, 79, 91, 156, 157, 159, 163, 168, 172, 173, 175–177
diversity, 3, 5, 6, 81, 89, 99, 108, 112, 113, 124, 150, 197, 201
divorce, 9, 17, 161
doctor, 50, 92, 93, 183, 184
doctoral program, 9, 16, 17, 21, 22, 40, 42, 43, 76, 90, 195
domestic violence, 78, 127
double-dutch, 99
dystopia, 182, 189

E

educator, 9, 78, 86, 96, 147–150, 193
election, 3–5, 187, 188, 202
elementary school, 88, 89
emotion, 188
empathize, 172
empowerment, 39, 127, 151
enslavement, 8
equity, 83, 88–90, 104, 105, 107–110, 113, 115, 128
ethic/ethics/ethical, 34, 35, 66, 80
ethnicity, 5
Eurocentrism, 139
exam, 18, 39, 169
exhaustion, 172, 182
expectations, 2, 16, 30, 32, 56, 58, 79, 93, 146, 159, 170
experience, 19, 22, 38, 45, 47, 50, 61, 67–69, 72, 77, 79, 81, 82, 90, 91, 94, 106, 114, 118–121, 123, 125–128, 133, 137, 138, 148, 156–158, 171–173, 176, 177, 197

F

failure, 4, 39, 42, 56, 57, 71, 170, 171, 176, 178
family, 1, 7, 15–17, 19, 20, 22, 27–29, 32–35, 43, 45, 58, 59, 63, 64, 66–69, 79, 83, 84, 87, 92, 118–120, 129, 132, 150, 157, 160, 162, 165, 169, 180, 186, 189, 197, 201
father, 20, 34, 40, 78, 83, 173, 189
feminine, 9, 38, 146, 187
feminism, 4, 5, 75, 182, 185, 188, 202
feminist, 4–6, 26, 28, 38, 42, 163, 179–186, 188, 190
fertility, 39
fight, 58, 121, 126, 128, 133, 138, 170
first-generation, 2
flowers, 54, 117
friend, 26, 51, 53, 139, 140, 149, 158, 159, 172

G

gender, 19, 45, 47, 67, 81, 84, 86, 93, 118, 122, 123, 128, 129, 133–135, 146, 147, 149, 150, 157–159, 194, 196, 198, 201
gender expression, 5, 149
gender identity, 5, 86, 146, 149
gender studies, 151, 181
gente, 123
Gilman, Charlotte Perkins, 180, 183–186

grade, 15, 55, 58, 82, 88, 89, 95, 120, 168, 169, 182
graduate school, 1, 7, 31, 53, 75, 78, 79, 83, 121, 168–174, 176–178
graduate student, 7, 76, 98, 123
grandmother, 87, 117, 179
Great Depression, 77
grief, 9, 32, 126, 127
guilt, 18, 20, 30, 45, 46, 141, 161, 176
gynecologist, 39

H
harassment, 197, 202
health, 21, 53, 57, 68, 71, 77, 92, 115, 118, 162, 171, 177
hearing aid, 107
heteronormativity, 67
heteropatriarchy, 124
heterosexual, 3, 47, 107, 148, 158
higher education, 2, 3, 5–10, 27, 31, 35, 78, 81, 83, 90, 92, 93, 118, 122, 124, 128, 129, 131, 135–137, 139, 151, 196, 202
high school, 15, 29, 39, 50, 53, 64, 71, 77, 79, 82, 87, 169
Hill-Collins, Patricia, 98
history, 4, 76, 77, 95, 96, 184, 202
home, 9, 17, 19, 20, 26, 30, 32, 33, 39, 42, 44–46, 49–53, 55, 57, 58, 61, 63, 65, 67, 69–71, 92, 107, 115, 117–120, 125, 132, 149, 156–158, 162, 165, 171, 181, 184
hometown, 27, 32, 33, 171
hooks, bell, 98, 99, 133
hope, 71, 109, 147–149, 186, 195–198, 202
hospital, 29, 40, 49, 59
husband, 7, 15, 17–20, 42, 44, 51, 61, 63–65, 67, 78, 79, 81–83, 88, 91, 132–134, 156–161, 164, 165, 180, 183, 184, 187
hygiene, 163, 175

I
identity, 5, 9, 17, 32, 55, 59, 113, 118, 120, 121, 145, 146, 150, 151, 161, 169, 173, 174, 193, 196
immigrant, 9, 124, 196
imposter syndrome, 16, 21, 30, 163
inclusion, 106, 108, 109, 111–116, 147
income, 50, 64, 83, 161
independence, 79, 119, 120
indigenous, 79, 193
inequality, 137, 138
infection, 53
inheritance, 181, 187, 188
institution, 9, 16, 38, 43, 66, 69, 85, 93, 105, 107, 110, 113, 198
Institutional Review Board (IRB), 197
Intersectionality(ies), 3, 5, 8–10, 115, 134, 147, 150, 151, 202
Italy, 82, 83
ivory tower, 198

J
James, C.L.R., 76, 79
job, 2, 15, 19, 21, 23, 37, 42, 43, 45, 46, 50, 54, 55, 57, 65, 66, 86, 89–93, 98, 107, 108, 112, 164, 165, 181, 182, 196
job market, 90–92
journey, 1, 8, 25–29, 32, 33, 35, 70, 76, 78, 79, 83–86, 156, 172, 196

K
K-12, 50, 64–66, 68, 92, 118, 126

Kenya, 77, 79, 84, 132

L
labor, 6, 98, 99, 123, 125, 127, 168, 175
language, 2, 6, 19, 77, 82, 107, 110, 115, 157
Latinx, 118, 120–122, 125
law, 76, 80, 88, 108, 109, 111, 148, 169
leadership, 31, 66, 79, 85, 89–91, 93, 125, 128
leave of absence, 57, 77, 78
lecture, 138, 148
LGBTQ/LGBTQ+, 6, 146
liberal arts, 107, 108
liberation, 68, 72, 76, 127, 137
loneliness, 77
Lou Gehrig's disease, 25
love, 7, 21, 22, 28, 38, 45, 47, 51, 57, 59, 66, 69–71, 83, 88, 104, 107–109, 118, 121, 127, 146, 150, 161, 173, 176, 182
low-income, 4, 83, 87

M
map, 26–28, 32, 84, 97, 98, 188
marginalized, 86, 93, 108, 113, 124, 157, 195
marriage, 7, 17, 21, 22, 54, 79, 89, 91, 92, 117, 118, 160, 161, 164, 165, 195
marry/married, 3, 15, 17, 77, 119, 120, 132, 133, 159–161, 163
matriarchy, 117, 119, 120
meditation, 21, 87, 175
memory, 33, 35, 71, 168, 169, 176, 177
mentorship, 123, 129, 190
#MeToo Campaign, 202

methodologies/methodologist, 37, 45, 123, 158, 177
microaggression, 121, 129, 196, 198
microphone, 103–105, 107, 109
middle school, 15, 88, 90, 155, 165
minoritized, 113
misogyny, 146, 147
mixed-race, 132, 133
mommy guilt, 2
money, 65–67, 69, 83, 87, 135, 161
Monster, 80
mother, 2, 7, 15, 25–28, 30–35, 37, 38, 42, 44, 45, 72, 78, 83, 87, 92, 96, 98, 99, 118–120, 132, 163, 172, 179, 187
motherhood, 2, 3, 5, 7, 26, 37, 39, 42, 46–48, 157, 160
Mother Scholar/motherscholar, 193, 194
multicultural, 88
Muslim, 4

N
narrative, 3, 6–10, 22, 27–29, 33, 34, 68–70, 86, 92, 108, 119, 120, 167, 195
navigate, 7, 25, 26, 31, 34, 48, 120, 126, 164, 187
newborn, 51
New York, 17–19, 22, 27–29, 32, 169

O
Obama, Barack, 194
office, 9, 17, 19, 20, 30, 31, 39, 42, 44, 47, 55, 58, 76, 88, 98, 110, 180, 181, 190, 194, 197
old maid, 119
oppression, 68, 76, 81, 84, 86, 125, 127, 129, 134, 180, 184

P

parent, 46, 50, 51, 53, 54, 56, 133, 134
partner, 17–19, 39, 43, 51, 53, 65, 78, 88, 92, 132, 186
pathway, 2, 85, 86
patriarchy, 9, 19, 21, 68, 119, 129, 134, 194, 195
pedagogy, 127
peer, 90
perfection/perfectionism/perfectionist, 56, 68, 114, 174, 176–178
personal life, 2, 51, 91, 134, 147, 161, 164, 165
Ph.D., 1, 2, 26, 33, 78, 79, 88, 89, 122, 155–160, 162, 164, 165, 194
phallogocentric, 38
phoenix, 10, 198, 202
politics, 26, 86, 88, 185
poll, 4
positionality, 129
power, 6, 53, 54, 57, 79, 80, 108, 111, 118–121, 123, 129, 134–137, 139, 178, 195, 202
pregnancy/pregnant, 40–42, 50, 51, 54, 197
presentation, 40, 137, 148, 149, 197
president, 4, 92, 113, 194, 202
privilege, 9, 18, 58, 69, 105, 107, 114, 123, 129, 132–135, 138, 140, 159, 181, 182, 196
productivity, 56, 58, 66, 115, 170, 173, 177
professional, 2, 7–10, 19, 22, 50–52, 56, 57, 67–69, 75, 78–80, 82–87, 90, 91, 93, 114, 115, 122, 129, 133, 149, 158, 160–162, 164, 165, 168
professor, 42, 43, 45, 53, 54, 56, 57, 59, 60, 64, 66, 76, 80, 85, 90, 91, 93, 95, 107, 108, 155, 163–165, 169, 193, 194
protest, 187
public school, 88, 90
publish, 90
Puerto Rican, 118–121, 125, 127
pussy hat, 188

Q

qualitative, 32, 108, 158
queer, 4, 182

R

race, 5, 9, 76, 81, 84, 113, 118, 121, 122, 132–135, 139, 146, 147, 150, 157, 161, 167, 185, 186, 196–198, 202
racial equity, 8, 75, 113
racially minoritized, 4, 6
racism, 9, 124, 132–135, 141, 146, 147, 185, 186, 197
rainbowism, 133
rape, 180, 187, 188, 195
read, 38, 46, 49, 51, 76, 112, 141, 172, 176, 180, 184, 185, 187–190, 201
recording, 110
rejection, 16
relationship, 22, 23, 27, 28, 51, 54, 55, 58, 60, 91, 92, 117, 119, 156, 158, 160, 164, 173, 180
remember, 26, 29–31, 38, 40, 41, 43, 44, 61, 63, 87, 98, 99, 103, 104, 133, 159, 163, 165, 170, 172
research, 1, 7, 8, 16, 32, 35, 37, 40, 42–45, 48, 51, 65, 69, 75–79, 82, 85, 93, 95, 108, 123, 124, 128, 131, 140, 157–160, 172, 177, 190, 193, 194, 198

resentment, 113
risk, 85–88, 91–94, 173
rural, 4, 29, 63

S
sadness, 35, 170
safety, 112, 126, 156, 197
salary, 57, 64, 66, 68
scholar, 2, 26, 32, 34, 35, 38, 75, 193, 197
school, 17, 18, 20, 29, 30, 32, 47, 55, 57, 59, 66, 76, 82, 88–90, 95, 108, 111, 118, 120, 123, 129, 133, 155, 159, 160, 162, 164, 165, 168, 169
science, 50, 51, 87, 88, 180
self-care, 86, 157, 158, 161, 162, 164, 165, 176, 201
self-doubt, 8, 20, 86, 170
self-loathing, 173, 178
sexism/sexist, 4, 19, 67, 68, 86, 124, 135, 194
sexuality, 135, 146, 159
sexual orientation, 6, 157
shame, 140, 141, 172, 173, 176, 178
Sharpe, Christina, 95–98
single-axis framework, 6, 10
single mother/single parent, 9, 77, 82, 169
sister, 32, 34, 159, 161, 163, 183, 202
slavery, 95–97, 126, 127, 180, 187, 189
Slavery and Civil War Museum, 125
sleep, 41, 51–58, 71, 161, 177
small town, 30, 32
sociality, 86
social justice, 6, 9, 76, 107, 124, 131, 195, 196
social network, 18, 19
social studies, 88
socioeconomic, 5, 6, 87, 146, 157

South Africa, 9, 131–136, 140
Southeastern U.S., 146
Spanish, 110, 120
spouse, 19, 40, 45, 65
spouse, trailing, 7, 19, 22, 78
status quo, 4, 18, 124
Steinem, Gloria, 5
story, 16–19, 22, 23, 28, 34, 66, 76, 86, 87, 97, 103, 114, 120, 126, 134, 156, 158, 162, 171, 183–185, 195, 198
storytelling, 22, 97
stress, 19, 77, 92, 93
student, 16, 18, 27, 31, 32, 35, 37, 41, 46, 50, 59, 60, 76, 80, 87, 89, 95, 105, 110, 111, 114, 120, 121, 124, 125, 148–150, 158, 161, 162, 172, 182, 186
suburban, 15
suicide, 140, 180
superwoman, 67, 68
support, 2, 5, 18, 26, 31, 43, 58, 65, 82, 83, 88, 98, 104, 110, 114, 121–123, 129, 132, 135, 149, 150, 174, 190, 197, 198, 202

T
teacher preparation, 108
teaching, 1, 16, 20, 39, 40, 42, 44–46, 48–51, 53, 58, 65, 66, 75, 77–80, 83, 88–91, 93, 96, 108, 125, 128, 136, 148, 155, 160, 162, 165, 183, 185, 189–191, 193
team, 17, 89, 125, 140
temporality, 86
tenure, 6, 40, 41, 43, 44, 46, 66, 71, 75, 84, 92, 93, 97, 103, 107, 108, 157, 160, 167, 181, 182, 190, 193–195, 198
theory, 67, 76

third shift, 20
time travel, 180
tough guy, 19
trailing spouse, 7, 19, 22, 78
training, 55, 147, 148, 174, 190
trans, 4, 9, 87, 145–151
transgender, 149
Trans Miami, 147
transwoman, 9
trauma, 95, 147, 167, 168, 177, 179
travel, 20, 40, 55, 56, 61, 62, 65, 69, 70, 84, 88, 97
Trump, Donald J., 4
Twitter, 167, 168
typology, 195

U
Uganda, 78, 81, 84
undergraduate, 43, 76, 119, 159
university, 2, 18, 28, 32, 37, 52, 62, 66, 75–78, 80, 81, 83–85, 87, 89–93, 122, 128, 132, 135, 147, 148, 157, 159, 170, 182, 183, 190, 197
urban, 85, 87, 88, 91

V
violence, 118, 139, 140, 146, 188, 189
vocabulary, 21
vulnerable/vulnerability, 9, 10, 21, 59, 111, 114, 139, 140, 165, 172–174, 177, 178, 201

W
weight, 52, 78, 96, 126, 162
White Feminism, 4–6, 185, 186, 190
Whiteness, 120, 121, 124, 131, 132, 136–141, 193–198
white supremacy, 121, 122, 125, 128, 129, 138, 186, 188, 195–197
White women, 4, 6, 134, 139, 148, 157, 188, 189
wife, 3, 7, 17, 31, 49, 51, 54–59
Wizard of Oz, 156, 158, 162, 165
woman, 1, 3, 7, 9, 19, 20, 25–27, 29–33, 35, 38, 40, 47, 67–69, 72, 80, 93, 98, 99, 111, 113, 119, 127, 132, 139, 145–147, 157, 158, 161, 163–165, 168, 180, 183, 185, 188, 189, 194, 202
womanhood, 3, 5, 10, 25, 26, 33, 48, 97, 157, 158, 162, 169, 185
women of color, 127, 147, 148, 151, 185, 188, 189, 194, 195, 198
Women's March, 202
workshop, 81, 139
writing, 6, 7, 15, 20, 32–34, 38, 42, 43, 51, 55, 58, 65, 69, 80, 82, 86, 90, 93, 111, 112, 131, 148, 157, 160, 162, 163, 165, 171–173, 176, 183, 185, 190, 201

Z
zombie, 181

The manufacturer's authorised representative in the EU is Springer Nature Customer Service Centre GmbH, Europaplatz 3, 69115 Heidelberg, Germany. If you have any concerns regarding our products, please contact ProductSafety@springernature.com

Printed and bound by CPI Group (UK) Ltd, Croydon, CR0 4YY
23/03/2026
02076672-0003